NIGERIAN FILM CULTURE AND THE IDEA OF THE NATION

Nollywood and National Narration

Edited by

James Tar Tsaaior and Françoise Ugochukwu

Adonis & Abbey Publishers Ltd

St James House
13 Kensington Square,
London, W8 5HD
United Kingdom

Website: http://www.adonis-abbey.com
E-mail Address: editor@adonis-abbey.com

Nigeria:
Suites C4 & C5 J-Plus Plaza
Asokoro, Abuja, Nigeria
Tel: +234 (0) 7058078841/08052035034

British Library Cataloguing-in-Publication Data
A catalogue record for this book is available from the British Library

ISBN: 978-1-909112-74-2

NIGERIAN FILM CULTURE AND THE IDEA OF THE NATION

Nollywood and National Narration

Edited by

James Tar Tsaaior and Françoise Ugochukwu

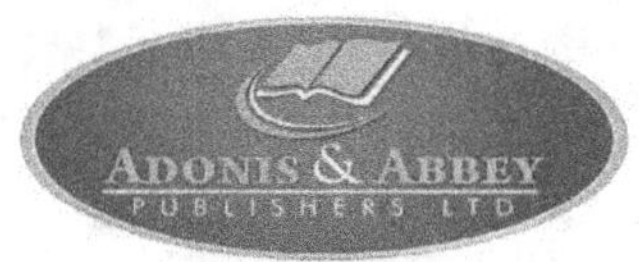

Table of Contents

Dedication

For
Abike
and the
children:
Aôndodoo,
Doosuur,
Terungwa and
Terzungwe;
and to the
cherished
memory
of Sarah
Tsaaior:
lasting
love

Acknowledgements

Let me begin with a brutal and candid confession: this book 'happened' to me more than I contributed to it. In 2011, the School of Media and Communication, Pan-African University (now Pan-Atlantic University), Lagos, Nigeria, my university, jointly organised an international conference with the Centre of African Studies, University of Cambridge, United Kingdom. Known as the Cambridge/Africa Collaborative Research Conference, the event was the culmination of my six-month visiting research fellowship in Cambridge as a Leverhulme Trust and Isaac Newton Fellow. The central theme of the fellowship was "Myth and Modernity in African Literature". This collaborative conference provided an academic site for five of us who participated in the Cambridge fellowship to share our research with Africa-based Africanist scholars and others from around the world who attended the conference event in Lagos.

The modest success of that joint conference gave birth to the annual SMC Media and Culture International Conference which I first convened in 2012. Since then, there have been two successive conferences, one in 2013 and the other in 2014, focusing on different themes. Intriguingly, a trajectory seems to have been established with the call for the conferences. Nollywood has not yet taken centre stage as the main theme for the conference: this belongs to the near future. I have, however, observed with interest and satisfaction that in each of the conferences, Nollywood has always featured as one of the sub-themes. This sub-thematic status is significant in the sense that a number of the essays in this book were inspired by these conferences, while the fortune of some led them elsewhere to be published in the School's online journal, the SMC *Journal of Cultural and Media Studies,* which I edit.

For the opportunity to collaborate in hosting the conference which led to our own international conference in SMC-PAU, I want to thank immensely colleagues from the Centre of African Studies in Cambridge. I thank especially Dr. Chris Warnes, from the Faculty of English, who coordinated the 2010 – 2011 Cambridge fellowship, for his collegial support and cooperation. I am also grateful to my colleagues for the research comradeship we shared in Cambridge and for the lasting collaborations we forged. I also thank them for graciously conceding the hosting right of the Cambridge/Africa Collaborative Research Conference to me and my university.

At the Pan-Atlantic University, I have always enjoyed the unfailing goodwill of the vice-chancellor, Professor Juan Manuel Elegido, whose interest in my professional work and career over the years has been truly stimulating. I thank him for the constant encouragement I have received from him. In the School of Media and Communication (SMC), the pioneer dean, Professor Emevwo Anselm Biakolo, has remained a pillar of support, both as a colleague and a family friend. Apart from tending SMC from the very beginning as a sapling in the undergrowth of the forest floor and nurturing it to its present sturdy growth, Prof. Biakolo provided seminal academic and sterling administrative leadership which challenged my sense of duty and commitment, and I am deeply grateful to him for this.

I have watched with great fascination how my research interests, like a kaleidoscope, have shifted over time, from literary studies to critical theory, folklore/cultural communication and now new/media and film studies. But this is the age of multidisciplinarity, in which disciplinary boundaries and practices have largely become fluid, indistinct and uncharted. I am now getting 'hypnotised' by cultural studies, particularly by the idea of the popular and the way culture shapes reality and is in turn shaped and reshaped by everyday life. New musical expressions, the global spectacle of sports and other performative arts, have become increasingly appealing to me in this regard. This book, therefore, finds its firm anchorage in this fixation with the episteme of the popular and the cultural sites for its materiality and performativity.

Three institutions on three continents provided a congenial and enabling milieu for me to work on the final draft of this book at various times in 2014. The first was Qatar University, Doha, where I attended a conference on: "Writing Back: Language, Identity, Culture, and Difference" organised by the Department of English Literature and Linguistics, during which I found the time, after the sessions, to revise some of the ideas and strengthen the arguments. I sincerely thank the organisers for their warmth and for providing the opportunity to get away from my normal call of duty to devote time to the project.

The other institution was Cairo University, Egypt, where I spent a few days, after the conference on "The Literature and Language of Resistance" organised by the Department of English Language and Literature, to script the first draft of the introduction to the book. I want to express my profound gratitude to the faculty, staff and students of the Department for hosting the event. In particular, my warm thanks go to

Prof. Abdalla Mohamed who drove me round the famous Tahrir Square in Cairo one boisterous night and also took me downtown Cairo for some rare sights and sounds of the city. Some of the students took hospitality and cultural tourism a notch higher by organising a train ride and a tour of Cairo for me to visit some of the sites the city is famous for. They crowned the expedition with a boat ride on the legendary Nile River. I am sincerely appreciative for this genuine expression of love and affection. Do accept my *Shukran!*

The third institution was Princeton University, New Jersey, USA, where I was a visiting scholar in the Centre for African American Studies in 2014. With a team of other Africanist scholars, we jointly worked on papers for a special issue of *Research in African Literatures* which centred on the theme: "Queer Readings in African Literature and Culture". I am indebted to this research collective, particularly to Professor Wendy Belcher of Princeton University and Dr. Tunji Osinubi of Western Ontario University, Canada, for the great effort and for the unexpected Christmas shopping that followed for my family. That experience will remain indelibly inscribed in my memory.

Thanks, too, to the individual contributors to the project for their patience and understanding, especially during moments of eloquent silence on my part when there was no cheering or uplifting news about progress on the project as the gestation period wore on. But you still believed. The materiality of the book is a product of your conviction, determination and confidence in me, and I am grateful for this demonstration of scholarly solidarity. My special thanks go to Professor Françoise Ugochukwu who arrived at the most auspicious moment for the much needed editorial interventions.

My immediate family was away most of the time in the course of this project. However, I drew inspiration from this absence with the realisation that I would hand this book to them on their safe return. For their encouragement and support in absentia, I thank my wife and friend, Abike, and the children: Aôndodoo, Doosuur, Terungwa and Terzungwe, for being part of my life. Your absence strengthened my faith and challenged me to believe more than ever before in the inscrutable ways of Providence. Together, we will continue to enjoy the warmth at the hearth, stoke the flames and offer the obese yam to the live coals for a sumptuous meal. And together, we will harvest the pollen of the dreams as they have begun to ripen.

Finally, all thanksgiving, praise and glory to Providence for the plenitude of grace, for life and for the good health to accomplish this project. *Aondo u hemba; Ungu Tor tswen. Or kuma we ga!*

List of Contributors

Allen ADUM holds a PhD from Nnamdi Azikiwe University, Awka. His research interests include health communication and media research methodologies.

Aje-ori AGBESE joined the Department of Communication Studies, University of Texas, in the fall of 2006 after two years at Salve Regina University in Newport, R.I. She received her doctorate in communication studies, with an emphasis in mass communication and intercultural communication (and African history and politics) from Bowling Green State University in 2004. Prior to that, she received her Masters, also in communication studies, from the University of Northern Iowa and a B.Sc. Honours in Mass Communication from the University of Lagos, Nigeria. Her research interests include Nigerian media history, African media and politics, global mass media, intercultural communication, Nigerian movies, and women and the media. She has worked in different capacities in public relations, journalism and social organisations in Nigeria and the United States. In 2006, Routledge published her book, *The Role of the Press and Communication Technology in Democratization: The Nigerian Story.*

Philip Onoriode AGHOGHOWVIA holds a PhD in English from Stellenbosch University, and teaches English and Cultural Studies at University of the Free State, South Africa. A fellow of African Humanities Programme of the American Council of Learned Societies (ACLS), he is completing a book manuscript titled "Reading Petrocultures in Nigeria's Niger Delta."

Damian AMANA is a lecturer with the Department of Mass Communication, Kogi State University, Anyigba.

Ogochukwu EKWENCHI is a Commonwealth scholar and holds a PhD from the University of Westminster, England. Her research interests include popular culture and critical approaches to the media.

Yusuf Baba GAR obtained a BA (Hons) Linguistics & Hausa from the University of Maiduguri, Nigeria and an MA in General Linguistics from the same University. Currently, he teaches at the Department of African

Studies, Humboldt University Berlin, Germany. Besides teaching, he is a doctoral candidate in the same department. His thesis is on a variant of the Nigerian video film known as Kannywood. His publications include: "Hausa Monosyllabic Words and their Semantic Distributions" (2006) in *Ibadan Journal of European Studies*; "Hausa Idiomatic Expressions: The Semantic View" (2010) in *Maiduguri Journal of Linguistics and Literary Studies*, and "Sociosymbolic Function of Language in Hausa Man's Spoken English" (2006) in *Azare Journal of Education.* His two articles: "Written Political Poetry in Hausa and the Change in Defining Characteristics: The Example of Aminu Shatima" and "Vanishing Tongue: A Case of Laɓur as a Dying Language in Bauchi State, Nigeria" are in press.

Alessandro JEDLOWSKI is a Marie Curie COFUND postdoctoral fellow in anthropology at the University of Liège, Belgium. His current research analyses the political and economic dimensions of film production in the Nigerian video film industry (Nollywood) and compares them with those of other video film industries emerging in sub-Saharan Africa. His main publications include the essays "From Nollywood to Nollyworld: Processes of Transnationalization in the Nigerian Video Film Industry" (in Krings and Okome, *Global Nollywood*, 2013), "Nigerian Videos in the Global Arena: The Postcolonial Exotic Revisited" (*The Global South*, 2013), and "On the Periphery of Nollywood: Nigerian Video Filmmaking in Italy and the Emergence of Intercultural Aesthetics" (in Lombardi-Diop and Romeo, *Postcolonial Italy*, 2012).

Nkechinyere MBAKWE was educated at the University of Hanover for her Master of Arts in Social Science and Media Communications and the Technical University, Berlin both in Germany for the Doctor of Philosophy in Communication and Media Studies. On her return to Nigeria, she became a research fellow in the Nollywood Studies Centre, School of Media and Communication, Pan-Atlantic University, Lagos. She is also the founder of Chi's Yoga and a trainer with the Delegation of German Industry and Commerce in Nigeria. One of her publications is *Oral Nollywood: Trauma and Healing* (2011).

Nomusa MAKHUBU lectures Art History at the Michaelis School of Fine Art, University of Cape Town. She has a PhD in Art History and Visual Culture, Rhodes University. She is also an artist whose artworks have been exhibited in South Africa, France, Germany, Italy, Austria, Swaziland, China and Reunion Island after receiving the *ABSA L'Atelier Gerard Sekoto Award* in 2006, the *Rhodes Amnesty International Woman of the Year Award* (Art) and the *Studio National des Arts Contemporains, Le Fresnoy* prize at the Dak'Art Biennale in 2014. She was nominated as the presenting artist for the *Business Day: Business and Art South Africa (BASA) Awards* in 2008 and was awarded the Purvis Prize for Academic Achievement in Fine Art, Rhodes University. Makhubu became an Abe Bailey fellow in 2008. In 2010, she completed her fellowship with the Omooba Yemisi Adedoyin Shyllon Art Foundation (OYASAF) in Nigeria. Her current research focuses on African Popular Culture. She has worked as a *Cue* reviewer for the National Arts Festival (2007, 2010, and 2012) in Grahamstown and was appointed to the National Arts Festival committee in 2011.

Osakue Stevenson OMOERA completed his PhD in Film and Media Studies at the University of Ibadan, Nigeria. He is currently affiliated to the Ambrose Alli University, Ekpoma, Nigeria, where he teaches film and media studies, theatre studies and African performance and the dynamics of culture. Having pioneered scholarly inquiry into the Benin video film segment of Nollywood studies, he continues to probe the culture and practice of Nigerian video cinema. Among his publications are *Contemporary Discourses on Media and Theatre Arts Studies in Nigeria* – co-edited with Hyginus O. Ekwuazi and Charles O. Aluede, 2012, and *A Gazelle of the Savannah: Sunday Ododo and the Framing of Techno-Cultural Performance in Nigeria* – co-edited with Sola Adeyemi and Benedict Benebai, 2012. Osakue is a member of the Society of Nigerian Theatre Artistes (SONTA), the Institute of Mass Communication and Information Management of Nigeria (IMIM), and the Association for Cultural Studies (ACS), Finland. Apart from publishing widely in leading journals and books across the globe, this eclectic scholar does community service with orphanages under the aegis of the Osakue Omoera Foundation (OOF) in various communities in Edo State of Nigeria. He is blissfully married, with lovely children.

Tunde ONIKOYI teaches Film Production and Studies in Digital Culture in the School of Visual Arts, Kwara State University, Malete-Ilorin, Nigeria. He is a film critic, scholar, reviewer and an oral interpreter. Apart from his doctoral research in film authorship, he is also compiling a book on videographers in Nigeria. He has published essays in journals some of which include *African Theatre, The Performer* and also has chapters in books.

James Tar TSAAIOR is Professor and Chair of the Department of Mass Media and Writing in the School of Media and Communication, Pan-Atlantic (formerly Pan-African) University, Lagos, Nigeria where he teaches creative writing, media/cultural studies and postcolonial writing. He is also the Director, Academic Planning of the University and editor, *Journal of Cultural and Media Studies.* In 2010 – 2011, he was a visiting Leverhulme Trust and Isaac Newton Research Fellow, Centre of African Studies, University of Cambridge, United Kingdom and a participant in the International Faculty Programme, University of Navarre's IESE Business School, Barcelona, Spain. He was also a visiting scholar, Centre for African American Studies, Princeton University, USA in 2014. His recent publications include: *African Literature and the Politics of Culture* (Cambridge Scholars Publishing, 2013), and *Politics of the Postcolonial Text: Africa and Its Diasporas* (LimCom Europa, 2010). In addition he has published over fifty chapters in books and articles in local and international peer-reviewed journals.

Françoise UGOCHUKWU, a Senior Research Fellow, IFRA, Ibadan, and a retired Professor from the University of Nigeria, Nsukka, is currently affiliated to the Open University (UK) and an external collaborator to the French National Centre for Scientific Research (CNRS)-LLACAN, with special interest in Nigerian (Igbo), Nollywood and Intercultural Studies. She is the author of the first Igbo-French dictionary, of several books including one on Nollywood (2013) and two on the Biafran war, and more than 155 book chapters and articles in journals worldwide. Her qualifications, professional career path and area of expertise have placed her at the crossroads between language studies, literature, anthropology, cinema and translation, as evidenced by her publications, PhD supervisions and external examinerships. Her pioneering work in the field and her longstanding contribution to the strengthening of cultural and educational ties between France and Nigeria awarded her the French national distinction of Chevalier des Palmes Académiques in 1994.

Asabe Kabir USMAN, a professor of Oral and African Literatures, is a lecturer in the Department of Modern European Languages and Linguistics, Usmanu Danfodiyo University, Sokoto, Sokoto state, Nigeria. Her research areas include: Oral literature, African literature, popular culture (with passion in film studies and Hausa popular fictional writings); creative writing as well as women studies. She is a member of the following academic associations: National president, Literary Society of Nigeria, (LSN); National vice president, Nigerian Folklore Society, (NFS); National vice President, Nigeria English Studies Association, (NESA); Association of Nigerian Authors (ANA); Nigerian Oral Literature Association, (NOLA); Linguistics Association of Nigeria (LAN); vice president of the Sokoto state branch of Forum for African Women Educationalists (FAWE). She is the author of *Destinies of Life*, a novel published by Caltop Publishers in 2005 and the revised version published by Kraft Books in 2014.

INTRODUCTION

Filmic Texts and Their Social/Cultural Contexts - Nollywood as Site for National Narrativisation

James Tar Tsaaior

In thinking and visualising the sociology and anthropology of texts and textuality, it is an epistemological given that texts are socially conditioned and culturally constructed. It is, therefore, appropriate to argue that texts – whether spoken, printed, photographic or digital, cinematic, canonical or apocryphal, dominant or subversive, official or popular – have been enabling the expression of social conditions and cultural processes constitutive of particular geographies, communities, societies or cultures. As a filmic text, Nollywood, the Nigerian video film tradition, is equally rooted in the sub-soil of its social and cultural surroundings.

The centrality of the circumstances surrounding the making of the text is important in a number of ways. First, these social and cultural contingencies actively mediate the very processes of textual production, circulation and consumption across time and space. Inherent in these conditions can be the people's grammar of values, traditions and customs, belief systems, political institutions, class formations and gender relations, among other historical and cultural experiences in the spatio-temporal continuum. Film cultures, including that of Nollywood, find their moorings in this complex web of conditions which constitutes the very furrow they elect to plough. Nollywood video films, for instance, are engaged in the relentless re/negotiation of the everyday lives of the people against the backdrop of their cultural traditions, cosmologies, social contradictions and the politics of their ethnic/national identity longing and belonging as they define themselves in an age of global flows amidst the challenges of post/modernity.

Karin Barber's insistence that the anthropology of texts is intimately connected with the everyday episteme of a people's ontology and existence is crucial to the understanding and appreciation of texts produced by such a people (Barber 1997). The significant issues to be addressed here are wide-ranging. For instance, it is important to understand how texts are constituted by the societies that produce them and how the texts themselves constitute those societies. The concerns here relate to the nature and structure of the societies: their social organisation, political institutions, religious and cultural practices as well as their modes of economic production. Of equal concern are the history of the societies in question and its impact on the texts they produce. How, for instance, are texts of Nollywood video films conditioned by Nigerian history?

It is equally strategic to know the source of texts and the individuals and communities from which they emanate, because these offer vital information which further illuminates the complex issues that mediate the actual gestalt of textual production. What type of occupational work are the people engaged in, for instance? Are they farmers, fishermen, traders, blacksmiths or artists? Do they have a war-like tradition or a history of peaceful coexistence? Do they survive and thrive on a subsistent or developed economy? What is their vision of life? What is their national or ethnic identity and how does this modulate their sense of existence? In what ways does their idea of themselves as a social group shape and reshape the texts they produce? These issues are also relevant in the constitution and interpretation of Nollywood video films as textual entities.

But beyond this, it is also important to understand the intertextual relations among texts within cultures and establish how such relations are part of the syntax of everyday existence in such cultures. It is important to state that, just like stars and other heavenly bodies exist in families, constellations or galaxies, texts do share certain qualities and attributes which unite them and define them as belonging to a cultural tradition. Nollywood video films, for instance, draw heavily from the inexhaustible fountain of vernacular traditions; they benefit from folktales, legends, epics, myths, songs, proverbs and sagas, and retell their stories.

The dialectic between the filmic text and the agency of the narrative voice, on the one hand, and the instrumentality of oral tradition, on the other, is important. For instance, in what significant ways can the intertextual encounters between these oral forms and Nollywood video films be established, and what are the nature and strategic relevance of this interaction? Do Nollywood texts get enriched, reinforced or impoverished by these intertextual dialogues? How do these encounters help the travelling patterns of orality and how do they deepen and strengthen the transmission of folk wisdom in the age of (post)modernity?

It is within this cultural schema that the idea of canon-formation and the politics which undergird it take place. The politics of canons and their formation determine how and why certain texts are privileged while others are apportioned marginal or less relevant status. Against this significant backdrop, it is imperative to be aware of the network of relations surrounding the texts in a particular culture, and of the transactions they are involved in. How do texts live their lives in this complex network of relations? What are the implications of intertextuality on the overall cultural tradition that produces the texts? In specific terms, what intertextual exchanges take place between Nollywood video films and other film cultures? On the other hand, what are the interfaces, if any, between Nollywood filmic texts and texts within the Nigerian and African literary traditions? Is there any history or legacy of adaptations between these two modes of cultural production? Does Nollywood have a canon of film texts and, if it does, what are the politics which mediate this canonisation process?

Deeply implicated in the discussion on texts, textuality and their contexts is also their capacity to generate a meaning susceptible to negotiations and renegotiations. What, for instance, is the morphology of a text, and what range of meanings does it offer? What does the text, as a meaning event, communicate about the society? How does the text negotiate the social and cultural contexts and the semantic possibilities embedded in it as a communal property? How do texts interrogate their societies? As a film culture, does Nollywood engage in such interrogations of Nigeria's postcoloniality in its narrative procedures?

Indeed, it is important for us to understand what texts choose to reveal and to conceal about the individuals and societies that produce them. What, for instance, are the revelatory potentials which texts harbour about their individual producers and the social realities within the communities or nations that gave them birth? What are the dominant concerns of Nollywood video films as they engage with the everyday physical and metaphysical existence of Nigerian/African societies? Why is Nollywood almost fixated with magic, rituals, voodoo practices, fantasia and exotica against the paradoxical backdrop of Pentecostalist religiosity? Why does this film tradition sometimes choose to emphasise certain aspects of indigenous cultural practices which are considered less than affirmative and salutary, thereby unwittingly falling into the formulaic pattern of western narrativisations and mis/representations of Africa?

The relevance of these issues can be summarised in the fact that they help in crystallising the very nature of texts, their production patterns, their constitutive properties and their functions within specific social and cultural contexts. Nollywood video films are not immune to these. Magic, voodoo, ritual killings, occultism, sorcery, sacrifices to gods, and the craze for ill-gotten wealth, are everyday occurrences in many Nigerian and African societies, and to ensure verisimilitude, the film text must focus on these realities as an essential aspect of the people's daily lives. The new wave of religion is also an integral part of individual and collective existence, especially in the urban spaces of Nigeria and Africa, and Nollywood beams its searchlight on it as an inevitable part of the African modernity.

This enduring concern with texts and textuality is underscored by the fact that, by their very nature, texts do not exist in a vacuum: they owe their material existence to concrete contexts. In this regard, texts are not soulless, meaningless or thoughtless entities. They are living tissues with capillaries, muscles and veins. Thus, the life-blood of texts runs through the complex arteries of contexts within societies and communities, highlighting issues which are vital to the conditions and lives of societies concerned, as they secrete meanings in dynamic ways.

Ngugi wa Thiong'o argues that the processes at work in textual production are resident within society and are immanently tied with prevailing ruling ideologies and other regimes of organised values and interests (Ngugi 1971). The Kenyan writer's formulation on the location of texts impresses on us their very sociality and culturality, based on the material conditions which over-determine their production. Chidi Amuta, the Nigerian socialist critic, also identifies the material conditions and patterns of social and economic production as playing a crucial role in the process of textual fabrication (Amuta 1989).

Locating Nollywood: The Past in the Present and the Present in the Past

The textual universe of Nollywood has its genealogy located in the peculiar social, economic and cultural conditions which precipitated its emergence. This genealogy, rooted in Nigeria's sub-soil, is both diachronic and synchronic. Diachronically, Nollywood's history casts its shadows onto the remote traditional African past when groups, communities and ethnicities organised various festivals, ceremonies, rituals and other rites of passage which dominated their cultural calendars. These rituals, ceremonies and festivals had their distinctive names in these cultures, and so there were no anxieties about naming them in a formal sense as dictated by the modern culture of print and digital technology.

These cultural activities were largely performed for utilitarian purposes. As such, they served the vital functions of entertainment and relaxation, usually after the day's enervating drudgeries. They were also useful for their didactic content, and served as instruments of pedagogy for the communal good. Societies deployed them also because of their capacity for social protest or criticism, moral suasion and the instruction of both young and old. Economic or mercantilist interests were usually peripheral to these cultural performances and ceremonies. Wherever business tendencies appeared to be fore-grounded, it was merely incidental, not the impetus or driving concern, although this did not preclude the patron or patroness of a particular artist or performer from rewarding such a performer financially when the need arose.

It is, therefore, imperative to state that the governing concerns and motivations of these cultural festivals and social events were generally altruistic, and not personal economic gratifications. What informed them principally were the imperatives for cultural transmission and preservation and the possibilities they held for cultural cohesion, social/political commentary and the regulation of behavioural tendencies within the structures of communities and societies. In this regard, pecuniary gains, where they were considered at all, did not rank high in the hierarchy of needs, since they were not usually intentional but tangential to the overall interests and communal good of society. Part of the reason for this is that traditional African economies were largely subsistent in nature and their modes of economic production were inchoate, collectivised or aggregated as belonging to the societal whole. Even though individual wealth was valued as a mark of social rank and distinction, the communal principle was promoted over the cult of individuality.

In another fundamental diachronic dimension, the ideational import of national narrativity, with its architecture of meanings, gestures back to history in its oral manifestations. Oral tradition is composed of texts which are both fixed and free but are nevertheless mobilised for the articulation of perspectives on human life (Ayakoroma 113). It is this oral history that invites us to reminisce on the creative stirrings of individual ethnic nationalities in African indigenous societies which produced texts in local performances within the dynamic of live, performing audiences who constituted the performance ensemble as an informed jury.

Imbued with a sense of urgency, audiences participated in the communal negotiation of nationhood through their running commentaries. The village square usually served as performance space for the purpose. As a civilised and knowledgeable jury, the people argued for and insisted on the accurate rendering of shared historical accounts and the sanctity of their minute details, the propriety of social conventions and the strict observance of moral and cultural codes. They also sanctioned aberrant behaviour, mounted opposition to tendencies of a despotic nature, especially from royalty, and deplored attitudes which sought to place the individual over and above the group interest.

In this regard, the agency of the oral word has always been central to the performance process. Indigenous African societies were not immune to this reality either. The quality and texture of the human voice and its creative manipulation played a decisive role in establishing the virtuosity and accomplishment of artists. The expansiveness of the repertoire of individual performers was also an asset in their honour. However, it must be observed that, during performance, the oral voice competed - and still competes – intensely with other voices which sometimes challenge, subvert and deconstruct the performative voice. These other voices may belong to the audience. They happen to the performance event, based on their social location which may be class interest, political ideology, religious persuasion, gender/sexuality or generational divide. These alternative and competing voices are all strategic to the performance and strain for their perspectives to be heard and reckoned with.

At other times, voices are fluid in their resonance and exist in other spheres like history and collective memory archives. What is, however, consistent with such oral performances is that the audience, in appropriating their prerogatives as an immediate jury, may respond through running commentaries, remarks, interpolations, laughter or grimaces generated with the dual purpose of approbation or reprobation. Interventions by the audience function as a strategy for ensuring the coherence and integrity of the text, re/shaping it and placing it within its proper cultural context. These spontaneous interventions add value to the overall text of the performance as a cultural product which participates in the narration of the nation as an entity in traditional life.

The traditional perspective to the development of cultural performance was to be taken over by modernity, especially with the colonising, civilising and evangelising mission. The instrumental role of the Church and the colonial authorities in the implantation of a film culture in Nigeria following the first film exhibition at Glover Memorial Hall, Lagos, in 1903, has been examined by many scholars and critics (Opubor et al 1979; Ekwuazi 1987; Mgbejume 1989; Okome and Haynes 1995; Adesanya 1997; Enahoro 1997; Haynes 1997; Shaka 2004 and Layiwola 2014). However, the film tradition received a major boost with the establishment of universities during and after the colonial encounter, and with the training of qualified manpower having the requisite capacity to produce stage productions.

In many African countries, universities were an imperial creation for the training of personnel for the public service interests of the soon-to-be new nations on the continent. The public service was crucial to the colonial arrangement and the development of the nations in all ramifications, including education, culture, politics, economy and international diplomacy. But it was also in the universities that drama and theatre departments emerged and later became hubs for cultural creative activities which produced generations of culture practitioners. Many of these later became instrumental to the emergence and flourishing of Nollywood, and some of them still function within Nollywood's formal and informal structures.

The African Cinema which prefigured Nollywood harboured political aspirations and sought to perform an interventionist role in the public domain. This cinema tradition was decidedly ideological, and nourished partisan interests aimed at strategically freeing the manacled African spirit politically, culturally and epistemologically. Sembene Ousmane, the Senegalese novelist and filmmaker, was one of the leading lights who mobilised the powerful influence of the cinema to undermine the assumptions and dominant corrupting influence of colonialism on the African continent. Though distinctively different from Nollywood because of its progressive pretensions, the African Cinema also had a genre of filmmaking that was popular and interested in entertaining and educating its audiences (Diawara 141 – 143). While not commercially-oriented, some practitioners of the celluloid culture of filmmaking, especially those of the first generation, were not averse to commercial interests (Saul 153).

Even though the celluloid film culture is locked in binary opposition to Nollywood – "High-low, elite-popular, art-business, political-entertaining, progressive-regressive, celluloid-video" (Krings and Okome 14) – because of the inherent differences between them, the latter is an heir, in a historical sense, to the rich legacies of the former as it staked the African film landscape and served as a forerunner to Nollywood. Nollywood has since effectively overtaken the scene with its popular appeal and mass consciousness, its bold experimentation with themes of local valuation which celluloid overlooked, and with its distribution patterns, which have succeeded in mapping the African film hemisphere to reach wider target audiences. According to Monica Dipio (53), Nollywood, as a filmic culture, is "popular in the sense that it traverses the immediate culture in which it is set, and people beyond the borders of the immediate community can identify with it."

Nollywood and the Imperative of Postnationality

No doubt, African Cinema culture had a pan-Africanist vision as it engaged with issues which were central to the black personality. However, it is Nollywood which has, through its wide circulation, reached a wider audience in communicating the panafricanist ideal in a truly global manner. The debate among practitioners and critics of these two film formations endures, but it seems that the future belongs to the video film, with Nollywood as its major exponent on the continent and beyond. In their unique narrativisations of nationhood and reality on the continent, Nollywood video films have announced the nation as a modern construct with its corpus of paradoxes. The invention of nationhood in Africa is consistent with European imperial interests through what one critic calls "the curse of Berlin" (Adebajo 2010). It is this curse that continues, in a number of ways, to over-determine postcolonial be/longing and becoming in Africa and to structure the nature of textual production and the character of its narrativisations of a continent in endless, relentless transition.

In telling and retelling the nation in Africa, Nollywood is positioned to embed its texts with signifying systems or codes which bear the marks of the remarkable shifts and detours that characterise African history and cultures. Indeed, Nollywood is unbound. It is interesting that the Nollywood filmic text has increasingly transgressed national territorial boundaries in its migratory rhythms, to become a truly transnational and global film culture. This film tradition is, perhaps, much more popular and appreciated outside Nigeria, as its social and cultural appeal has become as universally acknowledged as other film traditions such as Hollywood and Bollywood. On the African continent, as Matthias Krings and Onookome Okome have observed, Nollywood has influenced other film cultures including those of Ghana, Tanzania, Malawi, Namibia, Kenya and South Africa. According to these two film critics, this cinematic aesthetic "has become the most viable form of cultural machine on the African continent" and it "emerged before our very eyes, in our time" (Krings and Okome 1).

Commenting further on the provenance of Nollywood and its impactful spread on the continent, now reaching a global dimension, they affirm:

> Beginning life in an uncharacteristic manner in Nigeria about twenty years ago, Nollywood has become a truly pan-African affair…Nigerian video films travel the length and breadth of the continent, connecting Africa, particularly Nigeria, to its diverse and far-flung diasporas elsewhere. Satellite television, the Internet, and piracy – at once Nollywood's boon and bane – facilitate the spread of its films across linguistic, cultural, and national boundaries…. The continent-wide influence of Nollywood, however, does not stop at this level. In Tanzania, Kenya, Uganda, and South Africa, for example, Nollywood has served as a model film production and inspired the growth of local film industries…This diasporic influence of Nollywood – its spread across the continent and the fostering of localised versions of this mode of filmmaking – constitutes two dimensions of Nollywood's transnationality…. (2).

It is, however, among black diaspora communities that this impact is truly phenomenal, as many people find themselves home abroad while interacting with Nollywood as they watch the films thousands of kilometres away from 'home'. Such an experience afforded by the Nollywood film texts in their "travel all over the world", provides a veritable avenue for connecting with African cultures and social systems which helps in strengthening the bond between the diasporic personality and the idea of the indigenous (Jedlowski 25). This also helps in the process of identity formation and construction across a generational trajectory, even as a planetary consciousness in a multicultural world order is being negotiated and renegotiated. Through the films, the diaspora individual is also vicariously integrated into the process of national narrativisation and its protocols as they are summoned to intervene in the historic task of rescuing the continent from the interminable treacheries and perfidies of Africa's political establishment and business elite who take turns in pillaging the homeland.

In the present circumstances, Nollywood's dynamic and phenomenal transportability has culminated in the emergence of a diasporic generic typology. This is what Jonathan Haynes calls the "Nollywood Diaspora", which is "the spread of Nollywood filmmaking around the world" and the participation of "Nigerian expatriate communities…in this most powerful of Nigerian cultural forms" (Haynes 73). Even though Nollywood has expanded beyond Nigeria's national frontiers to acquire the character of transnationality, like the fish which, having grown bigger, departs the pond for a larger body of waters, its locus remains Nigeria, which is its natural and aboriginal *habitus*.

The globality of Nollywood as we know it today cannot be reasonably doubted, because this film culture has acquired a solid reputation which transcends fixed national boundaries. But for something to be global, it first has to be local. Indeed, there is nothing that is truly global without first having to be local. It is this local specificity, this situated particularity within a locale, which gives Nollywood a truly universal appeal and endows it with authenticity. Indeed, the true value and significance of this film culture is "its grassroots status, and that the people themselves create it represents at once a confluence of folkloric traditions and practices while also engaging with ideas of what might constitute African modernity"(Mistry and Ellapen 46 – 47).

The formal emergence of Nollywood in the 1990s represented a different kind of social and economic ethos. This is an age which is consistent with, and celebrates, post/modernity or what others call digimodernity, a dispensation where digital and satellite communication and the global media have reached vertiginous heights and where their sheer ubiquity transcends physical cartographic limitations. It is an age which luxuriates in virtual spaces with virtual communities which inhabit the digital ecosystem. In an age of global flows, Nollywood's fortunes cannot be compromised, as they are radically enhanced beyond the limitations that held back indigenous cultural production initiatives and African auteur films. The current dispersal of Nollywood is immense. It exists on the internet, YouTube, mobile telephony and other social platforms which guarantee this film tradition an alternative mode of life beyond traditional formats.

Today, the possibilities for the growth and development of the Nigerian film phenomenon are limitless. Nollywood is consistently and excitingly remapping the culture and entertainment environment, not only in Nigeria but also in other African countries and beyond. The true worth of the industry and its capacity for growth in various sectors of the national life emerged recently with the rebasing of the Nigerian economy. It was recently confirmed that Nollywood is now a net contributor to the annual Gross Domestic Product. The prospects for the industry are, indeed, huge as it continues to be a powerful means of social mobility through employment opportunities and social security safety nets for many people.

Reassuringly too, the positive developments in Nollywood, the intractable debilities and pathologies associated with its phenomenal success notwithstanding, have impacted the industry in ways that inspire great optimism. One clear indication in this optimistic turn is the new wave within the industry, now characterised as the "new Nollywood". This new phase is not without its raft of controversies. One of these controversies originates from a formation within the industry which feels that this new wave will further factionalise Nollywood and compromise its cohesiveness and future integrity. But does Nollywood actually need to be cohesive in the sense of being monolithic? In a multiple ethnic and cultural configuration like that of Nigeria, such differences will always define cultural production initiatives. Such diversity can actually be an asset rather than a liability, as diversity can be a real source of unity and strength.

Ethno-religious and cultural binaries are, and should be, expected in Nollywood. Religious and cultural dichotomies have already been identified between the Muslim north and the Christian south, and these attitudinal antinomies have created an industry known as Kannywood. As Abdulla Adamu (287) observes,

> The cultural differences between predominantly Muslim northern Nigeria and mostly Christian southern Nigeria reflect the different perceptions of the secular state. These differences are reflected not only in matters of state and policy, but also in how members of each region relate to the outside world. The differences are even more vivid in the popular culture industries. While they share common interfaces in

> terms of Western cultural products, the regional differences emerge when visually representative popular culture products are taken into consideration.

Based on these differences, it may be safer to limit Nollywood, in its constitutive reaches, to southern Nigeria, as some contend that this naming rite does not apply to the Muslim north. There are also certain ethnicities in the north which will vehemently oppose their film cultures being called Kannywood, because they neither belong to an Islamic culture nor produce their films in Kano. In the Southwest, the brand known as Yollywood refers to Yoruba language films. The name Nollywood itself has now become problematic as a name representing the entire Nigerian home video film industry and film culture. Matthew Brown (260) raises the spectre of the debate when he observes:

> [.] There is the debate about whether "Nollywood" represents the entirety of filmmaking activities currently taking place in Nigeria, or whether it only represents English-language video films financed and distributed by marketers in southern cities. After all, from Kano's Hausa-language "Kannywood" to the southwest's Yoruba-language "Yollywood", Nigeria's indigenous-language filmmakers are referring to their own activities with their own names.

These differences notwithstanding, the new wave of Nollywood is a trajectory which inaugurates a new dispensation of excellence in sophisticated storytelling, complex and unpredictable plot structures, more accomplished characterisation, improved picture quality, greater directorial skills, scripts with more technical depth and cultural verisimilitude, higher professional acumen and integrity and more robust attention to the minutiae of post-production details. It also emphasises international collaborations with other film cultures, offshore production of Nollywood films using foreign locations, and the revival of cinema-viewing centres. This is also the moment of high budget Nollywood films, which invariably requires a higher financial lifeline. To appropriate local Nigerian parlance, "Better soup na money makam". This roughly translates to mean that if you want a soup which tastes well, you will need a great deal of money. This is the financial challenge which faces Nollywood.

Admittedly, cultures are infinitely elastic, perpetually dynamic and in a state of flux. As such, African indigenous cultures have yielded to modernity and its habits. They have lent their energies to the screen culture so as to assume an alternative mode of existence. This transformation ensures that indigenous oral cultures and their histories will benefit from memory alcoves, new modes of storytelling, languages and other cultural expressions of longevity in a post/modern era - a dispensation which fosters the homogeneity of cultures and speaks of a difference in the constitution of a truly global culture.

Nollywood, therefore, becomes a powerful and defining receptacle of culture. Indeed, it constitutes a cultural mosaic, a filmic text, which homogenises and synthesises the local and the global, the traditional and the modern, the specific and the general, the marginal and the metropolitan, as well as the oral and the filmic. Local stories acquire a modern valency and achieve global relevance. Similarly, old tales are narrativised in a new mode and infused with fresh life and energy. Nollywood harbours both sameness and difference through the unique textual production processes and protocols of storytelling, manipulation of performance space, acting, directing, song, music and dance, among other technical details which are critical to the narrativisation of nationhood. This has serious implications on the continued interrogation of postcolonial belonging/becoming in Africa, a continent struggling with the inherent contradictions of history.

Nollywood is now contextually positioned as a veritable cultural lectionary. This film culture is a textual testament whose legibility in social and cultural significations negotiates nationhood on the continent as it seeks to validate African cultural systems in a postmodern turn, with its accompanying corpus of contradictions. On the subject of film aesthetics, Nollywood also strains to achieve cultural re/lexification and to distil strident commentaries which interrogate some of the paradoxes which have come to define Africa's modernity and postcolonial longing. In telling and re-telling the nation, Nollywood is involved in what can be called *cultural inform-nation* which is a programme intended to inform the nation in Africa, to convince, to convict and to convert it from its developmental arrest and daily realities caused by *politicide* (politics of wilful self-annihilation) to a more secure and assured future where participatory democracy, the rule of law and the respect for freedoms and the sanctity of human life will find a firm anchorage.

The film critical establishment may find something of a void in terms of politics and ideology in relation to Nollywood, especially against the backdrop of the ideological positionality and political engagement of

Nollywood's *other*, African Cinema. In this regard, any political/ideological readings of the Nigerian film may be considered as an imposition. But the supreme truth remains that there are occasional lineaments of a political/ideological nature in Nollywood as its video films "negotiate the politics of postcolonial representation" (Tanimonure 299). Even though Nollywood emerged essentially based on economic/business contingencies in the deregulated economic heydays of military dictatorship in Nigeria, political themes have also provided a fertile ground for the film tradition to till. Some of the themes are historical while others have a contemporary character.

Thus in re/telling the nation through the filmic text, Nollywood executes a project which engages nationhood in Africa through the instrumentality of filmic narrativisations that seek to trigger a cultural awareness and social consciousness aimed at validating African modes of cultural expression in a global milieu. If globalisation is the marketplace of ideas, it, therefore, follows that every society that desires to act the script of globalisation must come to the event with its goatskin of ideas. Ideas rule the world in an increasingly globalised order because they matter and have validity and consequence. It is, therefore, incumbent on Nollywood to embody ideas which can participate in globalisation and its political and cultural regimes.

In seeking to present the nation on the African continent, Nollywood is also involved in revealing Africa's rich legacies in the area of culture and civilisation, her history of violence and the violence of history especially in the cruel hands of Europe and the world. While doing that, it shows the prevailing pathologies of *African* modernity, *our* modernity and its interminable entanglements with *other* modernities and the possibilities of transcending these contradictions which define modern nationhood in Africa.

Gravitating to the idea of modernity

The essays in this book, in varying degrees and emphases, focus penetratingly on the range of issues and concerns sketched above. Their animating force gravitates to the idea of modernity and how the nation, as a signifier of modernity, can distil valuable and relevant meaning systems from filmic texts or narratives to help negotiate coherent nationhood on the continent. On their own, video films do not possess the exclusive capacity to change the world. However, they can function as surrogates of positive change and transformation as they help in the process of enlightenment and education, the fostering of cultural literacy, the empowerment of subaltern groups and the privileging of minority discourses which are critical to a new society on the African continent. It must be emphasised that in all of this, language is a critical concern and an important analytic category.

In particular, indigenous Nigerian languages constitute an integral part of cultural production, circulation and consumption in Nigeria. They are also involved in the same process of national narrativisation as Nollywood. This is without prejudice to the role of English as an official language which also functions as the language of commerce, jurisprudence and international diplomacy. Implicated in the discourse on language are also the place, agency and instrumental part pidgin, as a language of convenience, plays in the communication of culture through filmic/cinematic representation. Language also constitutes a contentious and contestable site in Nollywood. For instance, what is the language of Nollywood? Is the filmic message better communicated in the local languages or in English? Indeed, can films produced in English, an imperial language, be validly categorised as indigenous Nigerian films? The politics of language and the issues of authenticity in filmic as well as literary/cultural studies, endure and continue to be vexatious and unsettled.

James Tar Tsaaior addresses the issue of the language/s of Nollywood in a paper he provocatively titles: “Another Tower of Babel or a Future of Possibilities?” in which he argues for Nollywood films in indigenous Nigerian languages to help underwrite and define national cultural sovereignty and authenticity. He problematises the language question, not only in relation to the Nollywood film culture, but also to literature and other cultural production protocols which are similarly implicated in the complex and enduring linguistic challenge Africa is confronted with. He argues that, even though Nollywood is mired in challenges, the most redoubtable seems to be that of its language/s, because of the centrality and instrumentality of language to art, communication and culture.

Language, he argues, is also important in the articulation of the message of Nollywood, because embedded in its structures are power and hegemony with their constitutive social/cultural hierarchies and ideological representational practices which serve as sites of domination and political control. In specific reference to the language of Nollywood,

Tsaaior launches the debate by asking a set of thought-provoking questions: "why the imperative for Nollywood films in indigenous Nigerian languages? Is Nollywood any less Nollywood without indigenous languages? Is Nollywood a better cultural receptacle and expressive site when articulated in the indigenous languages? Who are the ultimate beneficiaries of this cultural project of linguistic indigenisation and acculturation?" Using an film in Tiv language to demonstrate the centrality of local languages to the understanding and appreciation of cultural products, he concludes that, because the discourse on language is, inevitably, a discourse on power, culture and social hierarchies in a modern world, indigenous languages are better equipped to narrativise the stories of the people who are the true creators of history and culture and the true custodians of their traditions.

The ritualised presence of the witch in Nollywood films is at the centre of Françoise Ugochukwu's paper, titled: "Changing Nigerian Cultures: Two Films against Witchcraft and an Impossible Dialogue." The witch as metaphor has generated a whole critical discourse in Nollywood. As agency of subjectivity in traditional feminist reflection, it illustrates a transgressive and counter-hegemonic tendency against patriarchal institutions and phallic power structures. In such a knowledge schema, the witch houses redemptive potentials for women. However, in the dominant masculinist imagination, it incarnates a reprehensible image and is viewed pejoratively within society. Ugochukwu critically examines the personhood of the witch in relation to its potentialities in forging a cultural dialogue between postcolonial societies and their western counterparts. Through a close reading of two Nollywood films, *The End of the Wicked* and *The Fake Prophet,* she offers a masterful commentary "on the difficulty of intercultural communication" on the subject, as demonstrated by the controversy sparked by a British NGO's discovery of Nollywood in 2008. What is most fascinating about the paper is that it foregrounds the transnationality of Nollywood in its travelling habits and its (sometimes conflictual) engagement with other world cultures.

Aje-Ori Agbese's essay enters the debate by invoking the document from the United Nations Organisation on the millennium development goals, to demonstrate how the world body can intersect with creative industries to foster cultural production efforts on the African continent with specific reflections on Nollywood. According to her, "One of the United Nations' millennium development goals is the promotion of gender equality and women's empowerment. To achieve this goal, organisations around the world are using various tools to inform, educate and sensitise people on its benefits. One such tool is film." Agbese relies on the instrumentality of Nollywood video films like *Women's Cot, Women in Power* and *The Bank Manager* as analytic paradigms to demonstrate that women have crossed the threshold of domesticity, cultural and political subordination, and have now appropriated domains of a public nature in their sustained quest for liberation and empowerment, in conformity with the Beijing declaration on women's rights and freedoms and as inscribed in the protocols of the UN-MDGs (Millennium Development Goals). As she argues persuasively, "Film is a very powerful cultural tool, as people can learn values and norms from it. The Nigerian film industry … has become more than just an entertainment tool. Its audiences are informed, educated, sensitised and sometimes persuaded on Nigerian issues. One could argue that Nigerian movies which use Nigerian cultural values and norms to address an issue would be accepted as more authentic and representative than one that incorporates foreign values and norms."

The United Nations declaration on women's rights is unambiguous and unequivocal about the paramount need to treat women's rights as human rights. The Beijing Women's conference further galvanised the campaign through the phenomenally exceptional manner it pursued the idea of radicalising women's consciousness around the world concerning issues of equality, justice, women's health, empowerment, affirmative action, unrestricted access and active participation to public life. Thus, beyond the complacency associated with being confined to domesticity, women became acutely aware of the need to step beyond the domestic frontier and embrace a programme aimed at achieving the occupation of public spaces including participation in public governance. They also realised that the liberated woman is educated, enlightened and gainfully employed, that she complements efforts in family support, and is aware of her environment, even though some of these expectations seem to privilege patriarchy.

Asabe Kabir Usman's contribution devotes its attention to the Hausa folktale, *Tatsuniya*, and examines how the sub-generic folkloric typology functions in unique and dynamic ways in the documentation and transmission of culture and civilisation through the generations. This dynamism is expressed in the capacity of the folktale, in its essentially oral manifestation, to transgress generic boundaries and travel as an oral text to assume the status of a filmic/cinematic text.

What is intriguing is that the transformation of the Hausa folktale from its oral *locus* to a filmic expressive medium does not diminish its functionality within the structures of the society. It still partakes in viable ways in the construction of Hausa modernity. Additionally, the folktale is increasingly vital in the recuperation, consolidation and representation of Hausa culture even in a new form, *film*, thereby making it still relevant within a post-industrial society and cultural ethos. In the essay titled: "Archiving Hausa Popular Entertainment through New Media Technology: An Assessment of the Recreation of *Ruwan Bagaja* into Video Movie", Usman grapples with some of these issues, especially the travelling habits of primary orality to a screen or visual culture in an increasingly globalised environment. In this interstitial schema, she "attempts an appraisal of the adaptation and recreation of a popular Hausa folktale *Ruwan Bagaja* into movie with the sole aim of preserving the genre". But beyond merely preserving the genre, the Hausa folktale does much more cultural service. It also promotes the culture and accomplishes the hybridisation of the two forms, *folktale* and *film*, into a harmonious whole, which, for want of a better characterisation, can be called *folkfilm,* and imbues it with the capacity to articulate issues of currency and great consequence within the culture.

The *Ruwan Bagaja* folktale is interestingly a fusion of Hausawa folkloric elements and the Cinderella typology of stories. The allusion to Cinderella is instructive, as the folktale typically engages with issues which are peculiarly feminine in nature. Feminine attitudes, beauty, morality, virtue and the cult of true womanhood are the dominant issues that structure the integral world of such tales. In this particular folktale, the plot is sustained by co-wife rivalry and conflict. This is the contentious relationship between two women, the *self* and the *other*, which is usually resolved with latent ambiguities, even though one of the rivals emerges triumphant while the other is humbled.

In this folktale, the plot is complicated by the Cinderella archetypal figure (a metaphoric extension of one of the daughters in the story) who embodies the paragon of feminine beauty and sense of morality as against her arrogant and self-conceited half-sister. In the end, inner beauty is rewarded and vainglorious life is punished, thereby un-problematically resolving the philosophical issue about appearance and reality, physical and inner/moral beauty. The problem about the tale here subsists in what feminists describe as the politics of patriarchal hegemony and its regime of representing women in an idealised and patronising manner which compromises their agency and subjectivity in a male-dominated world. The two daughters in *Ruwan Bagaje* typify two types of women: the ideal woman, loyal and obedient to tradition, and the wild and rebellious woman. This is a debate which Aje-Ori Agbese will later take up in her essay.

One remarkable feature of Hausa video films is that they belong to the category of Nollywood cinematic tradition referred to as Kannywood. Some puritanical formations have tried to resist this association of Kannywood with Nollywood, and figure it out as an act of violent yoking of two disparate filmic cultures. Kannywood itself is not without politics and controversies. But its naming rite is informed by the processes of production of these video films in the ancient city of Kano in Northern Nigeria. Kano is a densely populated industrial city and a centre of commercial activities extending to other parts of the West African sub-region and the Sahel. The city also featured prominently as one of the several trading centres along the famous trans-Saharan trade route linking the coast of West Africa and North Africa. Kano is also historically renowned as a centre of Islamic and Koranic education and for creativity in leather works and weaving. Indeed, as Françoise Ugochukwu shows, the city of Kano has inspired films, especially *Love in Vendetta* which negotiates the symmetry between film and history, appropriating the 1987 riots as a backdrop (Ugochukwu 125).

Kannywood films have a peculiar quality. They are modelled after Indian (Hindi) films and betray Bollywood influences, evident in the storylines, scenes, actions and sometimes musical accompaniment. Those films, therefore, reflect love, harem politics and intrigues, and issues bordering on domesticity. However, there is a growing tendency within Kannywood which emphasises bold experimentations with storylines of a public nature, away from the intimacies of the private frontier. Films from this tradition also promote a morality associated with Islamic religion, its tenets and culture, and which is somewhat distinct from the average Nollywood film set in Lagos or in any southern Nigerian city.

The issues Yusuf Baba Gar contends with in his paper, "Culture, Media Technology and Globalisation: Folktales in Kannywood Videos", are close to those touched on by Asabe Usman. Interestingly, both scholars have worked within the Kannywood film culture and have resorted to the use of the video film *Ruwan Bagaje* as an analytic category. However, Gar extends the critical limits and includes *Sangaya* as part of the analytic possibilities. He is essentially interested in investigating what constitutes the storyline in Kannywood videos, with the intent of establishing that "Folktales can be proven to be sources of the videos against the initial criticism that the videos are mere adaptations of Bollywood, in which case the Kannywood actors/actresses are described as the *Indiyawan Kano* (The Indians of Kano)."

His critical explorations gravitate towards identifying what elements are transformed in the plot structures of the film texts under investigation, particularly the elements that are added. These additions, he observes, help in critically assessing African culture in general, its flexibility and the impact of globalisation on Kannywood as an industry in particular. His discussion seeks to demonstrate that the inclusion of folktales in Kannywood has led to a cultural shift from orality to digital media and its subsequent preservation in the new mode. He concludes with a word for both the filmmakers and the critics of Kannywood. To the filmmakers, he observes that "If they had transformed much of other Hausa genres into videos, they would not have been accused of adaptation. On the part of the critics [...], it would be better to assess the videos based on their thematic details and also consider the fact that adaptation is a global phenomenon."

Philip Aghoghowvia's paper examines the cultural representation of the oil encounter in the Nollywood film *The Liquid Black Gold* (2010). It explores, among other things, the repercussions of oil politics on the social conditions and environmental structures in Nigeria, particularly the Niger Delta which is home to important oil resources. In the paper's appropriation of the trope of violence, both as a veritable commodity and promissory note of exchange which underwrites the agitation for environmental remediation and local control of the oil resources in the Delta region, Aghoghowvia draws attention to the various strategies mobilised by the competing social and political categories involved in the culture of commodifying violence as a means of resource husbandry.

Following the military interregnum, especially after the judicial murder of the environmental activist-writer Ken Saro-Wiwa and the Ogoni eight, Aghoghowvia argues that the dual role which violence plays in the oil politics of this region serves both as a transgressive strategy and as a tool of international monopoly capital and commodification. The belligerents are within the Niger Delta enclave and outside, but with interests under the alluvial earth which houses prodigious deposits of crude oil. As the author explains, "While the disgruntled Niger Delta people, especially the youths otherwise known as resource rebels, resort to violence as a desperate move to draw attention to their plight, government officials, some oil industry captains, local representatives and certain members within the ranks of the rebels, exploit this violence to distract the people" from the politics of exploitation and resistance enacted in and for the land.

Aghoghowvia considers the video film *The Liquid Black Gold* as a contextual backdrop and as an imaginative definition of what violence has come to signify in Nigeria's encounter with oil exploration and all its attendant politics. He insists that "Violence seems to have become a currency which circulates in exchange for the oil resource in the region. The atmosphere of agitation and rebellious mass action that the oil encounter galvanises ensures that only those who can afford this commodity of violence — either as resistance militant groups, state repressive forces, or those who flaunt environmental standards to maximise profit — can have access to the increasingly militarised oil wealth in the region."

In his contribution, Omoera Osakue also grapples with these language concerns in relation to Nollywood. He argues for the decolonisation of linguistic consciousness by advocating that greater critical attention be devoted, not only to the dominant indigenous languages, but also the so-called minority ones like his native Benin (Bini). According to him, "Apart from the usual Nigerian video films done in English language, Nollywood films are often addressed within the animated spectra of Hausa, Yoruba and Igbo language film studies, but new frontiers of the glocalised order such as Benin, Nupe, Afemai [and] Ibibio language films have yet to receive critical attention in popular culture discourse in Nigeria and elsewhere."

His approach is largely historical, through the deployment of analysis, interviews and document observation techniques which he uses in studying reviews of existing literature on Nigerian movies in indigenous languages. Of special interest to him is the Benin video film - one of the vibrant new frontiers which he examines against the significant backdrop of the Benin worldview that sets the sub-category apart from other Nigerian film cultures. He concludes by asserting that the burden of the study is "to dispel the notion by arguing that a considerable amount of filmmaking activities is taking place among other micro-national film cultures in Nollywood which remain generally underexplored and under-theorised".

In his paper, Damian Amana announces the paradoxical character of Nollywood in matters of religion, in relation to the logics of post/modernity. Following the disparate arguments by scholars ranging from Charles Taylor and Pope Benedict XVI's position on the entrenched culture of moral relativism and the increased secularisation of the structures and patterns of postmodern society, on one hand, to Jacques Derrida and Birgit Meyer's publications on the amplified religionisation of planetary consciousness and the proselytisation efforts of a new religion of a Pentecostalist bent, on the other, Amana volunteers to assume a *via media*, a philosophical perspective focusing on "a change in the modality of experience in religion in modern society."

This concern emphasises the changing dynamic of religious experience and its remediation through new media cultures and habits. The new media dispensation, with its knowledge infrastructure, celebrates new developments in visual memory and culture and impacts on the way religion is represented in the visual media, following a logic consistent with the new experience. This phenomenon of a new visuality is particularly evident in the language which has been constructed for the purpose of representations in fidelity to the modes of the *digimodern* culture with monopolistic, mercantilist fixity. As Amana concludes, "Religion's representations assume the language of the visual culture, therefore creating a fecund ground for the promotion of the very spectacular aspects of religious practices and silencing, through minimal reportage, aspects of religion that do not flow with the visual logic."

In the same line of thought, the paper postulates that representations of religion within an evolving "visual culture in the ambit of the predominance of visual media may follow the logic, language and profit of show-business globally." He refers to readings of select Nollywood film texts as well as Ghanaian videos to plough the furrow of his argument and put into perspective the dominant influence of visual media apparatuses on religious expression in a globalised world order.

The city of Lagos as the home of Nollywood is the primary concern of Alessandro Jedlowski's paper which he entitles: "Realism in Nollywood Films: The Materiality of Lagos and the Nigerian Video Film Industry". In it, he examines the social and material condition of Lagos as a city and its centrality as a site of cultural production in Nigeria. He traces the early beginnings of Nollywood as a video film tradition and presents Lagos as a major site of influence in its early life and continued efflorescence. In particular, he identifies the historical specificity of the structural adjustment programmes of the World Bank and the International Monetary Fund in the 1980s and 1990s as critical to the emergence of this film culture, arguing further that Lagos has always held a mirror to Nollywood, while Nollywood has reciprocated that gesture in a dialectical interaction.

The prominent place of Lagos in the life of Nollywood has led to what I choose to characterise as the *Lagosification* of Nollywood film production. This *Lagocentric* trajectory of Nollywood, especially of early Nollywood, becomes obvious when refracted through the high concentration of film production activities in the city as well as the informal distribution channels which have made Idumota and Alaba International markets famous as centres of Nollywood film activities. After affirming the crucial role of Lagos in the life of Nollywood, Jedlowski concludes with these words: "The megacity and the video industry are involved in an endless negotiation, in which they generate and regenerate each other constantly. Neither of them will ever have the last word. Neither of them will ever fully contain the other. But together they will allow us to better understand the material and emotional dimensions of everyday life in Nigeria."

Nomusa Makhubu, in her paper, argues that the increased fascination with Nollywood resides in the fact that, as an expression of local agency and subjectivity, it formulates a new paradigm, a new gaze and a fresh way of looking and seeing which is truly transnational and global in its reach. This confers on this film practice the status of first truly global pan-African film tradition, transcending social, cultural, economic and national boundaries. It is, therefore, reductionist to label Nollywood as an "essentially Nigerian" or "national" cinema, since that label is narrow and limiting, and since it is notoriously difficult and unconvincing to reduce filmic narratives and locate them within the construct and classificatory paradigm of nationhood.

She, however, interrogates the capacity of Nollywood as a social practice and cultural commodity called to service societal engineering in the domains of promoting peace, religious toleration and pan-African ideals on behalf of the nation-state. This, she argues, limits and impoverishes the Nollywood phenomenon and explains the initial rejection of Nollywood by scholars as a phenomenon lacking artistic and historical significance. Using what she characterises as the "Halleluiah" thematic trajectory, she discusses the concept of redemptive spaces created in the church and state and explores how these filmic narratives both affirm and subvert moral principles assumed to be receptacles of nationalist objectives. Her reading of Nollywood fiercely rejects the nationalist rubric which, nonetheless, constitutes a valid analytic protocol.

Notwithstanding critical arguments to the contrary like those of Makhubu, Nollywood is a social and cultural text with a national and pan-Africanist character. This also confers on the Nigerian cinematic tradition a political quality and allows it to partake in partisan engineering habits in sometimes subtle and ambiguous ways. It is becoming increasingly obvious that beyond merely contemplating local political currents, some of the practitioners, actors and actresses have shown more than passing interest in politics, have organised events during which they have demonstrated their sympathies for particular partisan formations and personalities, and often intervene directly in the political process by contesting elections for public office.

This interventionist dimension is another viable way of narrating the nation by other means, acting the script beyond the frozen confines of the screen by crossing into the public arena of political governance as a sure means of changing the society. Thus for Nollywood and its practitioners, film and politics are neither mutually exclusive nor irreconcilable but intimately connected as they reinforce each other for a better society.

Ogochukwu Ekwenchi and Allen Adum, the only co-authors of a paper in this volume, both explore the issue of globalisation and the inevitable consequences of living in a post/modern world where satellite and digital technology impact creative industries and those whose work and lives are intimately implicated in them. Like Mbakwe, they use an ethnographic approach to make bold commentaries on the impact of globalisation on Nollywood as a film tradition and on the dilemmas its practitioners are sometimes confronted with in the course of their cinematic practice. They affirm that Nollywood owes its existence to globalisation processes facilitating the availability and affordability of video technology, the ease in international travel and business. Thanks to globalisation, Nollywood has now toppled Hollywood as the premier provider of audio-visual entertainment in Nigeria.

It is the same technology, with its global aspirations, they reason, that also gave birth to other "woods" in sub-Saharan African countries such as Ghana, Kenya, Tanzania and Malawi. Technology is also the engine behind the revitalisation of Nigeria's and Ghana's previously comatose national film industries. In assessing the impact of globalisation, especially in relation to the issue of identity, using Segun Arinze and Steph-Nora Okere, two popular Nollywood actors, as paradigms, and drawing from interview excerpts with the two actors, the authors employ "critical discourse analysis to argue that a contradictory structure of feeling has developed in the actors in relation to Nollywood and social practices elsewhere, symbolised by Hollywood. This tension comes mainly from the reality of working in the country's video film industry and the global ideals as imagined by the actors." This imagination has combined with the wide availability of foreign cultural materials to foster what they call a "mental migration" in the two Nollywood actors.

Nkechinyere Mbakwe's paper employs a peculiar strategy, which is ethnographic in nature, to tease relevant information from Nigerian film producers/practitioners on an aspect of Nollywood which implicates what she characterises as the "healing powers of the African world". The focus adopted brings to the fore the agency of the oral word and its signifying properties in the negotiation of shared meanings and experiences with a historical backdrop. Nollywood, no doubt, mines the inexhaustible resources of orality in ways often largely unacknowledged. But what is even more intriguing and symbolically significant is the therapeutic value of the oral word, and the vast possibilities of healing it secretes in an attempt to transcend the pathology associated with postcolonial identities in Africa.

The discourse on the healing power of the spoken word foregrounds the oral world known to the guardians of the spoken word in Africa and shows how oral artists creatively manipulated the resources of orality in their performances and other expressive situations and practices. This was the familiar wor(l)d of town-criers, priests and priestesses, prophets and prophetesses, *vates*, *griots*, medicine-men and women, musicians and drummers, among other associated kindred souls of the sacred word who were in the vanguard of negotiating social and cultural realities for the benefit of the community. In their official capacities as mouthpieces of whole families, villages, hamlets and societies, these men and women occupied very important and respectable offices which conferred on them social and cultural capital on behalf of society.

As individuals, they did not merely operate in a void but as communal voices and consciences of their communities, approving of what was socially acceptable and censuring injustice and oppression. They sang the panegyrics of royalty and other patrons but were also unsparing in speaking the truth to those in power when that became imperative. In doing this, many paid the supreme price. However, what remains important is the appropriation of the oral word for performative possibilities which house the capacity to heal society and its maladies. Nollywood, as a filmic tradition, partakes in this interventionist programme of enlisting the word to heal society from social wounds inflicted by a violent history and the pathologies of modernity. Nollywood, therefore, serves a social and cultural function, not only in narrating the nation but also in participating in the resolving of its contradictions, ambivalences and ambiguities.

Linking the paper to the commemoration of Nigeria's 50th independence anniversary, Mbakwe explores the healing powers of the African word and argues that the history of that word has been greatly affected by the European colonisation of the continent. For her, the imposition of the Latin alphabet in many parts of Africa dramatically changed the very nature of verbal and non-verbal communication. In her words, "The nature of the Nigerian word is therefore explained using the example of Nollywood. The recovery of a pan-African experience is the subject of discussion in interviews conducted in Nigeria and [in] the African Diaspora with some forty experts including Nigerian filmmakers, producers, actors and viewers. Nigerian home videos effectively both support the decolonisation attempts by Africans everywhere" and contribute to the healing of collective traumas. "Thus, this study links postcolonial theories with the history of the Nigerian word. This is a story of healing."

Tunde Onikoyi examines the nature of the transition from literature to visuality in the form of literary adaptations to films and video films, and observes that this is a path rarely trodden in the Nigerian literary society. This mechanical distinction between literature and film is contingent on the strict hierarchies erected between the printed/written word and the screen as if the two categories were mutually antithetical. Literature is usually considered as a more serious domain of popular culture, reflecting as it does a poetic interpretation of life. Film, on the other hand, is often considered as a pure entertainment medium. But as Onikoyi argues, "Filmmaking also constitutes a form of discourse and practice that is not just artistic and cultural, but also intellectual and political. The video medium provides a very special opportunity for studying the transition of the same spectrum of creative arts." His paper, as such, re/imagines the relationship between film and literature, and also argues that both film and literature constitute aesthetic, cultural and (in the case of film) popular cultural discourse. It also investigates the reason why Nigerian literatures have not sufficiently lent themselves to film adaptations, and why people may prefer the film medium to that of literature.

Meta/narratives about Nollywood as a social and cultural narrative would be deficient and incomplete if they ignored Lagos, Nigeria's former political capital and now her commercial and business hub. This is because Lagos has always provided the geographic site for the setting of a range of cultural activities, from literary texts and musical compositions to artistic performances, paintings, sculptures, festivals (like the Festival of Arts and Culture, FESTAC 77) and, in this particular case, filmic productions. As one critic observes, "[W]e live in the age of the city. The city is everything to us — it consumes us, and for that reason we glorify it" (Okome 2002). Lagos is especially important because of its multi-ethnic, multilingual and multicultural constellations as well as its huge demography. John Campbell estimates that the city's population is about 21 million people (Campbell 2012).

Collectively, the essays which constitute the textual world of this book represent a discursive confluence on Nollywood as a local film culture with a global character, aspiration and reach. They engage the realities of language, culture, narrativity, history, nationhood and post/modernity, discuss how these realities structure film texts and how film texts, in turn, structure them. The book is about textual relations and the complex politics of representations within the texts as much as it is about the contextual circumstances the texts emanate from. It implicates the trajectory of language in cultural production practices, and Nollywood films in indigenous Nigerian languages which draw from the inexhaustible mine of local cultural histories/traditions in the telling and re-telling of stories with local and global relevance.

Narrativisations distilled by Nollywood films can best find validity in their capacity to negotiate and interrogate the local dynamics of politics and culture and relate these to global contingencies. It is this *glocal consciousness* which truly defines Nollywood as a filmic text capable of fashioning large commentaries about Nigeria and the world.

This is why the transnationality of Nollywood must not, and should not, be happening at the expense of its subnationality. Similarly, the globality of this film industry should not undermine its locality, which was the cultural site of its origins. Its transnational turn and global aspirations should rather release a galvanising force and impulse, a higher resolve which will call for the investment of narrative energies in the telling of local stories with global relevance and impact, a truly *glocal* text which is at home with both the local and the global in the narrativisation of 'everydayness' and nationhood in Africa. Whether or not Nollywood as a film culture will constitute itself as a cultural catechesis for the proselytisation and reawakening of Africa in the house of culture remains to be conjectured. Only time will tell, as it continues to bear testimony to past, present and future history.

Works Cited

Adamu, Abdalla Uba. "Transgressing Boundaries: Reinterpretation of Nollywood Films in Muslim Northern Nigeria". In Matthias Krings and Onookome Okome (eds.) *Global Nollywood: The Transnational Dimensions of an African Video Film Industry*. Bloomington and Indianapolis: Indiana University Press, 2013. 287 – 305.

Adesanya, Afolabi. "From Film to Video". In Jonathan Haynes (ed). *Nigerian Video Films*. Jos, Nigeria: Nigerian Film Corporation, 1997. 13 – 20.

Amuta, Chidi. *The Theory of African Literature*. London: Zed Books, 1989.

Ayakoroma, Barclays Foubiri. *Trends in Nollywood: A Study of Selected Genres*. Ibadan: Kraft Books Limited, 2014.

Barber, Karin. *The Anthropology of Texts, Persons and Publics*. Cambridge: Cambridge University Press, 2007.

Brown, Matthias. "The Crippled Cinema of a Crippled Nation? Preliminary Notes on Nollywood and the Nigerian State". In Adeshina Afolayan (ed.) *Auteuring Nollywood: Critical Perspectives on* The Figurine. Ibadan: University Press Plc, 2014. 257 – 297.

Campbell, John. "This is Africa's New Biggest City: Lagos, Nigeria, Population 21 Million", in *The Atlantic,* Jul 10 2012. Retrieved 10 December, 2014. http://www.theatlantic.com/international/archive /2012/07/this-is-africas-new-biggest-city-lagos-nig

Diawara, Manthia. *African Cinema: Politics and Culture*. Bloomington: Indiana University Press, 1992.

Dipio, Monica. "Ugandan Viewership of Nigerian Movies" in Foluke Ogunleye (ed.). *Africa through the Eye of the Video Camera*. Manzini, Switzerland: Academic Publishers, 2008. 52 – 78.

Enahoro, A. *Semiotics of an African Cinema: Xala as a Paradigm.* Lagos: Cinemarts Communications, 1997.

Ekwuazi, Hyginus. *Film in Nigeria.* Jos, Nigeria: Nigerian Film Corporation, 1987.

Haynes, Jonathan (ed). *Nigerian Video Films.* Jos, Nigeria: Nigerian Film Corporation, 1997.

______________. "The Nollywood Diaspora: A Nigerian Video Genre". In Matthias Krings and Onookome Okome (eds). *Global Nollywood: The Transnational Dimensions of an African Video Film Industry.* Bloomington and Indianapolis: Indiana University Press, 2013. 73 – 99.

Jedlowski, Alessandro. "From Nollywood to Nollyworld: Processes of Transnationalization in the Nigerian Video Film Industry". In Matthias Krings and Onookome Okome (eds). *Global Nollywood: The Transnational Dimensions of an African Video Film Industry.* Bloomington and Indianapolis: Indiana University Press, 2013. 25 – 45.

Krings, Matthias and Onookome Okome. "Nollywood and Its Diaspora: An Introduction". In Matthias Krings and Onookome Okome (eds). *Global Nollywood: The Transnational Dimensions of an African Video Film Industry.* Bloomington and Indianapolis: Indiana University Press, 2013. 1 – 22.

Layiwola, Dele. "The Home Video Industry and Nigeria's Cultural Development". In Adeshina Afolayan (ed). *Auteuring Nollywood: Critical Perspectives on* The Figurine. Ibadan: University Press Plc, 2014. 217 – 236.

Mgbejume, O. *Film in Nigeria: Development, Problems and Promise.* Nairobi: African Council on Communication Education, 1989.

Mistry, Jyoti and Jordache Ellapen. "Nollywood's Transportability: The Politics and Economics of Video Films as Cultural Products" in Matthias Krings and Onookome Okome (eds.). *Global Nollywood: The Transnational Dimensions of an African Video Film Industry.* Bloomington and Indianapolis: Indiana University Press, 2013. 46 – 69.

Okome, Onookome. "Writing in the Anxious City: Images of Lagos in Nigerian Home Video Films." *Under Siege: Four African Cities, Freetown, Johannesburg, Kinshasa, Lagos.* Germany/New York: Hatje Cantz Publisher, 2002. 315 – 334.

Okome, Onookome and Haynes, Jonathan (eds). *Cinema and Social Change in Nigeria.* Jos, Nigeria: Nigerian Film Corporation, 1995.

Opubor, A. E., Nwuneli, O. E. and Oreh, O. O. (eds). *The Development and Growth of the Film Industry in Nigeria.* Lagos: Third Press International, 1979.

Saul, Mahir. "Art, Politics, and Commerce in Francophone African Cinema." In Mahir Saul and Ralph A. Austen (eds.). *Viewing African Cinema in the Twenty-First Century: Art Films and the Nollywood Video Revolution.* Athens: Ohio University Press, 2010. 139 – 159.

Shaka, F. *Modernity and African Cinema.* Trenton, New Jersey: Africana Books, 2004.

Tanimonure, Gideon. "Nollywood and the Discursive Mediation of Identity, Nationhood and Social Anxiety". In Adeshina Afolayan (ed.) *Auteuring Nollywood: Critical Perspectives on* The Figurine. Ibadan: University Press Plc, 2014. 298 – 323.

Ugochukwu, Francoise. "Nigerian Video films on History: *Love in Vendetta* and the 1987 Kano Riots." In Foluke Ogunleye (ed.). African Film: Looking Back and Looking Forward. Newcastle upon Tyne: Cambridge Scholars Publishing, 2014. 125 – 135.

Wa Thiong'o, Ngugi. *Homecoming.* London: Heinemann, 1971

CHAPTER ONE

Another Tower Of Babel or a Future of Possibilities? The Language of Nollywood and the Politics of Cultural Communication in Postcolonial Nigeria

James Tar Tsaaior

Abstract

Artistic experiences, including literary and filmic/cinematic, are all expressed through language, using oral, written or visual communication media, but the linguistic medium deployed in these artistic expressions does not always constitute the critical discursive foreground. The discursive challenge I have elected to engage here is urgent. It concerns the imperative for a poetics of Nollywood video films in indigenous Nigerian languages and the contradictions which govern and define this filmic tradition. The urgency of this challenge can be summarised in the fact that language constitutes a veritable vehicle for the articulation of any grammar of culture and its transmission. I do this, fully realising the paradox of using English, a foreign language, to advocate the use of indigenous language in Nollywood films. Yet English is the official national language of Nigeria because of the contingencies of imperial history and its linguistic/cultural legacies.

This is not about the language alone, as film itself is not an autochthonous expressive medium, hence the contradictory nature of the cultural condition of postcolonial states including Nigeria. The questions to be asked here to tease our cultural imagination are wide-ranging: why the imperative for Nigerian films to choose indigenous languages? Are we suggesting that Nollywood cannot, and will not, survive and thrive without the indigenous languages? Is Nollywood any less Nollywood without indigenous languages? Is Nollywood a better cultural receptacle and expressive site when articulated in Nigerian indigenous languages? Who is the ultimate beneficiary of this cultural project of linguistic indigenisation and acculturation? This paper attempts to answer these questions by arguing that it is difficult to begin to imagine language without the embeddedness of politics, power relations and the complex representational practices integral to it.

> Languages as communication and as culture are then products of each other. Communication creates culture: culture is a means of communication. Language carries culture, and culture carries, particularly through orature and literature, the entire body of values by which we come to perceive ourselves and our place in the world. How people perceive themselves affects how they look at their culture, at their places, politics and at the social production of wealth, at their entire relationship to nature and to other beings. Language is thus inseparable from ourselves as a community of human beings with a specific form and character, a specific history, a specific relationship to the world (Ngugi, *Decolonising the Mind* 16).

Introduction

Language is crucial to the communication of individual agency, group interest or cultural identity. Indeed, language is culture-specific and this constitutes it as a unique vehicle for the transmission of culture. As such, whether verbal or non-verbal, language is deeply implicated in the politics and mediation of culture. However, the centrality of the role of language and its dynamic participation in culture are sometimes not given sufficient acknowledgement and attention. This is particularly so in cultural production processes like film cultures and traditions. Nollywood, Nigeria's video film industry, represents a constitutive cultural event whose language is not very often given the place it deserves in critical discourses. Francoise Ugochukwu corroborates this when she observes that "The language of Nollywood video films, its choices, and those of subtitling and dubbing, have long escaped scholars' attention" (1).

Apart from scanty scholarly attention given to the language/s of Nollywood by Barrot (2008), Ondego (2008), Ogunleye (2003), Larkin (2000) and Johnson (2000), detailed critical studies on Nollywood and its language/s have generally been lacking. Studies such as those of Adedun (2011) and Adejunmobi (2004 and 2007) which focus on the language of this film culture, are few and far between. Yet it is obvious that critical interventions on Nollywood will suffer a fundamental impoverishment if the language of its texts is ignored or bypassed in the hierarchy of concerns relating to this film culture.

The study of the language of Nollywood is, indeed, crucial. Nollywood, no doubt, has other real challenges such as its uncomplicated, predictable storylines and shallowness of characterisation. Other challenges include poor picture/voice quality, lack of directorial finesse, problems of cultural representativeness, social irrelevance and post-production matters, among other technical details. Add to these the problems created by piracy and poor, informal distribution patterns. However, the problem of language poses one of the single most important and stubborn challenges, because "Language, as an integral part of a people's culture and communication, is not only a unifying factor but also a vital contributive factor to the success and acceptability of the various genres of the video film production" (Oyewo 145). Similarly, "The language in which a film is produced has wider implications for its access, commercial success, relevance and cultural impact in a multi-ethnic, multicultural and multilingual nation like Nigeria" (Adeoti and Lawal 187).

The primary focus of this paper is to negotiate the language/s of Nollywood against the significant backdrop of Nigeria's heterogeneous cultures and rich legacy of historical experiences. The paper seeks to answer the following questions: what is the language of Nollywood? Does Nollywood have only one, unitary language? Indeed, does Nollywood have a language through which it articulates its message? Can we truly talk about the language of Nollywood? To be more brutal, is Nollywood another Tower of Babel? Can Nollywood be a better vector of national culture if its language is monolithic or multiple? What is the role of indigenous Nigerian languages in the future life of Nollywood? Is English language a better medium for Nollywood to convey its cultural message and aspirations? Why is the question of language relevant to Nollywood at all? The answers to these questions constitute the furrow which this paper intends to plough.

Nollywood and the Tower of Babel Metaphor

Whenever the language question is considered in relation to the plurality of the African linguistic experience, the metaphor of the Tower of Babel is used as a constitutive signifier. This refers to the notoriously difficult linguistic situation which Africa has been dragged into by what Adekeye Adebajo calls the "curse of Berlin", that is the arbitrary fabrication of nation-states following the European scramble for and partition of African territories between 1884 – 85.[1] With over 2000 languages, Africa stands out in the world as a continent whose linguistic diversity and cultural heterogeneity pose a huge challenge in terms of linguistic legibility, harmonious cultural relations and socio-political engineering.

In their book significantly entitled *The Tower of Babel*, Ali Mazrui and Alamin Mazrui negotiate Africa's heterogeneous linguistic heritage within the dynamic of its plural cultures. The book is a study of the African triple heritage of power, culture and modernity in relation to the continent's linguistic history and cultural experience. Implicated in their study also is the colonial determination of the language question. They argue that "[T]he linguistic balance sheet on the interplay between the indigenous and Western legacies in Africa so far has been decidedly in favour of the European languages that came to the continent as part of the colonial cultural package" (1).

To them, colonialism played a crucial role in the artificial and heuristic constitution of African nation-states to meet the European imperial programme. The imperial project, therefore, was intended to serve the hegemonic intentions of the colonial establishment without commensurate regard to the colonised territories and their linguistic and cultural peculiarities. But even before Europe's colonial programme of cultural erasure, the Arabs, through trade across the Sahara as well as through jihadist conquest, had some direct impact on African languages through the implantation of Arabic, another predatory language.

In a strikingly similar title to that of the Mazruis, though not specific to Africa, John McWhorter's *The Power of Babel: A Natural History of Language* navigates the phenomenon of human language as a means of social communication. Through the use of creoles, pidgins and dialects, McWhorter demonstrates how world languages represent the mobilisation of signs and symbols in ways which are species-specific. This means that as a science of signs, human language is an expressive and social interactional activity exclusive to humanity as against sub-species like lower animals and plants. The sociality of human language implies that it must be necessarily mutually intelligible for it to accomplish its communicative potentials.

What is particularly resonant and compelling about McWhorter's book is that it is articulate about the utilitarian functionality of human language. As he observes, human language is meant to "accomplish the tasks of communication of information, expression of emotion and attitude, commanding and requesting, social libation, calibration of power relations and poetic expression" (3). Of all these functions of language identified by McWhorter, the delineation of power relations and social hierarchies is the most integral to language. Indeed, embedded in all languages are potentials for domination by hegemonic power structures and rites of resistance to such dominant power mechanisms.

In the same way, Alain Ricard comments insightfully on this multiple linguistic reality which characterises Africa's cultural landscape. In his book, *African Languages and Literatures: The Sands of Babel,* he underscores the language problem on the continent as it intersects with colonial politics, power relations and cultural imperatives. The biblical myth of Babel equally resonates strongly as a metaphor which seeks to underwrite the conspiracies of history and culture in the determination of Africa's collective linguistic imaginary. This makes Africa a bewildering array of linguistic and cultural constellations. Such a multicultural mosaic militates against the emergence of local languages as strong national languages, hence the resort to the adoption of colonial languages as the preferred linguistic alternatives. While Ricard is specific about the language of African literatures, this linguistic conundrum is also present in Nollywood and other African film cultures.

Ricard's argument resonates precisely at the point where he posits that the implantation of the imperial languages in the African cultural sub-soil held obvious advantages over linguistic plurality but equally possessed certain disabling drawbacks. One of such limitations was the marginality imposed on indigenous African languages. This was so, even though the imperial enterprise was somehow simultaneously involved in the promotion of some of the African languages through the translation of Scripture and hymnals and the establishment of printing presses which encouraged the emergence of a print culture in indigenous languages. But language never ceased to be a double-edged sword. As Ricard argues, many Africans found that "their attachment to the European languages was always problematic" as language go-betweens (123). He further argues that,

> [.] They were sensitive to the advantages that their people could gain from the new forms of Western education, but they saw no reason why this education could not take place in their own languages, or any danger that it would ever make them forget the written and oral traditions of their own language (123).

The carving of colonial spheres of influence followed a fatalistic, deterministic path which necessarily privileged the Europeans and their administrative policies, which were meant to consolidate their stranglehold on the colonised populations. This meant that indigenous people's cultures and the languages critical to their transmission and sustenance ranked low in the British, French and Portuguese colonial policies of indirect rule and assimilation.[2] In any case, wherever and whenever local languages were given some attention, it was to promote Europe's imperial interests. The imposition of colonial languages as official means of communication in the public frontier and the educational system meant that indigenous languages were apportioned a marginal space and relegated to a subsidiary status in the colonial process.

Let us now return to Mazrui and Mazrui's framing argument, which is that the multiplicity of Africa's languages has also posed a challenge for the continent's cultural production processes and developmental initiatives. This lack of linguistic centre becomes reminiscent of the biblical Tower of Babel where a monolithic human language was confused due to the overarching ambition of the human race to erect a tower to reach God.[3] According to this mythological narrative, humanity was only defeated in its scheme when a single language which was mutually intelligible became confused and frustrated by the emergence of the various languages of the world. Africa has a fair share of these languages, thereby making it another Tower of Babel.

This situation comes with its formidable challenges, one of which is the difficulty to achieve mutual intelligibility in a trans/national dimension among African cultures and ethnicities. The only difference in this case is perhaps that these African languages are understood by their native speakers in a transcultural manner within specific spatialities. Instances of this case in relation to film include Hausa language films which can be understood in much of northern Nigeria and the Sahel region including Chad and Niger. This also applies to Yoruba films in western Nigeria, parts of Benin Republic and Togo. Igbo films, paradoxically, have increasingly gravitated to English, even though the first Nollywood film was in Igbo. Besides their immediate cultures, indigenous language Nigerian films do not find ready reception in other cultures except in Diaspora communities who understand those languages. These cultural antinomies and the dichotomous relations they institute interfere adversely with the cognitive reception of Nollywood films in Nigeria, and by extension with their commercial viability and success.

Nollywood and the Language Question

Nigeria's postcolonial condition has contributed to complicate the negotiation of the national language question and triggered the emergence of English, an imperial language imposed by the British colonial overlords, as an official language in which the business of government, trade and commerce, international diplomacy and education/instruction are conducted. This linguistic imperialism then led to the marginalisation of indigenous Nigerian languages.

The truth, however, is that when put together, the speakers of indigenous Nigerian languages prevail over English speakers. This demography is also true of Nollywood films in local languages, more common than those in English. The only drawback with the local languages is that their understanding is restricted to their local cultural domains. As such, they do not always travel beyond their immediate localities, thereby limiting the reach, popularity and, by implication, the commercial success of the films. This limited consumption pattern of Nollywood films in local languages is only helped through the transnational dynamics of diasporic categories in Europe, North America and the Caribbean.

The preeminence of the English language in Nigeria presents a real challenge for cultural production processes and consumption patterns, because English is an elitist language spoken by just the literate or western-educated fraction of the population. The majority of the populace is more familiar with their local languages, which reflect their existential, historical and cultural experiences. The real concern here is that history and culture are usually created and consumed by these ordinary people in their ordinary circumstances and everyday situations, using the local languages. This ordinariness and everydayness of the people's existential conditions are important, as they inscribe them in the making of history and culture. It also underscores the agency of local languages and the subjectivity of the indigenous population as repositories of traditional culture and agents of its transmission through the continuum of history.

It is, therefore, safe to argue that the presence of English language constitutes a huge paradox in Nigeria's linguistic experience and cultural history. While English lays claim to being an international language, it is merely a language of the elite, which alienates the bulk of the population, thereby making it a minority language. The real languages of the people are their local languages, which best articulate their individual and group experiences. It is also in these languages that they make sense of the material world around them and relate to it. The disadvantage only lies in the lack of capacity of those local languages to be widely spoken and accepted by the generality of Nigerians. This is the paradoxical challenge which Nollywood faces as a local video film culture with a global dimension and perspective.

Between Literature and Nollywood

In a formal sense, Nollywood began its life in Igbo, an indigenous Nigerian language, with the popular appeal of Kenneth Nnebue's *Living in Bondage* in 1992. It must, however, be stressed that the phenomenon of film and cinematic production in Nigeria can be traced to the trajectory of history before this date. This trajectory was present in the transition from the ecclesiastical and colonial domains to the secular stage, with the proliferation of theatre groups and dramatic arts departments in Nigerian universities, from the stage to the screen and from celluloid to the video film as we understand it today (Ekwuazi 333). It is, therefore, fallacious to say that the rootedness of Nollywood is exclusively located in the 1990s as if there was no prior history of filmic/cinematic practice in Nigeria, since, even before the evangelising and colonising mission, indigenous performances, widespread in Nigeria and Africa, remotely set the stage for the emergence of a modern performance and filmic culture.

The name Nollywood itself is not without its paradoxes and controversies. It represents a naming anxiety, as it is not indigenous but derived from a foreign model, Hollywood. Its inaugural use by Norimitsu Onishi in the *New York Times* in 2002 was also in a foreign medium. The only thing which unites it with Nigeria is the upper case "N". Indeed, as far as the politics of naming can determine, it is the N which differentiates Nollywood from Hollywood or Bollywood. However, the symbolic value of this naming rite underwrites the social and cultural significance of this film tradition as emanating from a concrete environment which constitutes the backdrop of its existence.

Owing to this controversial naming, critical intellection about Nollywood's authentic identity as a national film culture has also constituted a contested and contentious site. Does Nollywood represent the entire Nigerian national film culture or a particular part of it? In other words, is it regional, ethnic or linguistic? Opinion does not yet seem to be settled on this, even though the regional and linguistic categories appear to be more compelling constitutive identity markers. Nollywood, therefore, essentially designates the video film from southern Nigeria whose medium of expression is English language, as opposed to northern Nigeria where Hausa is the preferred language (Adamu 288). This is not to deny that Nollywood, in a formal sense, can be rooted in the historical contingencies of the early 1990s when Nnebue's video film in Igbo language became the watershed and fulcrum of attention. However, with time, English language appears to have taken over from the indigenous languages as the single most important medium of expression in Nollywood.

This challenge is not peculiar to the film tradition. Literary productions in Nigeria and Africa have also faced the same disquieting paradox before the formal emergence of Nollywood - and still face it. The language question has also been central to the discourse on what constitutes an authentic African literature. Is it literature written in English or other imperial languages with a discernible African experience and with African characters? Is it literature realised in indigenous languages by Africans? Or is it literature written by anybody including Europeans and Americans but which focuses on African issues, experiences, situations and contexts? What should be the language of this literature? Does Joseph Conrad's *Heart of Darkness* or Joyce Cary's *Mister Johnson* qualify as African literature?[4] Or is it African literature written in indigenous languages and translated into European languages? Or is it pidgin, a language of convenience which emerges in peculiar linguistic circumstances? What is the true character of African literature in relation to the language in which it is articulated?

The debate still rages on. Since the 1962 Kampala, Uganda conference which critically reflected on the issue of language and African literature, two critical formations have emerged. One formation has embraced English language while another has rejected it as a medium of literary creativity and expression. There is a third category, though, which advocates an eclectic linguistic approach and solution: the creative manipulation of European languages to achieve an idiom with a local flavour. Within African literature and cultural studies, there has been a huge debate on the verities of language and their fidelity to cultural expressions and the sovereignty of tradition. Beginning with Obi Wali's Kampala argument on the dead end of African literature, the language question has been critical to artistic production processes on the continent. Wali argued that the articulation of African literature in foreign languages will only come to grief, since such an African literature will lack cultural authenticity and rootedness in the local social sub-soil and historical experience.[5] What insights can we possibly glean from this argument in relation to Nollywood? Will Nollywood also cease to be authentically indigenous if we ignore our local languages? Is pidgin, which is also used in Nollywood, an indigenous language? How can Nollywood better benefit from pidgin as a medium of filmic expression?

The boundaries of the critical discourse on language and its impact on cultural production in Africa have since been widened, with culturalists like Chinua Achebe and Wole Soyinka arguing that English language is an imperial legacy which can be deterritorialised and made to serve local counter-imperial needs.[6] Achebe, in particular, proceeded to wean the language from its Indo-European roots and to temper it in the forge of his molten imagination to produce a peculiar Igbo idiom that is sometimes called *Engligbo*. On other occasions, Soyinka also advocated the adoption of Kiswahili, a language spoken in much of East Africa, as an African language, even though he himself has continued to use English. Can we successfully subject Nollywood to this experimental process in the cultural laboratory and still retain the authenticity of this film tradition? Or, to further problematise the issue, do we really need that testament of authenticity in Nollywood? And if we do, whose interests will this serve?

These two antagonistic positions have their strengths and limitations. The indigenous languages are the communal property of the local people and the fruit of history. They are the languages through which cultures and historical experiences are expressed and shared. Worldviews, philosophies of life and cosmologies receive validation and authentication from the languages people speak and interact in. However, these indigenous languages are severely limited in their travelling habits, especially in an age of global flows where globalisation has become the defining order of culture. This in turn affects the circulation of cultural productions including literature and film.

Similarly, English language, which is widely spoken as a world language, possesses the capacity to intervene productively in the process of circulation of cultural products. With local varieties described as "new Englishes" or "world Englishes" to emphasise "the diversity to be found in the language today", "English no longer has one single base of authority, prestige and normativity". The language has been domesticated in many cultures around the world, even though literacy levels are still a limiting consideration (Mesthrie and Bhatt 3). As such, the reality of *englification* is not without its complications and shortcomings. It shuts out the mass of the people who constitute the majority but lack literacy in English and other European languages, and this linguistic lack places them on the fringes of society and its linguistic discourses.

Cultural production, circulation and consumption are severely limited by these contradictions as African writers, filmmakers and other artists are confronted with challenging choices in an attempt to navigate their way through this beleaguered linguistic space. Albert Girard, quoted in Oliver Lovesey (2000), submits that this is thus a disquieting dilemma the African writer, also a man of culture, is enmeshed in:

> This is the dilemma of the African writer today: either he may use a European language and thus gain recognition (and financial reward) from a worldwide audience, but at the risk of cutting himself off from the very roots of all but the most esoteric creative flowering, the common experience of his own society; or he may use his own mother tongue, stoically shun the appeal of the world market, remain one of the inglorious Miltons of the present age, but help his own people's advance into the age of mass literacy and pave the way for future achievements and renown (15).

The fortunes of European languages, including English, translate to a crisis of local relevance for the indigenous population. Indeed, the major undoing of English (and other foreign languages) is its alienation of the people, the local people who are, indeed, the authentic producers of history, culture, tradition and the stories which constitute the raw resource for literature and film. This alienating influence of European languages is a real source of anxiety. The anxiety emerges from the fact that, as a foreign language in a postcolonial setting, English somehow interferes with the sanctity, sovereignty and inviolability of indigenous cultures and sometimes renders the people's experiences in distortive ways that do not represent them authentically. In this regard, English gives with one hand and takes back with the other.

The terrain of language is the terrain of power. Language is power and power is language. Against this backdrop, language can be understood as the domain of power and power relations. For whoever controls language controls the levers of power and exercises political and cultural hegemony over others. It is logical, then, that whoever lacks access to language and its vital and vitalising properties also lacks power and control over others. Therefore, the defining argument of this paper is that, because of the political and ideological power of language, the future of Nollywood resides in indigenous Nigerian languages as a strategy for achieving cultural power and authenticity. This treatise on language is also consistent with the received epistemology that language can be deployed for only two mutually exclusive and irreconcilable purposes or intentions: for domination and for liberation.

In the imperial cultural programme from the West, language is never neutral and ceases to be innocent. Indeed, language emerges as an engaged, indispensable ideological weapon, mobilised in the cultural war of attrition African/Black peoples are routinely subjected to in the world today. This is what the Kenyan writer, Ngugi wa Thiong'o, referred to as the decolonisation of the mind.[7] For him, the project of political liberation in Africa has been largely accomplished. What remains is cultural decolonisation which should begin with the mind. The motivation behind Nollywood needs to be broadened and located beyond commercial or mercantilist limits. Nollywood as a film tradition, like African Cinema and Third Cinema, can combine the quest for business or commercial success and cultural liberation so that it can continue "to be seen as contributing to the fight against *cultural imperialism* in tangible ways" (Esan 6).

Alamin Mazrui, in corroborating Ngugi's perspective, also asserts the instrumentality of language in the cultural resistance struggle when he talks about the place of language in the "quest for liberation".[8] For Nigeria, it will be a formidable way to begin the cultural warfare, deploying the arsenal of Nollywood, especially in the indigenous languages. This is essentially because Nollywood started in an indigenous Nigerian language and should continue to emphasise and promote the local linguistic options and possibilities to communicate its message. To achieve this cultural programme, a clear language policy will have to be articulated through constitutional means, which will privilege indigenous languages and legislate for their mandatory inclusion in school curricula at all levels in a manner that has not been previously contemplated. The urgency of such a parliamentary initiative is clear because Nollywood, literature and the other arts constitute a cultural space and a linguistic terrain where language can be used for national liberation and development.

Beyond its utilitarian value as an entertainment medium, Nollywood is also a counter-hegemonic programme which speaks back to the regimes of western cultural power and their empire-building machinations in Africa. By revising some of the flagrant misrepresentations of Africa and the Black race in dominant western filmic/cinematic traditions and media texts, Nollywood imposes on itself the cultural burden of undermining totalising forms of knowledge on Africa by Others. Implicated here are the ubiquitous Hollywood and media organisations like the BBC, CNN or VOA, whose "Focus on Africa", "Inside Africa" and the use of "African Voices" manipulate the image of the continent, misrepresent it and cast it as the vermin of the world.[9]

For the avoidance of reasonable doubt, Nollywood films can be produced in any language, local and global. The capacity of filmic texts to express realities which mediate the human condition cannot be totally vitiated by linguistic considerations alone. What makes a film sufficiently entertaining, instructive and expressive is not limited to the language through which it is produced. Its success is also function of the greatness and universality of the story it tells, the grandeur of the thematic concerns, and the fluidity of its plot and narrative kinesis. Equally important are the power of its vision for humanity, the consummate quality of the pictures, the profundity and complexity of the plot structure, the creative manipulation of the characterisation and the artistic talent of the directors/producers, as well as the details of production and post-production.

But for Nollywood films to reflect the Nigerian/African indigenous cultures and experiential realities, local languages are to be adopted, as better equipped to transmit peculiarly national micro and macro-histories, challenges and aspirations of people grappling with modernity in the (re)invention of nationhood. And if language is the terrain of power, mastery of indigenous languages gives an edge to Africans in their political negotiation of power and social relations in the house of culture.

Besides, the local population lacks a functional literacy in European languages like English, French, Portuguese, Spanish or German, and this conveniently screens most of the people out of discourses that validly concern them. This severely undercuts the robustness and inclusivity of the discourses in the first place. In the main, the population is denied entry into the portals of discourse and stands aloof, contemplating the temperamental discursive currents without meaningfully engaging in them. Nollywood as a popular cultural expressive mould is inhibited with such a wholesale erasure of interpretive voices which should participate in its reception.

Could subtitling or dubbing solve the problem? Subtitling is the translation of the spoken/written word of an audio-visual text, "usually at the bottom of the screen" (Luyken 31), while dubbing "consists in providing a film with a complete soundtrack in a different language" (Ugochukwu 6). The success here has also been less than impressive because of the challenges associated with managing "diverse disciplines" (McLoughlin, Biscio and Mhainnin 2011). In the first place, this experimentation would require proper literacy and the requisite capacity to read the translations. Again, most of the local population lack the education to achieve this. Besides, in most cases, people in charge of subtitling lack the required linguistic skills. Sometimes, the subtitling is faint and unreadable and the speech patterns are barely matched by the interpretive current embedded in the subtitles. Subtitles can equally be unusually fast-paced or annoyingly slow, thereby interfering with the message of the films. This greatly impacts the reception and cognitive responses of the audiences of Nollywood films.

Translation is also inherently fraught with its politics, which privilege one social or linguistic category over another. Moreover, no language is capable of retaining its potency and nuances when reduced to translation. Indeed, certain expressions simply refuse to yield themselves to translation into other languages, hence the phenomenon of *untranslatability*. In such gnawing, complex circumstances, the subtitling of Nollywood films only achieves a poor equivalent of the local expressions. The dilemma about translation, transliteration and transcription is not specific to Nollywood alone. It is equally embedded in literary texts, as Albert Girard notes:

> Does the author choose to work in a local language or a major European one? If the former — how does the work get translated and by whom? What might the translation have done to the work? What kind of semantic processes of abrogation/deformation and appropriation/reformation occur in the work? When a local language lends terms, in what context do they occur? Finally, what does the use of language imply about an implicit theory of resistance? (15)

Herein lies the imperative for a poetics of indigenous Nigerian Nollywood films. Nigerian films produced in indigenous languages will speak directly to the majority of the people in languages that they understand and can identify with. These languages will give them a voice and endow them with the power to negotiate their place in global culture and discuss it on their own terms. They can also give them a sense of their agency and subjectivity in a globalised order of power relations. In this regard, the subaltern voice will be enabled to speak, question and answer back as a subjugated knowledge form to the western order of knowledge in a language they are familiar with. Such films with an indigenous flavour bear the marks of the people's cultural experiences and social histories and tell their stories better to the various publics of the world.

This is important because every story is told from someone's perspective, using the person's language. If African stories are told by *others* using foreign languages, the perspectives of *others* will inevitably be privileged over those of the continent. Similarly, if African stories are told by Africans in a foreign language, such stories may not communicate as fully and forcefully as stories in indigenous languages would have done. As Terry Threadgold explains, the perspective from which a story is told is meant to privilege the subject who is the telling voice, even though such a perspective can be contested and changed, and, again, requires facility and competence in the target language.[10] To appropriate Chinua Achebe's famous statement, the story of the hunt will continue to be told from the hunter's perspective if the animals do not weave their alternative narratives. To achieve visibility in today's world, the *word* which best defines the Self must become the weapon for the ideological offensive in global cultural relations.

In the next section, I hope to use a Nigerian film in indigenous language to illustrate this imperative as a viable option out of the linguistic quagmire Nollywood has been driven into. This is because the people connect more readily with their history, cultural traditions and everyday experiences when these are rendered in the languages they are familiar with. They are more at home in their reception of, and responses to, the films and so become an integral part of the discourses generated. In such circumstances, they are more actively involved in the process of cultural production, circulation and patterns of consumption. This conclusion is based on my personal experience of watching a Tiv folkfilm with a group of Tiv old folks and my perception of their capacity for critical appreciation and reception of the film, essentially because the film was produced in the language they understood and so they could relate with it much more intimately than in any other language.

Ifan i Ngô and the Future Possibilities of Indigenous Language Nigerian Films

Ifan I Ngô (*A Mother's Curse*) is a film in Tiv language, structured around a folk narrative from the oral heritage of the Tiv of central Nigeria, present in Benue, Taraba, Nasarawa, Plateau and parts of Cross River States. The film is a tale within a tale. It begins with a mother-in-law telling one of her son's wives a story which teaches responsibility, obedience and deference to others, especially in-laws. The mother sends one of the wives on a domestic errand but the young lady blatantly refuses and abuses her. She, therefore, uses the occasion of the altercation to tell the disobedient wife a story about Meeme and the necessity of filial devotion, familial understanding and marital responsibility.

Meeme is an only son in a polygamous royal family where there is fierce co-wife rivalry and tension. His mother is the most junior of the wives but is much loved because she represents the king's hope for a future heir. This attracts the pathological jealousy and envy of many of the other wives. Intent on frustrating and destroying the favourite wife, her co-wives conspire and implicate her in the theft of a pendant belonging to the King, in a kingdom where theft is punishable by death. The co-wives steal the pendant and hide it in the junior wife's treasure chest; when it is discovered, the latter is unjustly condemned to death in accordance with the strict code of conduct of the land. However, the sentence is commuted to banishment from the royal court because the woman is found to be pregnant.

During her time of banishment, the junior wife gives birth to a son, Meeme, who is swiftly taken from her and given to the most senior wife, the arch-rival of the junior wife, as a foster-mother. Meeme grows up without knowing the true identity of his mother. He reaches his physical majority and becomes a sturdy, skilled and courageous hunter. On two occasions, Meeme's biological mother asks him to bring game for her from his hunting expeditions. As Meeme does not know that the requests are from her real mother, he treats her cruelly by wrapping human faeces as game for her.

His mother curses him in anger on the second occasion by saying that if she bore Meeme and gave him suck, he would not return alive from the next hunt. Meeme becomes an accursed son. His next hunt, true to his mother's curse, proves fatal as he is killed by a raging buffalo. All efforts to revive him prove futile until the oracle proclaims that his mother alone can revive him by removing the curse. As she reluctantly removes the curse, Meeme sneezes back to life and the film ends on a note of genuine reconciliation.

To properly understand this film, it is important to contextualise it within Tiv social and cultural life, values and mores. Traditional Tiv society is built around the family as the basic unit of social organisation. Such a family may be polygamous, composed of a man and his many wives, children and other relations. Rivalry, sometimes very unhealthy, is common among co-wives. Inherent in this arrangement is the role of the older members of the family who supervise its affairs in a network of relations with other families within specific communities. Decisions on juridical and political matters are also under the direction of gerontocrats who represent their families in quasi-democratic and representative manner and whose views are carefully weighed before decisions are taken. In that world, women are not always consulted. However, they can sometimes perform certain influential roles behind the scenes. A child, for instance, belongs to a particular family but is equally the child of the entire community and may be disciplined by all.

In the film, we find such a social organisation where a polygamous family provides a concrete canvas for the dramatisation of rivalries and jealousies. The film has a didactic, functional value as it uses a tale within the familiar world of folk narratives to underscore the paramount need for familial harmony, peace and good neighbourliness. It is fascinating to see that the tale is told by the matriarch of the family, a reality which underwrites the central role of women in the early education of the young. This foregrounds the relevance of matriarchal power and energies in the safeguarding of the community's future. Thus the film's main structural gestalt centres on the traditional typology of co-wives' rivalry and animosity within a polygamous system.

Co-wife relationships are usually governed and sustained by intrigues, subterfuges and treachery which, in many situations, inevitably bring about severe consequences including death. Many Nollywood films are structured around this thematic gravitation of co-wife rivalry. In some others, co-wife relationships function, not necessarily as the main plot, but as a sub-plot. This phenomenon operates mostly in patriarchal cultures where the patrilineal principle takes precedence over the matrilineal, and where the agency of women is significantly undermined by phallic hegemonic tendencies.

In this Tiv film, the co-wife is represented as the "other" woman, whose subjectivity and legitimacy come under intense scrutiny by co-wives who construct her identity in terms of otherness. This inscription of otherness leads to discrimination and institutes oppositional binaries between selfness and otherness, which ultimately privilege patriarchy. Co-wife rivalry helps in validating the patriarchal notion that women are their own problem as they cannot manage their own relational patterns, especially when they are involved in competition for the love and attention of men. This male perspective, however, overlooks the causes and motivations of co-wife acrimony. It is first a system willed into existence by patriarchy. Against this backdrop, patriarchy stands implicated and cannot absolve itself of responsibility and guilt.

Another causative agent of co-wife rivalry consists in the in/capacity of a woman to produce children, especially male children. In patriarchal societies, the male child is valued over and above the female, because the male child continues the genealogical line, while the female ends in another man's family. This makes wives without children, particularly male children, insecure and vulnerable in such societies. They, therefore, visit their insecurities and frustrations on "other" co-wives who have the fortune of producing male children who can become heirs. This causes phenomenal hostility and deadly conspiracies which sometimes lead to the death of children, co-wives, husbands and sometimes the disintegration of whole families.

In the Tiv film *Ifan i Ngô*, distilled from a Tiv folktale, we are led to a deeper appreciation of the role of oral traditions, especially folktales, an inexhaustible mine for artistic creativity, in artistic and cultural production processes. Many Nollywood films borrow from oral traditions in their choice of themes, characterisation, plot structures and perspective, and some of the characters in Nollywood films are "types" with their archetypal coefficients in African oral traditions. For instance, the actress Patience Ozokwor is a character type who functions either as a fastidious and confrontational wife, insolent co-wife or wicked mother-in-law in the Nollywood films she stars in. She epitomises the quintessential non-conformist, aggressive and counter-cultural woman who transgresses normative behavioural norms and subverts tradition.

While she confronts "other" women, men are not spared her tantrums and outbursts which disturb their masculinity. Ozokwor embodies the other co-wives in *Ifan i Ngô* as their construction of otherness in relation to other women reveals the intense susceptibilities of women in a patriarchal system which ranks them as a marginal category.

Aki (Chinedu Ikedieze) and Pawpaw (Osita Iheme), the diminutive characters acting in many Nollywood films, are metaphoric extensions of smaller animals such as Hare, Tortoise, Squirrel and Spider usually involved in relentless contestations with bigger animals like Tiger, Lion, Elephant and Buffalo in the universe of folktales. Just like Aki and Pawpaw outwit older people in Nollywood films they feature in with their daredevilry, the smaller animals also outdo the bigger ones with their craftiness, thereby underscoring the relevance of the philosophical question about appearance and reality, of sheer physicality and innate intelligence. In *Ifan i Ngô*, the dialectic between appearance and reality is represented in the jealous co-wives who outwit the men who consider themselves as the wise custodians of culture and tradition and dominate the society and its power relations. The women, who are marginal to the society's social and cultural organisation, succeed in wielding enormous powers in their conspiratorial role to cause chaos, with disastrous consequences.

Within Tiv society, matters which concern the physical world but cannot be neatly resolved because of their complexity are referred to the metaphysical universe, which intervenes to restore balance and order in human relations. This is precisely what happens in the film when Meeme loses his life as a result of an attack by a wild animal, following his mother's curse. The medicine-man is summoned to unravel the cause of death and administer a therapy to revive Meeme. Earlier, he is called upon to reveal the identity of the person who has stolen the King's pendant.

In both cases, the medicine-man functions as an intermediary between the known and the unknown worlds, a surrogate agent whose relevance to society becomes emphatic during moments of tension. The disruptions to society's delicate balance are a threat to harmony, hence the resort to the spiritual domain to restore the much needed balance. In Meeme's case, he is the only heir, though not to the throne (because the Tiv do not practice hereditary kingship), and his death triggers a major crisis affecting the continuity of the family line.

Even though co-wife politics may appear to be the governing concern in the film, its very title suggests otherwise: the major interest of the film lies in its treatment of a culture and tradition which enforce a strict code of filial obedience and subjection to parents and elders by younger members of society. Indeed, respect for one's parents and older members of society is enshrined in the canon of Tiv social codes. In this arrangement, youths are under strict obligation to honour their parents and respect their elders - who may not necessarily be biological parents. This is what constitutes the tragic dimension in the film.

In his brash and disdainful attitude to tradition, Meeme disrupts this code by repeatedly bringing home human waste to his estranged mother when she respectfully requests him to give her a piece of game from his hunt. The fact that Meeme does not realise the true identity of his mother does not really matter here, because society expects him to be civil to all family members and elders in the community. The theme of disobedience occurs in many African folk narratives and it is not strange that this film should appropriate it as its thematic preoccupation.

Oral traditions have equally provided literary creativity a stable source of tropes, metaphors and narrative strategies with which to construct literary worlds. Instances abound of this kinship between orality and written traditions, especially in the African novel, fed on folktales, myths, epics, legends and oral histories. The folktale plays a vital role in the narrative kinesis of Chinua Achebe's *Things Fall Apart*, as an instructional manual for the young members of the society. Isidore Okpewho's novel, *The Victims,* on the other hand, is modelled after a folktale primarily concerned with the theme of co-wife animosity. In this novel, the rivalry culminates in disastrous consequences for the family. Ngugi wa Thiong'o's *The River Between* and *A Grain of Wheat* are also heavily inspired by myths.

One progressive way Nollywood films in Nigerian languages can achieve cultural relevance and functionality is to turn to oral traditions, an inexhaustible quarry offering a wealth of resources to be mined for filmic purposes. Indeed, African oral traditions can yield a rich harvest of tropes, metaphors and cultural codes which are critical to the elaboration of themes, subject matters, structures, storylines and other textual resources. This will also confer authenticity on Nollywood films as avatars of positive indigenous cultural values and mores. Besides promoting and preserving indigenous languages, oral traditions can also serve as moral safeguards to the young and the old for a possible moral rearmament and cultural renaissance in society.

The centrality of oral traditions to Nollywood has been underscored by the continued appropriation of the infinite and prodigious resources they offer. Many of the films, in both foreign and indigenous languages, including *Oma tsen-tsen* and *Suara la*, two films in Itsekiri produced by Alex Eyengho, have benefitted from the fountainhead of oral tradition. Indeed, the nipple of oral tradition is readily available to be suckled and Nollywood producers and promoters should be encouraged to use it to boost their creativity. This is a service to indigenous cultural traditions, to modernity and to posterity.

A sure way of achieving cultural authenticity is to strive for representativeness in film texts. Films in indigenous languages can easily get entangled in the sticky web of generalisations and cultural tentativeness, especially if they are not representative of the local cultural condition. Representations of Africa in western films have at best been biased, prejudiced and racist. Africa is imagined and constructed in these films as a dense forest, a wilderness, the very heart of darkness, where barbarous beings engage in benighted and heathenish pastimes. There is already a tendency within Nollywood to unwittingly validate such politics of representation. Films in Nigerian languages must revise this trend, reimagine its assumptions and subvert its claims by representing our cultures boldly and positively.

The imperative for a poetics of Nollywood films in indigenous Nigerian languages is not the only functional and viable strategy for achieving cultural retrieval, but it represents an effective programme to ensure that Nigeria and Africa do not become linguistic and cultural dinosaurs. Nigeria as a nation must put its chaotic house of culture in order so as to shore up its cultural potentials. To achieve this, the understanding and perception of culture must be radically altered. Culture is more than mere dancing and public displays, although these can be its corporeal markers: it is an attitude which is integral to the aspirations of a people. It is a coherent ethos, a living tissue with tangible and intangible coefficients.

Notes

[1] Implicated in the African linguistic crisis are the issues of power, culture and modernity but also the focal role of history and its violence,

especially in the colonial legacies of the scramble for Africa and the partition of the continent by European imperial forces. See Adekeye Adebajo, *The Curse of Berlin: Africa After the Cold War*. London: Hurst and Company, 2010.

[2] Consistent with European colonial administrative systems on the continent were also their attitudes to language policies, which helped in the prosecution of the imperial project. In many cases, colonial languages were the preferred choice and the local languages consigned to the place of linguistic otherness.

[3] The biblical myth of Babel is found in Genesis, the first book of the Bible. But it is important to observe that this myth belongs to the Jewish culture and valorises a specific perspective, even though Babel has now acquired universal relevance.

[4] These texts are assumed to be foundational narratives which are misrepresentations of African traditional life through the imperial gaze. It was to these narratives and their politics of representation that African writers like Chinua Achebe and Ngugi wa Thiong'o responded.

[5] Obi Wali summed up his argument on the language question in the essay, "The Dead-End of African Literature" when he argued that: "… any true African literature has to be written in an African language" and that the "uncritical acceptance of English and French as the inevitable medium for educated African writing is misdirected and has no chance of advancing African literature". He concludes that "Until these writers and their Western midwives accept the fact that any true African literature must be written in African languages, they would be merely pursuing a dead end, which can only lead to sterility, uncreativity and frustration."

[6] Achebe argued in this regard that the English language had been bequeathed to him as a colonial legacy and that he intended to use it. In an interview with Gallagher, he stated: "The British did not push language into my face while I was growing up... Language is a weapon, and we use it... There's no point in fighting a language" (Gallagher, Susan van Zanten. "Linguistic Power: Encounter with Chinua Achebe." *The Christian Century* 12 March 1997, 260). Similarly, Soyinka apprehends English as a language for the articulation of African culture, though he

has at other times advocated the adoption of Kiswahili as a language for Africa.

[7] See Ngugi wa Thiong'o, *Decolonizing the Mind: The Politics of Language in African Literature, London: James Currey and Nairobi: Heinemann,* 1986.

[8] Alamin Mazrui, "Language & the Quest for Liberation: The Legacy of Frantz Fanon", in *The Power of Babel: Language and Governance in the African Experience,* Oxford and Chicago: James Currey and University of Chicago Press, 1998. 53 – 62.

[9] These western media organisations have programmes such as "Focus on Africa", "Inside Africa" and "African Voices" which purport to represent the continent in a fair manner but end up being the patronising and condescending reproduction of the image of Africa they want to see through their imperial eyes.

[10] See Terry Threadgold, *Feminist Poetics: Poiesis, Performance, Histories,* London: Taylor and Francis, 1997.

Works Cited

Adamu, Abdalla Uba. "Transgressing Boundaries: Reinterpretation of Nollywood Films in Muslim Northern Nigeria." In Matthias Krings and Onookome Okome (eds.) *Global Nollywood: The Transnational Dimensions of an African Video Film Industry.* Bloomington and Indianapolis: Indiana University Press, 2013. 287 – 305.

Adedun, E. A. "From Yoruba to English: The Untranslatable in Selected Nollywood Movies." Being a Paper Presented at the Symposium on "Reading and Producing Nollywood" Lagos, 2011.

Adejunmobi, Moradewun. "Nigerian Video Film as Minor Transnational Practice." *Postcolonial Text* 3 (2) 2007. http://journals.sfu.ca

______________. "Foreign Languages, Local Audiences: The Case of Nigerian Video Film in English." In Moradewun Adejunmobi (ed). *Vernacular Palaver. Imaginations of the Local and Non-native Languages in West Africa.* Clevedon, UK: Multilingual Matters, 2004. 101 – 130.

Adeoti, Gbemisola and Abdullahi Lawal. "Nigerian Video Film and the Conundrum of Language: Observatory Notes on Kunle Afolayan's *Araromire* and *Irapada*". In Adeshina Afolayan (ed.) *Auteuring*

Nollywood: Critical Perspectives on The Figurine. Ibadan: University Press Plc, 2014. 187 – 213.

Barrot, Pierre. (ed). *Nollywood: The Video Phenomenon in Nigeria.* Oxford: James Currey and Bloomington: Indiana University Press, 2008.

Ekwuazi, Hyginus. "Nollywood: How Far? How Much Further". In Adeshina Afolayan (ed.) *Auteuring Nollywood: Critical Perspectives on The Figurine.* Ibadan: University Press Plc, 2014. 332 – 349.

Esan, Oluyinka. "Appreciating Nollywood: Audiences and Nigerian 'Films'". *Particip@tions* 5 (1), 2008.

Johnson, Dul. "Culture and Art in Hausa Video Films." In Jonathan Haynes (ed). *Nigerian Video Films.* Athens: Ohio University Center for International Studies, 2000. 200 – 208.

Larkin, Brian. "Hausa Dramas and the Rise of Video Culture in Nigeria." In Jonathan Haynes (ed). *Nigerian Video Films.* Athens: Ohio University Center for International Studies, 2000. 209 – 241.

Lovesey, Oliver. *Ngũgĩ wa Thiong'o.* New York: Twayne Publishers, 2000.

Luyken, Georg-Michael et al. *Overcoming Language Barriers in Television: Dubbing and Subtitling for the European Audience.* Dusseldorf: The European Institute for the Media, 1991.

Mazrui, Ali and Mazrui, Alamin. "Introduction: Africa's Linguistic Legacy between Expansionism & Nationalism". In Ali Mazrui and Alamin Mazrui. *The Tower of Babel: Language and Governance in the African Experience.* Illinois: University of Chicago Press, 1998. 1 – 4.

Mazrui, Alamin. "Language & the Quest for Liberation: The Legacy of Frantz Fanon". In Ali Mazrui and Alamin Mazrui. *The Power of Babel: Language and Governance in the African Experience,* Oxford and Chicago: James Currey and University of Chicago Press, 1998. 53 – 62.

McLoughlin, Laura, Marie Biscio and M. A. Mhainnin. *Audio-visual Translation Subtitles and Subtitling: Theory and Practice.* Frankfurt: Peter Lang, 2011.

McWhorter, John. *The Power of Babel: A Natural History of Language.* New York: HarperCollins, 2001.

Mesthrie, Rajend and Rakesh M. Bhatt. *World Englishes: The Study of New Linguistic Varieties.* Cambridge: Cambridge University Press, 2008.

Ngugi, wa Thiong'o. *Decolonising the Mind: the Politics of Language in African Literature.* Oxford: James Currey, 1986.

Ogunleye, Foluke (ed). *Africa through the Eye of the Video Camera.* Manzini, Swaziland: Academic Publisher, 2008.

Ondego, Ogova. "Kenya and Nollywood: A State of Dependence." In P. Barrot (ed). *Nollywood, the Video Phenomenon in Nigeria.* Oxford: James Currey and Bloomington: Indiana University Press, 2008. 114 – 117.

Oyewo, Gabriel. "The Yoruba Video Film: Cinematic Language and the Socio-Aesthetic Ideal." In Foluke Ogunleye (ed). Manzini, Swaziland: Academic Publisher, 2008. 141 – 157.

Ricard, Alain. *The Languages and Literatures of Africa: The Sands of Babel.* London: James Currey Publishers, 2004.

Threadgold, Terry. *Feminist Poetics: Poiesis, Performance, Histories,* London: Taylor and Francis, 1997.

Ugochukwu, Francoise. "Nollywood across Languages: Issues in Dubbing and Subtitling". http://imme.se/intercultural/nr33/ugochukwu.html accessed on 22 January, 2014.

CHAPTER TWO

Changing Nigerian Cultures: Two Films against Witchcraft and an Impossible Dialogue

Françoise Ugochukwu

Abstract

The prominent place of witchcraft in Nollywood films produced in the 1990s is widely acknowledged, and has prompted a number of comments from critics. While filmmakers' opinion is divided on the subject, these films obviously echo familiar situations. The dissemination of Nigerian films outside Africa and their entering new geographical and cultural areas, and the didactic nature of Nollywood, have led to a clash between Nigerian and British cultures in the bid to fight the widespread practice of witchcraft and its attendant casualties, which now affect both worlds. This paper reflects on the difficulty of intercultural communication on the subject, as illustrated by the recent controversy sparked by a British NGO's discovery of Nollywood in 2008. The film born out of this culture-shock presents a novel way of dealing with screen-mediated witchcraft and its impact.

Introduction

Today, Nigerian video films are part of the African cultural landscape, and their "characters, plots, and themes are now part of the everyday discourse of farmers, taxi drivers, market women, urban professionals, and native doctors" (McCall 92). The hugely popular success of Nollywood is mostly due to the fact that this production is

> Defined and sustained by Nigerians. The commercial success and popularity of Nigerian films stem from their stories, which the audience finds fascinating and consonant with their expectations. The thematic and aesthetic choices of Nollywood are determined to a large extent by the preferences of its audience, [...] subjects such as infidelity, treachery, lust, hypocrisy, armed robbery, marital problems, murder, cultism and occultism, witchcraft, polygamy [...]. The themes are indeed broad and mirror Nigerian society (Alamu 166).

One of the themes mentioned above, witchcraft, based on "the belief that the spirits of living human beings can be sent out of the body on errands of doing havoc to other persons in body, mind or estate" (Idowu 175, quoted in Awolalu 247), has challenged scholars' reflection. Filmmakers' opinion is divided on the subject, but, as one of them, Emem Isong, recognises in an interview with Okome (48): "I tried as much as possible to deviate from the normal Nigerian video films of magic, witchcraft and violence. The response from the audience tells me otherwise" (quoted in Ugor 20). Kumwenda (ii) agrees: "Whilst some scholars and filmmakers criticise the prevalence of themes of witchcraft, magic and the supernatural, it is these very themes that draw local audiences."

Yet, both in Nigeria and beyond, there are some who feel ill at ease with what they perceive as "too much witchcraft and black magic" (Onuzulike 29).[1] Some do not watch those films "because many a time they clash with [their] Christian beliefs" (Onuzulike 36). Others fear that those storylines may reinforce western stereotypes about Africa:

> Films of this type have painted an even more negative image of Nigeria than it already has, making it appear to be a nation bogged down by superstitions and primitive beliefs. Furthermore, traditional Igbo spirituality is demonised by people who have little knowledge or understanding of it, and who are spreading this misinformation to the entire world. Isn't it bad enough for the West to demonise every aspect of our traditions, and now we are doing it to ourselves? Does anyone seriously think that all our ancestors did was sit around performing so called satanic rituals all day? (Onyiiboy, 23/01/2008)[2].

The dissemination of Nigerian films outside Africa and their entering new geographical and cultural areas, and the didactic nature of Nollywood, have led to a clash between Nigerian and British cultures in the bid to fight the widespread practice of witchcraft and its attendant casualties, which affect both worlds. This paper reflects on the difficulty of intercultural communication on the subject, as illustrated by the recent controversy sparked by a British NGO's discovery of Nollywood in 2008. The film born of this culture-shock presents a novel way of dealing with screen-mediated witchcraft and its impact.

Nollywood's treatment of witchcraft

A cursory glance at four Nollywood films will give an idea of the various cinematic treatments of witchcraft, illustrating its definition as "a concealed practice of spiritual attack, torture, and misfortune against life in order to withhold progress of people or diminish success through misfortune on eating life out" (Iroegbu 201). Most video films only place this practice on the screen for all to see, forcing it into the open and punishing the culprits in a bid to trigger a public debate on it and possibly discourage the practice.[3] This is illustrated here by four examples:

- The Yoruba film *Alade Ikunkun* (Prince of Darkness, 1995) presents witchcraft as a skilled status passed on from one generation to the next through blood, and affecting children, presented as innocent victims: a lady doctor, who is also a practicing witch, sucks the blood of one of her patients' baby and so initiates the little girl into witchcraft. The girl grows to become a threat to her family but will eventually be delivered and converted.[4]
- In *Evil Men* (1998), where some male elders terrorise a village, holding the Chief's Council and local church to ransom in their bid to monopolise land and power, witchcraft is used separately by an uncle and an aunt to kill a newborn baby and cause miscarriage, in order to block the families' lineage and prevent their economic and social progress.
- In *Evil Seed* (2001), the witch is a grandfather, whose activities bring death to his family and community: a young bride dies and several boys are sacrificed. The old man's syncretism will be his doom: he dies suddenly after attending mass. In the end, the priest will succeed in breaking the curse affecting the family.
- In *Tears of Love* (2007), the witch is, again, a woman, who, out of jealousy, torments her brother's wife, causing her to suffer repeated miscarriages. The wife is then accused of being a witch herself, and persecuted.

From these and other films, "viewers get the impression that witchcraft is a prevalent practice in Nigeria" (Dipio, 2008: 61). One thing is sure: it had always been regarded as "social violence" (Iroegbu 201) and an abomination in the country because of its blood-drinking practice, as confirmed by Basden (418) who compared it with the same practice in England at the time:

> The Ibos have no love towards such people, especially in respect of witches ("amosu"), and used not to hesitate to ill-treat, drive away, or even kill them. This, of course, only tallies with the prevalent custom in England up to comparatively recent times, and the fear of witches is by no means extinct in parts of Europe to this day, and there is the same tendency to penalise the witch rather than the wizard.

Yet, in Nigeria and elsewhere on the African continent, such practices remain a thriving business, as "Christian converts have never made a clear-cut disconnection with their traditional cultural heritage. Even among the educated elite, the boundary between traditional religious practices and Christianity is rather fluid, characterised by crossovers according to convenience and expediency" (Dipio 2007: 78).

The grave consequences of this practice determined Christian filmmakers and directors to take the crusade against witchcraft a step further, not just placing it on the screen but using the screen as "a medium in which Africans generally, and Nigerians especially, can face their fears of witchcraft" (Kumwenda 47) and offering a solution. In an interview, Pastor Ukpabio explains her use of video films: "As ministers of God, we preach the gospel by different means… and we also discovered that this video film is a new thing in Nigeria and a lot of people are watching" (Kumwenda 61). Mike Bamiloye "contends that most Nigerian films teach the society how to become witches and wizards apart from other vices. This conviction led him to design his films to fight what he regards as 'pollutants to the society' "(Ogunleye 2003: 109).[5]

The same treatment of the theme has been adopted in a number of other films where "Christianity is presented as the panacea to all the social problems experimented in the narrative, and evil […] completely destroyed" (Dipio 2007: 73-76). *Cassandra* (2000) stages a romance between a rich girl and a poor boy, John. One of Cassandra's university colleagues tries to separate the two by inflicting a deadly and incurable disease on Cassandra through the use of witchcraft. Then, John is accidentally knocked down by a car driven by a pastor, who will lead both John and Cassandra to full recovery. The film ends with the witch's death and the lovers' wedding. In *A Cry for Help* (2001), the main character, an orphan girl, suffers continuous hardship at the hands of her aunt who had previously used witchcraft to kill the girl's parents. With the help of the pastor, the aunt's powers are destroyed "in the final showdown between the power of witchcraft and Jesus-Christ" (Dipio 2007: 74). McCall (88) confirms that

> Some of these movies are backed by well-financed evangelical institutions, but many simply appeal to the widespread Christian values in southern Nigeria. In these videos, the plots inevitably lead to the same Christian dénouement. An evangelist enters to exorcise the demons, whether of capitalist greed, traditional paganism, or, frequently, some noxious mixture of both. Whatever complex and cruel fate befalls the protagonists, in the end all is remedied by repetition of the phrase "In the name of Jesus!"

The End of the Wicked

One of these films is *The End of the Wicked*, directed and produced in 1999 by Teco Benson, and distributed by a Nigerian pastor from Akwa Ibom State of Nigeria, Helen Ukpabio. Kumwenda (47), who devoted some two chapters (pp.55-81) of her master's dissertation to an in-depth study of the film, rightly summarises it as a battle between good and evil:

> The story of the film centres on the Amadi family. Chris Amadi, husband to Stella and father of their two children, lives in an urban area in Nigeria. The family lives with Chris's mother who, unknown to any member of the family, is a witch who belongs to a coven. [...] The children are influenced to join the cult. [...] The story ends with witchcraft exposed, destroyed and put to shame. The pastor and Stella triumph with their religion and beliefs. The ending of the narrative positions Christianity as morally superior, better and capable of destroying all sources of witchcraft. [...] The exposition merely achieves to portray the exposed witchcraft in *End of the Wicked* as being evil whilst Christianity is being the answer to all the misfortunes that may be caused by witchcraft (65-69).[6]

This comprehensive reading of the film brings to the fore the mother-in-law's criminal witchcraft and reveals children as passive victims lured into the coven through shared snacks. They will be initiated and used as hypnotised, programmed agents.

For Okome, who interviewed Ukpabio on several occasions, "*The End of the Wicked* is [...] a gripping story of the coven of witches, blood-sucking and flesh-eating vampires. [...] Chris Amadi, husband and father, now oversees a home torn apart by the forces of darkness. It is not clear how his worries began. It is not obvious either why the coven of witches is after him but the aim is to destroy all that [he] has achieved in life" (2004: 9). The film, centred around "the diabolical image of the mother as the witch of the family" (11), shows the mother-in-law and sole real culprit coaxing her son to consult a native doctor to try and solve his domestic problems, after successfully turning him away from his wife and causing him to lose his job. Okome examines this episode of the film in detail, highlighting the native doctor's potency and revered status in the local traditional society. The pastor arrives at the end and "meets Chris at that point of ultimate distress, when everything about the medicine man has failed" (11).

A third source, coming from a film review website, confirms the two readings above. For the reviewer, *End of the Wicked* shows "a firm moral compass and a distinctive West African vision of the occult":

> The story focuses on acolyte Lady Destroyer's machinations to wipe out her son's happiness. [...] The coven assembles in a wooden grove of some sort around Beelzebub's wooden throne and various pots and bubbling cauldrons. The look of the witches themselves has parallels with the crones of European folklore, as they range from scraggily crones with dirt smeared faces to fresh initiates who look normal.
>
> With the focus upon harvesting blood for the coven, two instances of blood-letting stick out mainly for linking it to the menstrual cycle. In both, female characters awake from nightmares with bloody groins. Lady Destroyer rapes her own daughter-in-law with a mystical phallus she has grown in one sequence, and steals the womb of her daughter in the other. As a further cruelty, the stolen womb is then hung from a tree at the coven as a trophy of their wickedness. Organ stealing also happens elsewhere in one of the sub-plots where a man's eyes are stolen by the coven and the man awakes to find himself still in possession of his eyes but inexplicably blind.
>
> Unlike many other Nollywood films, *End of the Wicked* tackles witchcraft head on, in the usual popular morality tale framework. The extra blend in the mix being the introduction of Christianity as an alternative cure: a stark contrast to the casual inclusion of the occult in many other films likely caused by the religious backing of the film. [...] Its violence is akin to that of a morality play. Here blood is split and a reason however tenuous is given for it. The effect is disarmingly unsettling.[7]

Crossed wires in-between cultures

After years, and with the film now practically out of stock[8], the interest in its storyline was unexpectedly revived following a chance intercultural encounter. Foxcroft, a Briton, now the director of a UK-based NGO, 'Stepping Stones Nigeria' (SSN), explains what happened:

> SSN began in 2005 after I had spent three months in the Niger Delta researching community perceptions of the oil industry in 2003. I met and became friends with a local head teacher – Grace Udua – during this trip and she offered to donate her family land if I could help with building a school for disadvantaged children. It was first launched in Akwa Ibom State and is focused on the Niger Delta since there are a wide range of child rights abuses that take place in the region and very little interventions by government or other NGOs.

The NGO, trying to make sense of the child abuse reported as taking place in the region at the time, was made aware of allegations that "one of the primary contributory factors in the belief in child witches was the widely viewed Nollywood film – *End of the Wicked*."[9] This encounter opened a new chapter in the complex dialogue between Nollywood films and their audiences, projecting the 1999 Christian film on the international scene by proxy. A recent online commentary by Cussans (2011) on the film agrees with previous studies that it "was made specifically to promote evangelism, the Liberty Foundation Gospel Ministries church, headed by Pastor Helen Ukpabio, and to 'reach out' to the misguided." But, judging from his comments, Cussans seems not to have watched the same film: for him,

> Here, Ukpabio and director Teco Benson use the conventions of horror filmmaking […] to tell a moral story that warns against the evils of witchcraft, where children are the main perpetrators. Coincidentally or not, at the time of its release, the belief in child witches and wizards began to increase - particularly around the Niger Delta. The film, and films like it, have been seen by child protection organisations in Nigeria as fuelling beliefs in witchcraft that lead to ongoing child abuse.[10]

Having heard rumours that "many Nollywood films have capitalised on the belief in child witchcraft, with some depicting children eating human flesh and using their power to wreak havoc over communities", the British NGO came to believe that *The End of the Wicked* "had helped to spread the belief in child witches" (Beletre 2010).[11] This conviction soon reached a worldwide audience through the uploading of the November 2008 TV documentary reporting their trip to Nigeria, and prompted a militant response from groups bent on using the screen and the web to wage war on child abuse through the maligning of the Nollywood film believed to be at the root of it all.[12] The same November 2008, *FalseprophetNigeria*, a UK-based website hosted by *World News* (www.wn.com) and whose aim seemed to be that of denouncing deviant church leadership practices, uploaded a carefully crafted yet controversial 9'18" horror video, markedly different from the 51' original 1999 movie trailer and combining clips taken in disorder from various segments of *The End of the Wicked* part I (1999).[13] The video ended with the following text: "In religion, the term false prophet is a label given to a person who is viewed as illegitimately claiming (charismatic authority) within a religious group. The individual may be seen as one who falsely claims the gift of prophecy."[14] This video was introduced on the website itself with these words: "Religious nut Helen Ukpabio makes these films designed to brainwash people into believing that child witches exist. In truth she makes money off the back of child suffering caused by her video as preaching."[15] This short but incriminating introduction and the sequencing of the video were clearly part of a concerted attack on the prominent Nigerian pastor's ministry, hitherto unknown to *YouTube* viewers outside Nigeria, as Ukpabio's expository films, sold on VCDs and DVDs in her country, have never been freely available on the Web, for technical reasons.

The uploading of the video *The End of the Wicked* to a growing number of websites[16], and its express mention of Helen Ukpabio, provide a link between issues highlighted in the November 2008 "Saving Africa's Witch Children" *Channel 4* documentary prepared by SSN, international bodies like the Institute for Ethics & Emerging Technologies or the International Humanist and Ethical Union, and the Nigerian pastor and evangelist who, like many other pastors, had been making use of video films to support her ministry. This video alludes to the film with the same title considered above, produced in 1999 by Teco Benson and featuring Helen Ukpabio herself in a pastor's role. Yet, regrettably, the unauthorised use of the title from the 1999 film by the authors of the video is highly misleading, as the skipping of both the beginning and the end of the film and the focusing instead on the few scenes involving children, prevent viewers from getting the intended message. This doctoring of the original film radically changes its storyline and message: the elderly woman's role (the only criminal in the film) is totally occulted, with viewers made to see children as active witches instead of involuntary actors; the role of the pastor (played by Ukpabio) as an adviser restoring the family's peace in a non-threatening way is equally occulted. The viewing of the online video had an immediate impact: repeated verbal attacks on Ukpabio were indirectly encouraged by online postings and the launching of a petition against her in a bid to prevent her from holding crusades in Akwa Ibom and the United States, fearing that this might lead to more child abuse. These postings and petition in turn seem to have led to the closure of Ukpabio's personal website, www.helen-ukpabio.com.

The 1999 film explained

On September 1, 2009, *Onlinenigeria.com* published a long interview with Helen Ukpabio, conducted by its assistant editor, Emmanuel Uffot, and triggered by the fact that, "ever since the documentary on how children branded witches by pastors in Akwa Ibom are maltreated, the evangelist has been at the centre of the storm, following allegation that her movies encourage the stigmatisation of witches."[17] Early in the interview, Ukpabio, confronted with the comment that "there are lots of write-ups posted on the Internet saying your film, 'End of the Wicked' promoted the branding of children as witches in Akwa Ibom State", expressed her dismay at the sudden accusations against her film after nearly ten years of silence, accusations which, with hindsight, might have been explained by *Falseprophetnigeria/YouTube's* uploading of the incriminating video mentioned above and its borrowed title, coupled with the fact that, in the absence of any uploading of the film itself, viewers might have readily accepted that this video was the original trailer of *The End of the Wicked* suddenly out online.[18] For Ukpabio,

> It is surprising that nine years after, somebody is having a problem with a film that has delivered a lot of families. The storyline of *End of the Wicked* has nothing to do with children. [...] I didn't see the people that the film branded witches. Rather, we saw children who were greedy and were contaminated by other children who were witches in the school.

> That is what the film did. […] I don't see anything in *End of the Wicked* that brands a child a witch.

She insisted: "I am not in support of the torture of witches, whether adult or children. I don't subscribe to that. I have well over 10,000 children in my ministry and they are being handled the way children should be. I have done a film called *Child Rescue* in 2001. […] In the film, I said if you have any problem and are tortured anywhere, call me or come to this address. I put the address there at the end of the film." She then went further and accused the leader of the Child Rights and Rehabilitation Network (CRARN), at that time SSN's main partner on the ground[19], of turning the orphanage they were running into a refuge for children accused of witchcraft – "suddenly, because the UK government voted so much money to fight child abuse over the problem that the Congolese government had with children, he decided to tap into it."[20] She denied receiving money for her deliverance sessions, complained about her life being now in danger because of the British documentary, and advised not to treat genuine and counterfeit coins alike. Ukpabio sued SSN for defamation, accusing the organisation of misrepresenting her ministry. In March 2011, the *News magazine* ran a feature on Foxcroft, accusing him and his colleagues of being scam artists exploiting a relatively minor phenomenon to raise funds and fleece donors. Foxcroft later commented: "It is clear that our work with so-called child witches in Nigeria has upset many powerful people who would prefer that this issue had never been brought to the attention of the International community. Such people, some of them who have made a great deal of money from spreading the mythical belief in child witches, will often use everything in their power to protect their interests".[21]

Joining forces against witchcraft

SSN then decided to further explore the use of films in the fight against child abuse. As its director said at the time, "the £200,000 that we received in donations has given us the opportunity to further expand the facilities at the CRARN children's centre, establish another street children project in Oron […] and produce a Nollywood film for distribution throughout Africa that strongly challenges the belief in child witches" (Foxcroft 2009).[22] Persuaded of the influential role played by

Church leaders in a country known to be deeply religious, Foxcroft contacted the renown Nigerian film maker Teco Benson, the same who directed and produced Ukpabio's 1999 *End of the Wicked*, and together they produced a typical Nollywood film, *The Fake Prophet*, intended to carry the message on child protection to every home and church in Nigeria and throughout the Nigerian Diaspora.

> The film was made after we came to the realisation that one of the primary contributory factors in the belief in child witches was the widely viewed Nollywood film – *End of the Wicked.* We therefore thought that we could make a similar film but with an entirely different message to reach out to community members that we may not be able to reach with other advocacy tools. We contacted Teco via *Facebook* and asked if he would be willing to work with us to develop the concept. We then worked closely with him to draft the storyline. The main content was provided by me and a scriptwriter then put this into a draft script, which was then edited by me and Nigerian partners over a period of time.[23]

A crucial point made by Foxcroft, and which distinguishes *The Fake Prophet* from most of Nollywood films, is the close-knit cooperation between the British charity and the film director in the building of the storyline, with a clear and definite target and adequate facilities. In addition, and again unusually, the film was scripted and then tested on a carefully selected group of viewers. [24]

The SSN director acknowledged that "there have been a number of challenges. These mainly relate to some people seeing the film as being anti-Christian, which we do not feel it is. Also the use of some Efik in the film has been seen by some as casting a slur on the Akwa Ibom community. This then led us to re-editing the film again in order to take much of this content out." The trailer, which features on *Falseprophetnigeria*, first presents "the UK-based child rights charity Stepping Stones Nigeria (SSN) who works with partner organisations to prevent the abuse of innocent children who have been stigmatized as witches", adding that "the film acts as a key component of the 'Prevent Abuse of Children Today' (PACT) campaign which SSN launched in 2006 in partnership with the Child Rights and Rehabilitation Network (CRARN). […] This film is aimed at all Nigerians but particularly those non-literate communities who are unable to access billboards and newspaper articles."

According to Cussans (2011), Teco Benson "joined forces with child protection charity Stepping Stones Nigeria […] and made *The Fake Prophet* that perhaps can be seen as […] an interesting homage to the belief in the power of film to change opinion. Benson considers this film, which aims to expose the truth about a widespread situation, as 'the first truly socially responsible Nollywood film.' "[25] *The Fake Prophet* was widely advertised and premiered in cinemas, on March 12, 2011 in New York, June 14, 2011 in Abuja (Nigeria) and June 24-25, 2011 in London – a huge success every time. Information on *The Fake Prophet* is now available on many websites; *Nollywood Gossip* for example features an interview, dated May 25, 2011, with the writer Nnorom Azuonye who considers that "by supporting this film, you will be supporting African cinema, making it possible for us to bring you more world class entertainment from Africa to the UK. Most importantly, you will be helping Stepping Stones Nigeria prevent the abuse and murder of children in Nigeria and elsewhere."[26]

The Fake Prophet

> Benson's two films follow the same Nollywood pattern, Socio-realist problems dramatised in a Manichean style where the good and the evil, the beautiful and the ugly, the true and the false are polarised with the intention to educate and entertain. Although there is a high degree of entertainment in these films, pleasure is never for its own sake; the moral lessons that are offered at the end of the narratives are always evident. The one who looks for entertainment in these films gets just as much as the one who looks for moral lessons. The films often end with a closure: almost always, the good characters are rewarded while the bad, irredeemable ones are punished. It is this clear characterisation driven by the desire to tell a story which can be followed without taxing the audience, that is partly responsible for the popularity of Nigerian cinema (Dipio 2007: 3).

Yet those two films are poles apart. Based on the premise that witchcraft did exist, *The End of the Wicked* (1999) treated the issue the traditional way and mostly from a family's viewpoint, showing how witchcraft silently wrecked both a family and an unsuspecting community, until prayer led to the witch's confession, leaving villagers in shock. *The Fake Prophet* (2010) on the other hand, while highlighting the havoc created by this traditional belief, turns the story upside down, with no description of witchcraft: all we witness is the sudden death of an elder and the ensuing public persecution of two pre-adolescents falsely accused of his death, with the self-proclaimed prophet being the only one to encourage villagers in their cruelty. As explained on the *Facebook* page of the film, "*The Fake Prophet* aims to […] expose the truth behind the so-called men and women of God who have made their wealth from branding children as witches, and highlight the legal consequences of child witch stigmatisation and abuse."[27] The text placed right at the beginning of the film clearly makes the point: "Each year, thousands of innocent children are abused and stigmatised as witches by so called men and women of God".

The storyline presents a man of dubious character involved in an international prostitution racket, who loses his 'job' after several botched 'operations'. Threatened by his boss and forced to leave Lagos, he is now faced with a question which will determine his next move: "how can I survive outside Lagos as an uneducated young man without any specific talent?" He moves back to his Akwa Ibom village to stay with his brother and, faced with imminent hunger, decides to open a church, seeing this as a business. Meanwhile, in that village, two young secondary school pupils (a boy and a girl) are being accused of active witchcraft following the girl's father death after a long illness with TB-like symptoms which defied all traditional remedies. At that time, the girl is taken to the fake prophet's church, which started growing through the systematic use of deception, and where she nearly gets raped by the 'man of God'.

The two children are eventually forced to leave their school and homes and fend for themselves on the street. The girl ends up falling in the hands of the prophet's former boss, who trafficks her to London for prostitution, while the boy gets imprisoned after stealing bread. While the fake prophet gets fat on people's money, a true pastor arrives on the scene and starts preaching against false prophets, providing the film with a welcome balanced viewpoint. He will turn out to be the instrument used to bring the fake prophet to book, with the support of the local population, fed up with being fleeced and deceived. The film ends on the reminder that things have now changed, with the passing the Child Rights bill into law allowing the successful prosecution of child abusers. The last screen, after dedicating the film to the memory of children who lost their lives through witchcraft-related abuse, invites audiences "to take action to stop the abuse of innocent children" by contacting www.makeapact.org.

The fight continues

The Fake Prophet got "a thumbs up" from reviewers.[28] At the time, its producer had great plans for the exploitation of the film, with its educational attempt "to change [its] audience behaviour for the sake of the community" (Sereda 206) in the tradition of Nollywood, and the jailing of the lead character meant as a deterrent to would-be abusers:

> I will not be satisfied with its impact until it has become a widely watched film in the Niger Delta region and there is still some way to go with this. Nollywood movies have immense moral power and huge potential to bring about positive change in the lives of vulnerable people. Unfortunately, many movies do not acknowledge this and seem to actively promote messages that do more harm than good [...].We will be distributing the movie for free throughout the region this year and will also be showing it at University campuses throughout Nigeria. We will then look to develop a training toolkit around it that can be used by community workers to help dispel the belief that children can be witches.

Unsurprisingly, since then, both films seem to have disappeared from radars. Meanwhile, for the ordinary Nigerian, not much seems to have changed:

> If Nollywood truly cared about showcasing Igbo culture instead of trying to disgrace it, they would include more movies that highlight the positive aspects of Igbo spirituality. [...] We should start taking Nollywood for what it is: pure fantasy. The Church is not 100% benevolent, and will certainly not solve all of your issues. Every problem does not have evil spirits behind it. The pastor is not always right, and will not always win. Traditional religion is a lot more than just witchcraft, juju and black magic. It is a deep part of our heritage that should at least be properly understood. People should stop letting their television sets be their textbook and go out and research things for themselves. If we continue to demonize our culture and traditions, we cannot be upset when others do the same (Onyiiboy, 23/01/2008).

Bibliography

Adesanya, A. From Film to Video, *Nigeria Video Film,* Ibadan: Kraft 1998.13-20.

Alamu, Olagoke. Narrative and style in Nigeria (Nollywood) films, *African Study Monographs*, 31(4), 2010. 163-171

Awolalu, J. Omosade & Dopamu, P. Adelumo. *West African Traditional Religion.* Ibadan: Onibonoje press and book industry, 1979. 310p.

Barrot, Pierre (ed). Nollywood. *The Video Phenomenon in Nigeria.* Oxford: James Currey, 2008. 147p. Translated by Lynn Taylor

Basden, George T. *Niger Ibos.* London: F. Cass. 1938 Reprint 1966, 456p.

Dipio, Dominica. Uganda viewership of Nigerian movies, in Foluke Ogunleye ed., *Africa through the Eye of the Video Camera.* Manzini (Swaziland): Academic Publisher, 2008, 52-73

Dipio, Dominica. Religion in Nigerian home video films, *Westminster Papers in Communication and Culture* 4(1), 2007. 65-82.

Harrison, David. Child-witches' of Nigeria seek refuge. *Telegraph.co.uk.* 2008, November 8.

Idowu, E.B., *African Traditional Religion,* London, SCM Press Ltd, 1973, 228p.

Iroegbu, Patrick E. *Healing Insanity: A Study of Igbo Medicine in Contemporary Nigeria.* Bloomington: XLibris, 2010. 558p.

Kumwenda, Grace. *The Portrayal of Witchcraft, Occults and Magic in Popular Nigerian Video Films.* Masters, University of Witwatersrand, Johannesburg, 2007. 109p.

Marti, Joseph. Witchcraft between tradition and modernity: the Ekong case in Equatorial Guinea, *The Scientific Journal of Humanistic Studies* 3(5), 2011. 11p.

McCall, John C. Madness, Money, and Movies: Watching a Nigerian Popular Video with the Guidance of a Native Doctor, *AfricaToday,* 2006. 79-94

Ogunleye, Foluke (ed). *Africa through the Eye of the Video Camera.* Manzini (Swaziland): Academic Publisher, 2008. 283p.

Ogunleye, Foluke. Christian Video Films in Nigeria: Dramatic Sermons through the Silver Screen, in Foluke Ogunleye (ed). *African Video Films today*, Manzini, Swaziland: Academic Publishers, 2003. 105-128

Ogunleye, Foluke (ed). *African Video Films today.* Manzini, Swaziland: Academic Publishers, 2003. 162p.

Okome, Onookome. Women, religion and the video film in Nigeria, *Film International* 7(1), 2004. 4-13

Okome, Onookome. Naming suffering and women in Nigeria video films: notes on the interview with Emem Isong, *Ndunode: Calabar Journal of Humanities* 3(1), 2000

Olayiwola, Abiodun. Nollywood at the Borders of History: Yoruba Travelling Theatre and Video Film Development in Nigeria, *The Journal of Pan African Studies* 4(5), 2011. 183-195

Ondego, Ogova. Kenya and Nollywood: a state of dependence, in P. Barrot (Ed), *Nollywood. The Video Phenomenon in Nigeria*, Oxford: James Currey, 2008. 114-117

Onuzulike, Uchenna. *Nollywood Video Film – Nigerian Movies as Indigenous Voice*, Saarbrűken: VDM Verlag, 2010. 126p.

Şaul, Mahir & Austen, Ralph A. (eds). *Viewing African Cinema in the Twenty-First Century – Art Films and the Nollywood Video Revolution.* Athens: Ohio University Press, 2010. 248p.

Sereda, Stefan. Curses, nightmares and realities. Cautionary pedagogy in FESPACO films and Igbo videos, in Mahir Şaul & Ralph A. Austen eds. (2010) *Viewing African Cinema in the Twenty-First Century – Art Films and the Nollywood Video Revolution*, Athens: Ohio University Press, 2010. 194-208

Ugor, Paul. Censorship and the content of Nigerian home video films, *Postcolonial text* 3(1), 2007.

Filmography (Main films)

The End of the Wicked (1999) part I & II
Director: Teco Benson
Producer: Teco Benson
Executive producer: Helen Ukpabio
Genre: Horror
Length: 2h47 (part I: 49:32mn; part II: 46:40mn)
Main actors: Charles Okafor, Hilda Dokubo, Ramsey Noah, Helen Ukpabio

The Fake Prophet (2010)
Director: Teco Benson
Producer: Gary Foxcroft
Genre: Drama

Length: 80mn
Main actors: Charles Okafor and Grace Amah

Notes

[1] Martin Mangenda, a Zambian, BBC interview, 2006

[2] http://www.naijaryders.com/forums/201667-traditional-igbo-religion-nollywood.html. The page is no longer available.

[3] Someone close to us once sent us a VHS of such a film to warn us about threats from home.

[4] Olayiwola (2011: 186) records Adesanya (1998)'s words of regret: "From the folkloric *Ajani Ogun*, the Yoruba film genre metamorphosed into the witchcraft-horror thriller introduced by Ogunde's *Aiye*, leading to a spate of witchcraft flicks that gave the Yoruba film genre a bad name."

[5] Quoted as coming from *Mount Zion Ministries* (Ile-Ife) website, http://www.mountzionfm.org, accessed 04/07/2016

[6] For the 0.51mn movie, see https://www.youtube.com/watch?v=VRivy uU151Y. Ukpabio was once a member of the Calabar-based Olumba Obu (O.O.O.) spiritual movement also known as the Brotherhood of the Cross and Star, and a practising witch, before she became a Christian (Okome 2004: 10). As often in such cases, her zeal in fighting witchcraft is fuelled by the inside knowledge she got on the subject.

[7] http://www.sneersnipe.co.uk/review_title.php?id=454. The page is no longer available.

[8] Producers do not seem to keep the originals of their films, and after a few years, it is usually impossible to get hold of any film or order copies. Copies of the film are now only available through the Liberty Foundation Gospel Ministries church.

[9] G. Foxcroft (2012), personal online interview, January 16, 2012. According to David Harrison (2008), "Gary Foxcroft, 29, programme

director for the UK charity Stepping Stones, Nigeria, first came to the country in 2003 to research the oil industry for his master's degree. But he was so shocked when he learned about the children's plight that he decided to help raise money for the refuge - the Child Rights and Rehabilitation Network (CRARN) - and try to persuade the parents to take their children back. He has also helped to build a school for the children who are refused places at local schools" (Telegraph, November 8, 2008).

[10] Comment on the advert for "Nollywood Free School at The Speaker Palace [Hackney, London] on Tuesday 1st March" posted on 23/02/2011 on http://freefreeschool.wordpress.com/2011/02/23/ nollywood-free-school-march-1st/ (page no longer available). The Kenyan scriptwriter Jane Mbiti had made a similar remark: according to her, "hitherto well-educated, progressive Christians no longer frown on notions of consulting witchdoctors, mediums or medicine men as was the case before the appearance of Nigerian videos in Kenya" (Ondego 2008: 116).

[11] http://www.balancingact-africa.com/news/broadcast/issue-no82/ content/nigeria-stepping-sto/bc, accessed 04/07/2016

[12] These attacks equally targeted the Christian ministry marketing the film, in a bid, no doubt, to block the sales.

[13] Part I of the 1999 film can be divided into 25 sequences. The video used segments 1 (title page), 10-12, 14-15, 19, 21, 25, 9 and the last screen shot of 22, thereby recomposing a storyline with the children sub-plot as main plot, evacuating the main story in its entirety and planting children as culprits in incidents which did not involve them.

[14] http://wn.com/false_prophet_nigeria. The same website featured a video presenting Leonardo Rocha dos Santos from UK, at that time a volunteer with CRARN (the Child Rights and Rehabilitation Network) and Stepping Stones Nigeria and a co-founder of the Brazilian NGO Ways to the Nations, talking about his work rescuing witch children in Nigeria and showing a booklet produced to correct false doctrines which led to child abuse (uploaded May 28, 2011). The page is no longer available.

[15] That same video was uploaded on http://www.youtube.com/user/FalsePropheTNigeria/feed (accessed 04/07/2016) and has since been posted on a number of other websites, resulting in its being accessed 100,737 times in three years (nearly 3,000/month), with the number of viewers growing by the day.

[16] http://ieet.org/index.php/IEET/more/helenukpabio20120212 (Institute for Ethics & Emerging Technologies 12/02/2012) accessed 04 /07/2016; http://videosift.com/video/Children-Killed-or-Abandoned-due-to-Film-End-of-the-Wicked accessed_4/07/2016;_http://www.veoh.com/watch/v166117854yQscr6k?rank=0&jsonParams=%7b%2522numResults%2522%253A20%252C%2522rlmin%2522%253A0%252C%2522query%2522%253A%2522end+of+the+wicked%2522%252C%2522rlmax%2522%253Anull%252C%2522veohOnly%2522%253Atrue%252C%2522order%2522%253A%2522default%2522%252C%2522range%2522%253A%2522a%2522%252C%2522sId%2522%253A%2522181158818257203647%2522%7d&searchId=181158818257203647&rank=1,accessed 04/07/2016. In addition, articles on the same have been posted on the website of the International Humanist and Ethical Union (http://www.iheu.org/node/2856, 23/11/2007, no longer available), that of the Institute for Ethics & Emerging Technologies (http://ieet.org/index.php/IEET/more/igwe20120212, 12/02/2012, accessed 04/07/2016) and on a parallel Wikipedia site (http://en.wikipedia.org/wiki/Helen_Ukpabio) supported by WikiProjectNigeria, last modified on 06/03/2012 and last accessed 04/07/2016.

[17] http://onlinenigeria.com/member/content.asp?contentid=1836, accessed 04/07/2016

[18] Cf. "The Hullabaloo About Child Witches" published in This Day Nigeria 7 May 2009, Lagos — "Following reports that children branded witches in Akwa Ibom were being maltreated, a couple of foreign TV stations ran a documentary which was allegedly named, styled and culled from a film made by a local foundation titled 'End of the Wicked'. The body claims the documentary has brought woes to the organisation." http://allafrica.com/stories/200905080092.html (This page is no longer available).

[19] Following a serious incident, SSN ended its five-year old collaboration with CRARN on February 18, January 2011.

[20] http://onlinenigeria.com/member/content.asp?contentid=1836, accessed 04/07/2016

[21] http://barthsnotes.com/2010/03/12/nigerian-journalist-backs-helen-ukpabio-with-attack-on-charity-protecting-children-accused-of-witchcraft/ accessed 04/07/2016

[22] http://www.channel4.com/programmes/dispatches/articles/return-to-africas-witch-children-stepping-stones (This page is no longer available).

[23] G. Foxcroft (2012), personal online interview, January 16, 2012.

[24] Most Nollywood films so far have been produced based on a loose storyline and rely heavily on actors' creativity.

[25] http://freefreeschool.wordpress.com/2011/02/23/nollywood-free-school-march-1st, accessed in 04/07/2016

[26] http://www.nollywoodgossip.net/2011/05/25/nigerian-writer-talks-fake-prophet-and-more-with-nollywoodgossip/ (this page is no longer available).

[27] https://es-la.facebook.com/africafilms.tv/posts/110596762320031, accessed 04/07/2016

[28] http://nollywoodforever.com/the-fake-prophet/ accessed 04/07/2016

CHAPTER THREE

Setting The Agenda for Women's Liberation and Empowerment in Nigeria through Movies: An Analysis of *Women's Cot*, *Women in Power* and *The Bank Manager*

Aje-Ori Agbese

Abstract

In September 2008, the United Nations' Secretary-General, Ban Ki Moon, addressed the organisation on the progress of the Millennium Development Goals regarding women's issues. In his address, he said: "The gender gaps remain considerable and the full potential of women is untapped" (5). This was not surprising, considering that various recent studies have shown an increase in the rate of domestic and gender-based violence (including honour killings, genital mutilation, trafficking and forced marriages), the victimisation of women and girls in conflicts, the lack of women in political and economic decision-making positions, and a refusal to consider women's reproductive rights, particularly in the area of abortion. One possible explanation for this increase might lie in media portrayals of women and women's issues. This study, therefore, investigates how the mass media present women issues. Specifically, the study examines how Nigerian video films have been setting the agenda for the 2015 UN goal of women's empowerment and gender equality through their definitions of women empowerment, gender equality and women's liberation. Agenda-setting scholars have argued for decades that the media can tell audiences what to think.

Introduction

In examining the relationship between mass media, women and society, scholars have argued for decades that media images of women are often negative and stereotypical. Even the 1995 Beijing Platform of Action recognised that "the lack of gender sensitivity in the media is evidenced by the failure to eliminate the gender-based stereotyping that can be found in the public and private, local, national and international media organisations" (Beijing Platform for Action, Section J, Women and the

Media, 1995). Issues of gender inequality are also narrowly constructed and presented in the media (Opoku-Mensah 2001). When these issues appeared, they "displayed ideological constructions" that "define women's understanding of their experiences in ways that guarantee the reproduction of patriarchal definitions of the social world" (Yunjuan & Xiaoming 282).

Additionally, media effect theories suggest that the mass media are not objective, stationary, facets of society. This is not to say, however, that they are the only institution responsible for creating such values about women. If anything, the media are capable of reinforcing the status quo, giving certain issues importance over others, distorting accounts and shaping people's notion of society and societal issues.

Contextualising Nollywood

Nigerian movies are called video films, or home videos, because they are traditionally shot directly on video (including digital) for home viewing (Larkin 2002). Known as Nollywood, the Nigerian video industry is the third largest in the world, following Bollywood (India) and Hollywood. Sold across the continent and beyond, these films "are one of the greatest explosions of popular culture the continent has ever seen" (Haynes 1) and have replaced television in many homes. Since mass media are cultural industries, Nigerian video films might be good sources for learning Nigerian cultural beliefs, values and attitudes regarding gender.

There are three reasons why this study is important from a Nigerian perspective, apart from the fact that women's empowerment and gender equality are part of the Millennium Development Goals (MDGs). One is that African women, "particularly at the grassroots level, are avid users of media despite a popular belief that they are too poor or busy with house chores" (Opoku-Mensah 26). Therefore, one can argue that the more women are exposed to these movies and their messages, the more likely they are to believe that what they see is what is expected of them. Jonathan Haynes also points out that Nigerian films are "oriented towards female viewers" (4) because the audience is predominantly female. However, very few screenplay writers, producers and directors of these movies are women.

A second reason for this study is that African communication and social change scholars have understudied the media aspects in the areas of empowerment and gender equality. With the spread of these movies across the continent and the rise in similar industries in other African nations, it is time to closely examine their contributions to nation-building. Lastly, it is important to understand the terms of women's empowerment and gender equality from a Nigerian perspective, because for decades, Nigerian women's rights advocates and foreign development agencies have advanced the participation of women as equal partners with men in achieving sustainable development, peace, security, and full respect for human rights. But can Nigerian women actively participate in development if they receive messages contrary to this goal, considering that African cultures are posited as being "hostile to women"? (Tamale 47) Understanding such definitions could also increase the success of programmes aimed at achieving the MDGs on women's empowerment and gender empowerment in Nigeria.

This paper will examine two questions: what is an empowered, liberated woman according to Nigerian video films? What is gender equality according to Nigerian video films? Guiding this study is the agenda-setting theory which posits that the media can tell people what and how to think of events and issues by the cues they deliver on such events and issues. Continuous coverage of such events and issues will put them on the political agenda, thereby influencing governmental policies (Wanta 1997). However, unlike previous agenda-setting studies that have focused on news events and issues and on the way news organisations and personnel select and present certain issues over others, this study applies this theory to film to learn how film can be used to build a public agenda and make societal issues politically relevant.

Considering that women's empowerment and gender equality are societal issues, one can presume that continuous and prominent media coverage of these issues could establish them as public priorities. Could filmmakers equally be considered as gatekeepers, since movies by popular producers and directors are newsworthy? If popular producers and directors make movies, one can assume that the news media would cover their work. Larosa and Wanta (1990), in their study on inter-media influence, found that, regardless of differences in size, audiences or influence, media agree on issues and events that appear on the media agenda, but present them differently to get different reactions from their audiences.

Movies on women's empowerment and gender equality could be seen as influential and timely, considering that UN member nations have them on their political and social agenda as part of the MDGs. Women's liberation, which is synonymous with the movement for equal rights, was added to the study because much of the literature and programmes in Nigeria never divorced women's empowerment and gender equality from women's liberation. In some cases, 'women's liberation' was used instead of 'equal rights'.

The Fight for Women's Empowerment and Gender Equality

Gender issues became one of the United Nations' top priorities following the Fourth World Conference on Women in Beijing in 1995 (Parliamentary Assembly 2005). More than one hundred countries promised to implement the Beijing Platform for Action, which required strong commitments from governments and international organisations and institutions to "advance the goals of equality, development, and peace for all women everywhere in the interest of humanity" (Nigeriafirst.org 2007, 1). The platform also asked signatory governments to recognise that "women's empowerment and their full participation on the basis of equality in all spheres of society, including participation in the decision-making process and access to power, are fundamental for the achievement of equality, development, and peace" (Nigeriafirst.org, 2007, 1). But how will these countries achieve these goals, considering that they might have different values, attitudes and beliefs about women, gender equality and empowerment?

Empowerment is generally defined as increasing the political, social or economic strength or capabilities of marginalised groups. However, definitions abound of empowerment, depending on whether the aim is empowering people on the basis of gender, politics, health, spirituality/religion, economics or social marginalisation. These definitions and perspectives make empowerment a touchy and conflict-ridden issue. For instance, "The phrase combines optimism with misgiving. It puts forth the claim that empowerment will bring about substantial benefits – but only as a claim, not as axiomatic truth" (Troutner & Smith 27).

One cannot also talk about empowerment without discussing power, its visibility and what it means – who holds it, who applies it, who loses it and who decides what struggles occur. Troutner and Smith (4) say that the concept of power "raises the question of empowerment, which can simply be defined as the process of accumulating power". Any empowerment programme or act presumes that some level of disadvantage and powerlessness exists. According to Nelson, Shanahan and Olivetti (228), "Empowerment begins with learning about one's own identity. This self-knowledge often leads to a concern for the empowerment of others and a commitment to promote change in society".

One is empowered when one can "solve problems, make decisions to be proactive, and have a sense of control, even in problematic situations" (Järvinen 174). For women, empowerment is defined as "the process of building a woman's capacity to be self-reliant and to develop her sense of inner strength" (Shefner-Rogers et al. 323). According to Nwaneri (40), "For a woman to be empowered, she has to be prepared for all forms of challenges; she has to know what she is actually struggling for". Women's empowerment symbolises "a more political and transformatory idea for struggles that challenges, not only patriarchy, but also the mediating structures of class, race, and ethnicity that determines the nature of women's position and condition in developing societies" (Batliwala 558). From an African perspective, empowerment is defined in the context of women having access and power in the areas of education, employment and politics, including decision-making positions at work (Longwe & Clarke 1999; Greig & Koopman 2004; Ravinder & Narayana 2006).

The emphasis here is on the act of putting women in charge of their own destiny, while recognising that if they want to be empowered, they can choose how they want this to happen. Of course, that begs the question of the standards that one must use to determine who is empowered and who is not. According to the United Nations Development Program (www.undp.org, 2010:1), women's empowerment, like gender equality, is a human right that "lies at the heart of development and the achievement of the Millennium Development Goals".

On the other hand, gender equality refers to "the right of women and men to have the same opportunities" to achieve "important goals in society, e.g. quality of life, education, employment and income" (Reddock 256). It is seen as a human right and a major goal of development because men and women need to actively participate in nation-building. Although gender and its roles are culturally and socially defined, signatory countries to the 1979 Convention on the Elimination of All Forms of Discrimination against Women (CEDAW) and to the 1995 Women's Conference in Beijing agreed that women had the short end of the stick because they were discriminated against in many ways. These countries agreed to find ways to not only empower women to participate in nation-building, but also create environments that would monitor, report and eliminate all forms of discrimination. To this end, gender equality is measured with indices like the Gender Equity Index and Gender Gap Index, which examine how well opportunities and resources are divided between men and women.

This is done by checking the progress or regression of nations at four levels – economy, education, empowerment, health and survival (Dijkstra 2006; www.choike.org; www.wefoum.org). But recent studies show that women and girls are still discriminated against in many ways, and "the most pervasive and persistent forms of inequality" include "gender-based violence, economic discrimination, reproductive health inequities, and harmful traditional practices," which remain the most pervasive and persistent form of inequality (UNFPA 1).

One reason for this, according to The International Centre for Research on Women (2005:1), is that "gender inequality is deeply rooted in entrenched attitudes, societal institutions and market forces that vary from community to community". Another reason could be the messages people receive concerning women and women's issues. What messages, therefore, are people receiving in their communities regarding the place and importance of women? One possible place to look for answers is in a country's mass media.

Women and the Mass Media

Mass communication scholars like Marshall McLuhan, Roger Everett and Daniel Lerner have argued since the 1950s that mass media are a powerful tool for national development and social change. This is because "Mass media are key components in any nation's culture" that are "so pervasive and touch so many people" (Ogan 294). Filmmaker David Putnam (1) also adds that "Stories and images are among the principal means by which societies transmit their values and beliefs from generation to generation, and [from] community to community". Furthermore, "How empowering messages are communicated, such as in a dialogic, rather than one-way, style, can itself be an empowering influence" (Shefner-Rogers & al. 1998).

However, the media have been criticised for stereotyping women as sexual objects, passive, evil and submissive, and underrepresenting them

(Yunjuan & Xiaoming 2007) in several countries. In the United States for instance, studies show that the media still perpetuate unhealthy and unrealistic images of women. Giffard, Cunningham and Van Leuven (2006) found in their study that the way the media frames women and women's issues help set the agenda for public discussion on the MDGs. One thing is sure: "Media have been defining power, whether we like it or not" (Fröhlich 161). The media are thus hypothesised to fulfil the structural needs of a patriarchal and capitalist society by reinforcing gender differences and inequalities (Yunjuan & Xiaoming 282). Take the medium of film for instance, which, according to Adenugba Olushola (2008), plays a vital role in social mobilisation and information. Owing to their ability to hold an audience captive, films are used more than any other means of mass communication to promote ideas of positive social transformation as well as to consolidate and build new relationships between culture and national development (2).

As Norma Iglesias (225) puts it, "Cinema creates and disseminates important symbols that we use to shape representations." However, film is a "gendered technology," controlled by men who equally control other mass media or technology. Though women are actors, they are more or less excluded from the ownership and production arenas (Iglesias 225). Many movie industries still perpetuate stereotypical images of women. From 1993 to 2003, women directed only 3% of the top 50 movies in Europe (ERICarts 2005). Byerly (226) explains that "women's marginalisation and stereotyping" in film is "the result of a patriarchal media system that has manifested male biases in neglecting and undervaluing women's experiences, meanings, ongoing daily contributions, and imagery".

But one must not conclude that women have not made any gains in the film industry. For example, Mexican women have produced films that challenge traditional notions, images and identities of women (Iglesias 2004). Organisations like 'Women in Film' actively support and promote the contributions of women in the film industry, with the purpose of empowering them. Its members' works have won awards and critical acclaim in several arenas. "Women's access to media and ICT is obviously crucial for their personal empowerment" (Steeves 192). Therefore, the image of women in film has changed over time. But Steeves (2007) warns that though women are present, content has not changed much. Also, regardless of the culture, media portrayals of women are "related to the broad socio-economic, political and cultural context of a society" (Yunjuan & Xiaoming 282). Therefore, significant studies on how films portray women must be "based on specific social, economic, political, and cultural conditions of a given country within a particular period of time" (Yunjuan & Xiaoming 282). Let us examine this issue in the Nigerian context.

The Nigerian Case

Nigeria, located in West Africa, is the most populous country on the continent. Women make up about 50 percent of its 140 million people. Men make up 30 percent, while children make up the remaining 20 percent (Onyedika, 2009). Women's liberation, empowerment and gender equality became a major part of Nigerian life following the Women's Conference in Beijing in 1995. Prior to that, Maryam Babangida, the nation's first lady from 1985 to 1993, created a Better Life for Rural Women Programme to address the issues of women's "unappreciated" and "marginal position" in the country (Babangida 1). The goal of the programme was to "empower rural women socially, economically and politically through adult education and training in the fields of education, agriculture, public health, arts and crafts, and food processing" (Nwonwu 1).

A National Commission for Women was created to oversee the programme, which later became the Ministry of Women's Affairs and Social Development under General Sani Abacha in 1997 to further "confer institutional recognition on the contribution of women to national development" (Mama 12). Since Babangida, other Nigerian first ladies have undertaken programmes geared directly towards women and such efforts have sparked feminism, which in this study refers to "the awareness of women's oppression in the society, within the family, the economy, the law, at work and elsewhere, and to the struggle by women and men to change the situation for a just and fairer society" (Adamu 3). Nigerian women today are more visibly recognised in the economic, educational and political spheres, but still fight patriarchy instituted through religion and tradition.

Many are also still disadvantaged by poverty (including the lack of ownership of the means of production), harmful traditional practices (genital mutilation, violence, inheritance and widowhood customs), religion, customary laws and illiteracy (Okunna 2002; Para-Mallam 2006). Some women have created non-governmental organisations at the grassroots, national and international levels to address these issues, which deal directly with empowerment and gender equality, and they have been effective in some areas. But what is really holding women back? Could it be the messages they are getting from the Nigerian mass media, which "men produce an overwhelming majority of" (Okunna 7)?

Nollywood – The Rebirth of Nigerian Cinema

The Nigerian movie industry, popularly called Nollywood, was resurrected in 1992 when Kenneth Nnebue produced *Living in Bondage* to sell a stock of blank video cassettes (Ebewo 2007). His company, NEK Videos, sold about 750,000 copies of the movie: this marked the beginning of a $200 million-$300 million industry that produces about 1,000 movies annually (Hays 2005). Prior to this, the Nigerian movie industry was almost dead. In the 1980s, soap operas and made-for-TV movies dominated the Nigerian television screen. In the late 1980s, a few film producers then turned to video production to stay in the movie business. However, they had limited funds and very small audiences. Nnebue's success provided an alternative. Moreover,

> with the global world united under the sway of visual culture, the emergence of the video film in Nigeria is timely and crucial as it serves as the voice of its people and responds to the drudgery of a socio-economic existence characterised by high unemployment and dwindling opportunities. It has taken all on board, including religious-minded people (Ebewo 47).

Nollywood movies differ from Hollywood movies, largely in terms of production and distribution. The movies are shot using video technology (including high-definition video technology) and shooting can take ten to fourteen days to complete on a $15,000 to $24,000 budget (Osifo-Dawodu 2007). The movies are commonly produced in multiple parts. It is not unusual to find a movie with four parts, most times under a different title. Movies are also re-released under different titles. More than 65 percent of them are produced in English and the rest in indigenous languages including Hausa, Yoruba, Tiv, Idoma, Bini and Pidgin English with English subtitles. Some of them have French subtitles to reach the Francophone audience. The industry's major sources of funding include marketers, individuals, non-governmental organisations and corporations.

In terms of distribution, television is the major channel for Nollywood. The movies come in video-cassettes, video CDs (VCD) and DVDs, which are intended for home use (hence its other name, home videos) for about $1 or less. There are many ways to watch the movies without buying them directly. State and private television stations in Ghana, Kenya, Cameroon and Uganda feature the movies on their programming schedules (Osei-Hwere & Osei-Hwere 2008). In the United States, Ireland and the United Kingdom, Nollywood channels are available through Dish Network and Sky, as well as through The African Channel, a video-on-demand channel. Some flights to Africa also feature Nollywood movies, and they are free through YouTube and sites like onlinenigeria.com and africanseer.com.

The movies are so popular that they have driven foreign films off the shelves in Nigeria (Ozele 2008). Ebewo (2007) explains that Nollywood movies are very popular because "they have indigenous content and address issues relevant to the audience" (47). As one critic observes, "In spite of the ethnic differences, there are core values that transcend ethnic and regional boundaries. These include religiosity, extended family, tradition and rituals, community, respect for elders and veneration of ancestors" (Ozele 14). The movies also feature the cultural hybridity of modern (Western) and traditional (African) cultures in Nigeria, as well as the resulting tensions between old and new, extending their appeal to an international audience. But filmmakers estimate that despite its success, the industry loses at least $20 million annually to piracy, duplication and online streams (Osifo-Dawodu 2007).

In terms of storylines, Nollywood tells melodramatic stories. According to Abah, "Melodrama is a powerfully conservative social artefact" that draws its audience "into both the prescriptions and the proscriptions of mainstream cultural values" (338). Another critic observes that "Nollywood films tend to be full of moralising messages, cautionary tales in which citizens are handed dire warnings about the perilous consequences of infidelity, crime and greed," a common trend in melodrama (Hays 2). Melodrama is a genre with local and international appeal (Haynes 2000; Casas-Perez 2005; Martin-Barbero 2006). The common themes deal with social and cultural issues, including religion, corruption, women's rights, materialism, culture, immigration, AIDS, marriage, unemployment, and gender roles. In its depiction of women, however, Nollywood is heavily criticised.

The Image of Women in Nollywood

According to Haynes (2007), Nollywood films are "oriented towards female viewers" because the audience is predominantly female. However, women account for less than one percent of producers, directors and writers. Abah (2008) observes that though Nollywood movies "celebrate African women of all shades, shapes, and sizes," and portray women in "varying professional roles" from wives and CEOs to prostitutes, many videos still show a stereotyped image of women (339).

An ideal woman is depicted as married, with children, and submissive. Women are considered as dangerous when they are "economically, socially, or politically independent" (Abah 339). Movies like *Unchained*, which deals with the political empowerment of women, thematically cast women in the "culture-bound definition of domestic roles for women" (Abah 353). Women who act outside expected and culturally defined gender roles are generally depicted as bad and doomed. In *Power Tussle*, a rich and single woman is portrayed as bad. She becomes good only after a male servant beats her daily into submission. In other movies like *Girls' Cot*, *Aristos*, *Be My Val*, *Sleep Walker I – IV*, *Fishers of Men*, *Koko Babes* and *Runs*, the Nigerian woman's "only asset is her sexuality" (Ozele 20). She is someone whom her fellow women cannot trust, and is frequently punished for doing the same things men are rewarded for.

This image of women as portrayed in Nigerian home video films is the same across the country, though with varying intensity, the only difference being that the rituals and murders which occur in Southern films do not yet appear in Northern movies. Still, women in the Northern films are not portrayed as any better; they are seen as greedy, fickle-minded, weak, unable to make their own marital decisions and available for purchase by the highest bidder (Anyanwu 84 – 85).

For instance, Chinyere Okunna (1996) finds Igbo movies' portrayals of women as "unrealistic," "counterproductive and damaging to the cause of women" (34). Furthermore, she argues that the movies could "lead to the subjugation of women because they can increase men's disdain for women, sow mistrust between women, undermine their confidence in themselves and strengthen the forces which push women to the background in this patriarchal society" (Okunna 34). She also finds that though none of the participants in her study knew women like these characters, many believe the depictions to be accurate. It appears "Nigerian movies perpetuate sex role stereotypes and reflect the patriarchal social values dominant in Nigerian society" (Ebewo 49). "The general impression is that women are negatively portrayed" to appeal to men (Ebewo 48). Unfortunately, there seems to be little or no studies on the audience to challenge that impression.

Ozele (2008) also criticises Nollywood's image of women, saying that "the industry has still to critically address fundamental issues of gender equality and equity, violations of women's rights, traditional stereotypes of females, and the struggles of female children for equal educational opportunities" (20). He adds that

> Such uncomplimentary depiction of the *'Africanness'* in women undermines the lofty virtues of the African woman, especially in other spheres of life. The influence of these negative portrayals on adolescent minds who view movie actors as their heroes could only be left to the imagination (20).

Methodology

To answer the research questions, I looked for Nigerian movies produced from 2000 onwards where women's empowerment, liberation and gender equality are the central themes. At first, I used the descriptions on the back covers to select a sample. Unfortunately, the descriptions on the back covers were inaccurate, as I discovered after watching ten movies that featured women stereotypically as suggested by previous research. Though seven movies carried important messages, they did not fit the criterion for this study and were excluded. These movies largely fit the city girl genre, which depicts women as prostitutes and gold-diggers. A future study would widen the criteria to include movies on women in general.

Though most movies did not have the desired concepts as themes, they carried powerful stereotypes of women that could influence women's understanding of empowerment and gender rights. Only three movies (which, technically, count as six as two had multiple parts) are centred on women's empowerment, liberation and gender equality. I had hoped to find more movies using these themes, because Nigerian women are committed to meeting the Millennium Development Goals (MDGs). While watching the movies, I categorised the portrayals of these issues according to the themes revealed by the data, since I could not replicate them from previous studies. Definitions and descriptions were then analysed and interpreted to describe and discuss the values women will imbibe about empowerment and gender equality from these movies and cultivate. The movies I used are *Women's Cot* (Parts 1, 2 and 3), *Women in Power* (Parts 1 and 2) and *The Bank Manager*. Each movie was at least 80 minutes long.

Women's Cot deals with an important issue facing women in Nigeria – widowhood. Many women are disenfranchised by customs and tradition when their husbands die, as in-laws seize whatever property exists (regardless of who owns what). In some cases, the relatives do not consider the children, especially if they are young or female, as beneficiaries. In other cases, relatives are allowed to inherit the widows. In one scene, we learn from a local king that women cannot inherit property because "widowhood and posterity do not sleep together. ...inheritance issues are never discussed in the kitchen."

Produced in 2005 and directed by Dickson Iroegbu, *Women's Cot* tells the story of two widows, Adamma and Joyce, and their efforts to fight the unfortunate plight of widows in Nigeria through the Widows' Cot organisation. Using their own experiences, they decide to "liberate" other widows facing the traditional predicaments of widowhood. The movie is full of messages, especially from Igbo culture, on the plight of widows.

Women in Power is about four women – Lois, Agatha, Stella and Maureen – who attended a women's conference in Canada. They belong to the Career Women's Forum, a non-governmental organisation that addresses issues facing women in Nigeria. Maureen, Lois and Agatha are married, with successful careers and successful husbands. Stella is a single "independent woman" with a very successful career as a personnel manager. Directed and produced by Adim C. Williams and released in 2005, this film, more than the others, directly addresses the issues of empowerment, liberation and gender equality. In the movie, we see that, although these women belong to the same organisation and attend the same conference, they return with different interpretations of women's empowerment and gender equality.

In *The Bank Manager*, also produced in 2005 but directed by Ugo Ugbor, we meet Nneka, a well-educated and career-driven woman with a PhD in banking and finance. She is the mother of two children, a boy and a girl, and is married to a very successful businessman, Evans. In the movie, she is so busy with work that she neglects her responsibilities as a mother and wife, with dire consequences.

Findings

To answer the first question - what is an empowered, liberated woman according to Nigerian films, I found that the various definitions offered by the films come with both negative and positive connotations, as can be seen in the characters' success and difficulties. These show what happens to women who act contrary to expectations as women, mothers and wives in Nigeria. Male characters, on the other hand, are not portrayed as being against women's empowerment, liberation or gender equality.

An Empowered and Liberated Woman is Free from Men

In all these movies, empowered and liberated women are portrayed as being free from male domination and independent. However, this definition carries negative connotations for women, as those who illustrate this definition believe that men control women through marriage and relationships. Therefore, they choose to have no husbands, and if there are men in their lives, including sons, they are aggressive towards them. These women are in charge of their relationships and rule with an iron fist. Men are unavoidable necessities, only good for sex, making babies and getting material commodities.

In *Women's Cot*, for example, Adamma tells Joyce, "Freedom from men is the preoccupation of womanhood." The movie's theme song also says a woman has "lots of freedom when she is nobody's wife." The movie also takes a very unusual turn when a powerful woman, Eze Nwanyi, tells Adamma that she must encourage women to be free from men. The way to do this? Kill your husband. Adamma then begins a crusade, attracting women into the organisation through materialism – expensive cars, monetary gifts, power and expensive clothes. Seduced by wealth, several women actually end up killing their husbands to join what later becomes the "Women's Cult."

In *Women in Power*, Stella and Lois also illustrate this definition. Stella believes that getting married would stop her from attaining the "corporate target" she sets for herself. Moreover, she is "an independent woman who functioned better as a single lady." On her part, Lois sees her husband, and men, as an obstacle. She constantly attacks men who work for and with her. However, she is not opposed to using them to get traditional honours which women would not receive without being married, or attaining certain political positions she could not get on merit. For instance, when village elders offer her husband a chieftaincy title, she nags him to accept, against his will: Lois is obsessed with status, and considers that as a married woman, any rise in her husband's status would benefit her. She constantly undermines her husband in public, even in front of elders.

An Empowered and Liberated Woman Has a Career

These movies also define an empowered and liberated woman as one who works outside the home. She is educated and trained to work outside the home while supporting the family. All the major characters in the movies have careers. This is a positive message, considering that in Nigerian society today, two-income households are becoming more common. However, there is a negative connotation attached to this definition when the women place their careers before their families. Take Nneka for instance in *The Bank Manager*. Nneka loves her career so much that she barely has time for the children. She returns from work late at night (often around 10 p.m.) when the children are in bed, and she constantly quarrels with her husband about her responsibilities.

Nneka believes that staying at home will prevent her from "reaping the fruit" of her labour, especially since she is well educated and advanced in her career. Her husband, Evans, constantly reminds her that she is a "mother and a housewife with children who need her." When her brother chides her on her attitude toward her husband and children, she replies: I have "laboured so hard to be where I am today, and I have a few more steps to go. So whoever loves me should stand by me." Soon, Evans gets tired, marries the maid and sends Nneka packing: she is punished for choosing her career at the expense of her family. She later goes mad and roams the streets. In one scene, the director mocks her choice by having her in her mad state believe she is in her office attending to customers.

In *Women in Power*, Agatha is also very focused about her business. She spends a lot of time travelling and making money. Her husband, Mavis, asks her to spend more time with him so they can start a family, to which she replies, "Those babies ain't coming. I can't sit at home brooding about it when my mates are out there making millions. Is it only men who have the prerogative to make money?" She interprets her husband's concerns as jealousy. In the end, she too loses her husband to a woman he married secretly. Agatha finds this out when she returns from a business trip and meets a pregnant woman. Mavis nonchalantly introduces the woman as his wife, a "nice, domestic, fertile" woman who "understands my needs." Overall, the women who exaggeratedly put careers before family lose what Nigerian society considers as valuable to women – their husbands. Both wives also deviate from the cultural definition of a good wife, one who is submissive to her husband and wants children.

In contrast, the movies also show other women with careers whose characters carry positive connotations. Positively, a liberated and empowered woman understands her role as a wife and a mother (if she had children) and puts her family before her career. She values her children and respects her husband. She does what bring honour to her husband. We see this in Maureen who cooks for the family despite being a minister of the federal government. She gives up any position that conflicts with her role as a mother and wife. As she put it, "Women's liberation and empowerment is all about understanding our roles as women and realising our talents and endowments and making sure there are no hindrances in achieving full potential." Her husband explains further that "A totally empowered woman does not allow emancipation to conflict with her God-given roles as mother and wife." Women like Maureen are constantly called "good wives" and "good women" in these movies.

An Empowered and Liberated Woman is Proud of Her Culture

Another quality of a liberated and empowered woman her cultural pride in her dressing. This is also an identity issue. In the Nigerian society, a good woman is expected to dress conservatively, with little or no makeup. If she is married, her body is for the eyes of her husband and she dresses mainly in traditional clothes that identify her as a married lady and as a mother. When she wears Western attire, she is also conservatively dressed. In the movies, liberated and empowered 'bad' women wear very tight, short and low-cut Western clothes, except when they are in traditional settings. They also wear heavy make-up and use blond or red hair extensions or wigs. It almost seems as if, for these women, being empowered or liberated means dressing like European or American (not Nigerian) women.

In a scene in *Women in Power* for instance, we meet Paulina, an obese mother of four who visits her friend in very tight jeans and blouse. No part of her is left to the imagination. Paulina calls her dressing "women's libe" (pronounced lee-bay), short for women's liberation. She tells her friend Ugomma that, according to a new government declaration, men and women are now equal and that women have now got power. As a result, she considers that she can dress as she likes, and that her husband himself cannot tell her what to do. Though the scene is comic, Paulina (notice the foreign name) is standing next to Ugomma, a married woman whose dressing suggests she is a good woman. Confirmation of this comes when Paulina's husband goes to Ugomma to complain (Nigerian husbands do not complain to their wives' friends unless they respect those ladies and see them as good women).

Ugomma explains that Paulina was simply "confused" because, as she explains, "some of our women do not understand the true meaning of women's liberation and empowerment. They think it's all about dressing anyhow, talking anyhow, and disrespecting their husbands." The way a woman dresses actually says a lot in Nigerian societies and often determines people's reactions to her. When the women who err change their behaviour and attitude, their dressing also changes. When Nneka is healed, she returns home dressed in traditional clothes with no makeup and with covered hair. Gone are the blond hair and tight trousers. When Paulina begs her husband to let her come back, she too covers her hair and dresses modestly in a blouse and wrappers. Overall, the movies teach that a truly liberated and empowered woman shows, through her choice of clothes, that she respects the traditions of her people regarding her role. One could say that she is proud to be Nigerian, and does not copy or embrace Western women and their concept of what is good for the world.

An Empowered and Liberated Woman Does Not Dominate Others

An empowered, liberated woman equally cares about others. She uses her power for the good of the less fortunate, and respects her subordinates. She seeks to empower others and pushes for social change, as defined in Shefner-Rogers et al. (1998). Joyce and Maureen are good examples of this definition. Whenever these women meet the less fortunate, they help them extensively. For example, although Maureen is a minister, she attends to women in her home, not just in her office. She is interested in their welfare, listens to them and even provides scholarships to less privileged girls because education and skill acquisition, she says, are "the first steps to self-empowerment." In her position, Joyce starts *Widows' Cot* to help fellow widows. Her goal is to get the government to recognise that certain cultural practices are unfair to widows. When the organisation raises millions of naira, she pushes the leaders to use funds to help orphans, the poor and the hungry, even though Adamma tells her "charity is not a cure for poverty."

One must recognise that there are women, in the movies, who dominate others, and this attitude carries negative connotations. If these women cannot dominate through money and political power, they use sex. They have no respect for men, other women, the poor or the powerless. This is a common theme in movies. In *Women's Cot*, Adamma advises a widow to exercise her "right to pleasure" by having sex with her three brothers-in-law, who want to dispossess her and yet, individually, want to have sex with her. The widow takes Adamma's advice and, as long as she sleeps with the men, they do not give her any trouble. When their wives become suspicious, Adamma tells the widow to kill them. One wonders why she does not advise her fellow widow to go to court and fight for her rights.

Adamma also uses her money and influence to seduce younger men into relationships, which she controls. The men are young enough to be her sons, but she does not care because they give her pleasure and she gives them money or cars in return. However, they cannot leave the relationship until she says so. When her young boyfriend in the movie ends the relationship, she kills him for his "ingratitude." Adamma also believes that the leader of the *Widows' Cot* should have absolute control – no debate, no votes. Lois, who arrogantly commands everyone to address her as Honourable Chief Mrs. Lois Collins, also takes pride in dominating men and other women. She believes that men and women are at war and that the only language men understand is "action and aggression." She calls Maureen a bad leader because, "A woman leader cannot be on good terms with her husband and take care of the family. A good woman leader must be hostile and uncompromising to the men folk." She believes there is no need being nice to men or empowering women through education and work, because their husbands would take the money away. For her, women must aggressively demand their rights from men, and not be nice to them or ask them for anything, because such a beggarly attitude is weak.

Domination is also displayed through wealth. Money is power. In *Women's Cot*, women are seduced to join the organisation through wealth. In her membership bid, Adamma uses some of the money they raise to buy exotic cars, expensive clothes and give monetary gifts. Every member of the more than 100-member organisation gives new widows a N50, 000 ($500) cash gift. Wealth attracts women so much that it does not take long for them to kill their husbands to join the cot. According to one woman, women will long to be widows after seeing its members. What those "women enjoy," she said, "no husband is worth it."

Nneka, in *The Bank Manager*, drives exotic cars, wears expensive clothes and attacks her maid physically and verbally. One gets the message here that men are not the only hindrances to women's empowerment and liberation. Women can be their own worst enemy. Domination in any form from women is portrayed as wrong and the women who dominate others suffer terrible consequences.

Lois's employers and seniors fire her for her aggressiveness and attitude towards men. She is also arrested for embezzling public funds and abusing her office. Even her husband divorces her and moves to Switzerland with the children, where he hopes to undo her evil influences. Just as the police officer comes to arrest her, she pleads with him to remain and help her, to which he replies: "You are an independent woman. I am sure you can take care of yourself, my dear". Eze Nwanyi kills Adamma and is herself destroyed by a man.

A Liberated and Empowered Woman Needs a Man

The movies teach that women need men, no matter how independent or liberated they are. The only women who are excluded from this rule are widows. Women who say that they do not need men are often reminded by their mothers, never by men or other women, that a man is necessary in a woman's life. For instance, though Stella wants to meet a corporate target before she gets married, her mother constantly reminds her to replace the stuffed bear she hugs every night with a man. After her third engagement ends, Julia, Lois's daughter, wonders why she cannot keep a man. She soon realises that, contrary to her mother's teaching, she wants marriage. Overall, these are the main definitions in the movies concerning what an empowered, liberated woman is. From the movies, it is clear that women fighting for their rights and empowerment have to balance their needs with those of their culture, family and tradition.

What is gender equality according to Nigerian video films? To answer this second research question, movies provide two definitions. The first definition of gender equality is that men and women are equal, have equal rights and are entitled to the same things, regardless of tradition. One could easily dismiss this definition as Western, since Nigerian women belong to a communal culture that recognises the importance of tradition and customs. In the movies, women who adopt this definition often express it as a competition between the sexes, and want to do as the men do.

For example, Julia tells her older brother to cook because she cannot cook all the time. "You men want to do the eating while we do the cooking," Lois retorts when her son complains. The chores must be shared equally. But Julia is never shown doing her brother's chores or paying on a date. Agatha never does the chores at home either. She never cleans or cooks, and leaves the house very early without seeing her husband or guests. You get the impression that she is a bad wife because she does not perform her duties as a wife. In one scene, Lois publicly defies the patriarchal structure of tradition.

At a meeting of the CWF, Maureen's husband, Chief Odensi, welcomes guests using the Igbo tradition of showing the men kola nuts in a covered bowl before they are broken. Seated at the table for honoured guests as well, Lois strains to look into the bowl when it is shown to the men at the table. But the presenter never shows them to her. Just before they are broken, Lois loudly demands to look into the bowl. The audience is stunned, including her ardent supporters. Odensi politely tells her that women do not see the kola nuts before they are broken. Lois haughtily replies that she must, because she is a chief, a minister, and equal to men. Odensi said, "Chief or no chief, you are still a woman and this is tradition." Lois then threatens that if she is not shown the kola nuts, she would leave with the members of her organisation. But she storms out alone as none of the women wants to break this patriarchal tradition. They are afraid of disturbing the status quo and obviously only take the fight for equality so far, for fear of annoying the men. Her strongest supporters later tell Lois that they would no longer support her because she does not know that "tradition must be followed". One of them even describes her as having "too much ambition." The women who adopt the definition of gender equality as men and women being equal are portrayed as bad and unsuccessful women.

The second definition of gender equality illustrated in the movies is that men and women, though created equal, have different abilities that complement each other and are not in competition with each other. Lois's husband gives this definition throughout *Women in Power.* When Julia expresses her confusion about the equality of the sexes, her father explains that "with equality comes the actual realisation of [your] responsibility as a man or woman. To usurp the other's role is to cause friction." This explanation falls in line with what many womanists and African feminists define as gender equality. The women who imbibe this definition are portrayed as successful and good women.

Conclusion

According to Romy Fröhlich, "the people who make decisions about media content, maybe news or entertainment, have defining power" (161). The people, here those in charge of the movies mentioned earlier, are men from the Igbo ethnic group of Nigeria, as the major owners of Nigerian mass media are men. Therefore, one could argue that these definitions of empowerment, liberation and gender equality are men's visions (based on Igbo culture). Men have thus used these films to set an agenda concerning women's empowerment, liberation and gender equality.

The definitions hint that men are not against women's empowerment or their fight for rights, but define the contexts in which they should be empowered or given equal rights (if at all). A woman who falls outside the roles which tradition assigned to her is not only bad, she is really bad. For example, though Nneka works outside the home, Evans still sees her as a housewife. Even in the context of gender equality, the message is that women should know their place. Women are not in competition with men, but if they want to be, they are doomed, and traditional roles are presented as more important.

Through the video films, women will learn that empowerment, liberation and gender equality are good if they can bear the consequences. In some ways, the movies' definitions and interpretations of these terms are unfair to women, and the portrayals of bad women are exaggerated. Lois's character for instance is too aggressive, rude and ambitious. It does not make sense either that Agatha, who should know that children are the foundation of marriage in Nigeria, is nonchalant about her childless state and does not care about her husband. In Nigerian societies, "Women are highly valued for their childbearing capabilities. Therefore, a childless woman [is of] little or no value to her husband, her family, or the community at large" (Wilson & Ngige 252).

One must add that, while tradition punishes women for their 'wayward' actions, the same tradition allows men to commit adultery. For example, though Evans blames Nneka for the family's breakup, he never takes responsibility for having an affair with the maid. He never even notices that his children are starving and unhappy. The movie excuses this as a voodoo or juju spell. But the viewer is not even aware that he is charmed until the end of the movie. In fact, the first time the husband has sex with the maid, he is not under any magical influence because he calls her to his bed after noticing the seductive negligee she wore to serve him breakfast. One might also interpret his actions as a punishment for Nneka because she is a bad wife.

In *Women in Power*, Agatha is another victim of tradition. When she does not play the wifely role expected of her, her husband does not divorce her but marries another wife, since tradition allows him to do so. His family is aware of this action and fully supports him, and his sister breaks the news to Agatha, telling her with glee that the new woman is "our wife. She has done for us what other women (meaning Agatha) have been unable to do in many years." Moreover, by getting another woman pregnant, Mavis shows that, in their couple, the infertile one is Agatha. Agatha is the 'man' she wanted to be after all. Women are apt to say that Agatha deserves what she got, because her career was more important to her than her "God-given roles."

The movies carry a serious warning for women about how dispensable they are. When they misbehave, a man can simply replace them. Women do not have that luxury. Moreover, in spite of his western education and his position as a senator, Joyce's husband does not leave a will or make arrangements to safeguard his wife and children's futures upon his demise. His brother explains that it is because he is "a traditional man" who understood the customary rules of inheritance. Why did he not plan for his family? Was he not willing to change the status quo? Do men approve the traditions that subjugate women in Nigeria? Are these not gender issues?

These movies also show the immense pressure that Nigerian women face in a world that wants to be modern but still holds on to its traditional past. Nigerian women must simultaneously achieve their goals of self-realisation and actualisation as women without being seen as anti-family or anti-men. They must maintain a balance between the two. They can get an education and job, but they must also be able to bear children, raise them, take care of their husbands, cook and clean, and be good at their jobs. Nigerian women must be superwomen. These movies also show that if a conflict arises between their lives as workers and their lives as wives and mothers, they are expected to give up their work and serve their families. Family comes first.

In addition, no matter how successful she is in her professional life, a Nigerian woman is incomplete until she has a husband and children of her own. When she gets them, she must do all she can to keep them, for a woman who puts her career before her family is heading for destruction, as Nneka's brother put it. These movies show that women might learn to look at their careers as hobbies - something to while away time, especially when you have a rich and hardworking husband who can provide for you. But what if you do not? What options do you have? How will tradition treat you?

Women's Cot could also have focused much more on widowhood and the fight to bring about social change through the organisation. The issue is trivialised with the addition of Eze Nwanyi. Does that mean that these unfair widowhood practices cannot be changed? The way the issue is handled shows how men view the issue, which is a serious one for Nigerian women. Widowhood disenfranchises many women, particularly in cultures where they are considered as property, and women's groups are fighting these customs. Another common stereotype in the movies is that women cannot trust other women. Nneka cannot trust her maid who starves her children and takes her husband. Lois cannot trust her friends, neither can Joyce trust Adamma.

In the end, Lois's husband may be right when he says that women must always apply what they learn realistically because, after all, "This is Nigeria." That excuse is difficult to swallow, and defeatist, considering all the efforts and contributions which Nigerian women have made to society. It is time for movie makers in Nigeria to tell stories that not only highlight the issues in society, but suggest ways to solve them.

Overall, these movies carry important messages about Nollywood's role in setting the media and political agenda and preparing Nigerian women to meet the MDGs. But since men are the dominant producers, directors and writers of these stories, they have maintained the status quo of portraying women negatively. Women's images in the context of these issues are very negative, subjective and even unrealistic in some cases. The danger here is that such images influence the perception of women, who are the dominant viewers of these movies, regarding women's empowerment, liberation and gender equality.

These images can also hinder the fledgling movement for women's empowerment and rights in Nigeria. When movies routinely exaggerate the negative aspects, the consequences could be devastating, not only for the group stereotyped, but for society as a whole. Nigerian women in the industry should also produce movies from within, to address "what is specifically female," because Nigerian men do not seem to get how important social change regarding women's issues is (Iglesias 226).

Works Cited

Abah, A. L. "One Step Forward, Two Steps Backward: African Women in Nigerian Video film". *Communication, Culture & Critique*, 1 (2008): 335 – 357.

Adamu, F. L. "Women's Struggles and the Politics of Difference in Nigeria". Retrieved April 11, 2008 from www.gwsafrica.org/african% 20feminist% 20thinkers/ adamu/ adamu%20publication5.

Adenugba, O. O. "The Role of Film in Development". Retrieved October 16, 2008 from http://filminnaija.blogspot.com/2008_06_01 _archive.html.

______________. Genres of the Nigerian Film. Retrieved October 16, 2008 from http://filminnaija.blogspot.com/2998/07/genres-of-nigerian-film.html.

Babangida, Mariam. Acceptance address for the Africa Prize for Leadership. Retrieved December 16, 2008 from www.thp.org/prize91/mb991.htm.

Bandura, A. "Social Cognitive Theory of Mass Communication." In J. Bryant and D. Zillman (eds.), *Media Effects: Advances in Theory and Research* Hillsdale, N.J.: Erlbaum, 1994. 61 – 90.

Batliwala, S. "Taking the Power out of Empowerment – An Experiential Account". *Development in Practice*, *17*:4-5 (2007): 557 – 565.

Byerly, C. M. 'Situating "the other": Women, racial and sexual minorities in the media'. In P. Creedon & J. Cramer (eds.), *Women in Mass Communication* (3rd. ed.), Thousand Oaks, CA: Sage, 2007. 221 – 232.

Casas Pérez, M. "Cultural Identity between Reality and Fiction: A Transformation of Genre and Roles in Mexican Telenovelas". *Television New Media, 6* (2005): 407-414.

Cohen, J., & Weimann, G. "Cultivation Revisited: Some Genres Have Some Effects on Some Viewers". *Communication Reports 12*:2 (2000): 99 – 114.

Cooke-Jackson, A., & Hansen, E. K. "Appalachian Culture and Reality TV: The Ethical Dilemma of Stereotyping Others. *Journal of Mass Media Ethics, 23*:3 (2008): 183-200.

Dijkstra, A. G. "Towards a Fresh Start in Measuring Gender Equality: A Contribution to the Debate". *Journal of Human Development, 7*:2 (2006): 275 – 283.

Ebewo, P. "The Emerging Video Film Industry in Nigeria: Challenges and Prospects. *Journal of Film and Video*, 59: 3 (2007): 46 – 57.

ERICarts. Retrieved March 6, 2010 from http://www.gender-research.net/web/index.php.

Fröhlich, R. "Three Steps Forward and Two Steps Back: Women Journalists in the Western World between Progress, Standstill, and Retreat". In P. Creedon & J. Cramer (eds.), *Women in Mass Communication* (3rd. ed.), Thousand Oaks, CA: Sage, 2007. 161 – 176.

Garritano, C. "Women, Melodrama and Political Critique: A Feminist Reading of *Hostages*, *Dust to Dust* and *True Confessions*". In J. Haynes (ed.), *Nigerian Video Films* Athens, OH: Ohio University Centre for International Studies, 2000. 165 – 191.

Gerbner, G. "Toward Cultural Indicators: The Analysis of Mass Mediated Message Systems. *AV Communication Review* 17 (1969): 137 – 148.

Gerbner, G. & Gross, L. "Living with Television: The Violence Profile. *Journal of Communication, 26* (1976): 173 - 199.

Giffard, C., Cunningham, S., & Van Leuven, N. "The Female Face of Poverty: Media and the Gender Divide in the Millennium Development Goals". Paper presented at the International Communication Association Conference, 2006.

Greig, F. G., & Koopman, C. "Multilevel Analysis of Women's Empowerment and HIV Prevention: Quantitative Survey Results from a Preliminary Study in Botswana". *AIDS and, 7:2* (2004): 195 – 208).

Haynes, Jonathan. "Video Boom: Nigeria and Ghana". *Postcolonial Text, 3: 2* (2007): 1-10.

Hays, M. "A Thousand Films and One Queen". *The Globe and Mail,* 2005. Retrieved December 20, 2010 from http://nigeriamovies.net/articles 1.htm.

Iglesias, Norma. "Women and the Cinema in Mexico". In P. H. Smith, J. L. Troutner, & C. Hünefeldt, (eds.), *Promises of Empowerment: Women in Asia and Latin America.* Lanham, MD: Rowan & Littlefield Publishers, 2004. 225 – 246.

International Center for Research on Women. "Toward Achieving Gender Equality and Empowering Women. Retrieved October 14, 2008 from www.icrw.org/docs/Task%20Force%20Brief.pdf

Järvinen, T. "Equipping and Empowering for God's Service: Empowerment: Sociological, Psychological, Organisational, and Biblical Perspectives for Empowering People and Organisations". *The Journal of the European Pentecostal Theological Association, 27: 2* (2007): 173 – 182.

Larkin, Brian. "Popular Video Film". In *African Film Festival,* New York: African Film Festival Inc., 2002. 1 – 4.

Larosa, D. L., & Wanta, W. "Effects of Personal, Interpersonal and Media Experiences on Issue Salience. *Journalism Quarterly, 67*, (1997): 804 – 813.

Longwe, S., & Clarke, R. *Towards Improved Leadership for Women's Empowerment in Africa: Measuring Progress and Improved Strategies.* Accra: Leadership Forum, 1999.

Mama, Amina. "Khaki in the Family: Gender Discourses and Militarism in Nigeria. *African Studies Review, 4: 2* (1998): 1-17.

Martin-Barbero, J. "The Processes: From Nationalisms to Transnationalisms. In M. G. Durham & D. Kellner, (eds.), *Media and Cultural Studies Key Works.* Malden, MA: Blackwell Publishing, 2006. 626 – 657.

MDGmonitor. Retrieved October 14, 2008 from www.mgdmonitor.org/aboutMDG.cfm

Moon, K. "High-level Event on the Millennium Development Goals: Key Action Points for Consideration by Government and Other Stakeholders", 2008.

Nelson, L. J., Shanahan, S. B., & Olivetti, J. "Power, Empowerment and Equality: Evidence for the Motives of Feminists, Nonfeminists and Antifeminists. *Sex Roles, 37:* 3-4 (1997): 227 – 277.

Nigeriafirst.org. (June 19, 2007). New opportunities in women empowerment. Retrieved October 1, 2008 from www.nigeriafirst.org/printer_7447.shtml

Nwaneri, H. (1997). "Nigeria: Gender Stereotypes and Power Equality". *Women's International Network News, 23:4* (1997): 40.

Nwonwu, F. "The Role of Adult Education in Women Empowerment: An Assessment of the Better Life for Rural Women Program in Nigeria". Paper presented at The Project for Literacy International Conference, South Africa, 2001. Retrieved December 16, 2008 from www.projectliteracy.org.za/tmpl/Frank%20Nwonwu.htm

Ogan, C. L. (2007). "Communication and Culture". In Y. R. Kamalipour (ed.), *Global Communication* (2nd ed.). Belmont, CA: Thomson Wadsworth, 2007. 293 – 318.

Ogunleye, Foluke. "Gender Stereotypes and Reconstruction: A Feminist Appraisal of Nigerian Video Films". *Sabinet, 37:3* (2005): 125 – 149.

Okome, Onookome. "Onome: Ethnicity, Class, Gender". In J. Haynes (ed.), *Nigerian Video Films.* Athens, OH: Ohio University Centre for International Studies, 2000. 148-164.

Okunna, C. S. "Portrayal of Women in Nigerian Home Video Films: Empowerment or Subjugation?" *Africa Media Review 10:3* (1996): 21-36.

______________. Gender and communication in Nigeria: Is this the twenty-first century? Retrieved August 9, 2009 from http://www.portalcomunicacion.com/bcn2002/n_eng/programme/prog_ind/papers/o/pdf/o005se04_okunn.pdf

Olushola, A. "The Role of Film in National Development". Retrieved 10/16/2008 from http://filminnaija.blogspot.com/2008/06/role-of-film-in-national-development.html

Onyedike, N. "Empower Women, Protect the Child to Achieve MDGs, Minister Pleads". Retrieved July 22, 2009 from http://news.onlinenigeria.com

Opoku-Mensah, A. "Marching on: African Feminist Media Studies". *Feminist Media Studies, 1: 1* (2001): 25-34.

Osei-Hwere, E., & Osei-Hwere, P. "Nollywood: A Multilevel Analysis of the International Flow of Nigerian Video Films". Paper Presented at the Annual Convention of International Communication Association, 2008.

Osifo-Dawodu, E. "WIFV-DC Member Promotes the Nigerian Film Industry in the U.S.", 2007. Retrieved January 10, 2010 from http://www.wifti.org/news.cfm?nf_nfid=51.

Ozele, A. "Representations of Cultural Resilience and Perceptions of Religiosity in Nigerian Movies and the Crisis of Personal Identity Among Nigerian Adolescents". Paper Presented at the Annual Meeting of the Religious Education Association, Chicago, IL. 2008.

Para-Mallam, O. J. "Faith, Gender and Development Agendas in Nigeria: Conflicts, Challenges and Opportunities. *Gender & Development, 14:3* (2006): 409 – 421.

Parliamentary Assembly Recommendation 1716. Promoting a United Nations World Conference on Women, 2005. Retrieved October 14, 2008 from http://assembly.coe.int/Documents/AdoptedText/TA05/EREC1716.htm

Patel, J. (2002). Review of Nigerian videos: *Born Again* and *Submission. Ijele: Art EJournal of the African World*, (5). Retrieved October 16, 2008 from www.africaresource.com/ijele/issue5/patel/html

Putnam, D. "Introduction at Proceedings of Audiovisual Conference". Luxembourg: Office for Official Publications of the European Communities, 1998.

Ravinder, R., & Narayana, N. "Gender Empowerment in Africa: An Analysis of Women Participation in the Eritrean Economy", 2007. Retrieved February 5, 2010 from http://mpra.ub.uni-muenchen.de/11081/2/MPRA_paper_11081.pdf

Reddock, Rhoda. "Gender Equality, Pan-Africanism and the Diaspora. *International Journal of African Renaissance Studies, 2:2* (2007): 255 – 267.

Shefner-Rogers C. L & al. Parasocial interaction with the television soap operas "Simplemente Maria" and "Oshin". *Keio Communication Review*, 20, 1998, 3-18

Shefner-Rogers C.L. and al The Empowerment of women dairy farmers in India. *Journal of Applied Communication Research* 26(3), 1998, 319-337

Steeves, H. L. "The Global Context of Women in Communication". In P. Creedon & J. Cramer (eds.), *Women in Mass Communication* (3rd. ed.) Thousand Oaks, CA: Sage, 2007. 191 – 206.

Tamale, Sylvia. "The Right to Culture and the Culture of Rights: A Critical Perspective on Women's Sexual Rights in Africa". *Feminist Legal Studies, 16*, (2008): 47 – 69.

Tan, A., Fujioka, Y., & Lucht, N. "Native American Stereotypes, TV Portrayals and Personal Contact". *Journalism & Mass Communication Quarterly* 74 (1997): 265 – 284.

Troutner, J. L., & Smith, P. H. "Empowering Women: Agency, Structure and Comparative Perspectives". In P. H. Smith, J. L. Troutner, & C. Hünefeldt, (eds.), *Promises of Empowerment: Women in Asia and Latin America.* Lanham, MD: Rowan & Littlefield Publishers, 2004. 1 – 30.

Wanta, W. *The Public and the National Agenda: How People Learn about Important Issues.* Mahwah, NJ: Lawrence Erlbaum Ass, 1997.

Wilson, S. M, & Ngige, L. (2006). "Families in Sub-Saharan Africa". In B. B. Goldsby & S.D. Smith (eds.), *Families in Global and Multicultural Perspective* (2nd ed.), Thousand Oaks, CA: Sage. 2006. 247 – 271.

www.choike.org

www.undp.org

www.wefoum.org

Yunjuan, L., & Xiaoming, H. "Media Portrayal of Women and Social Change: A Case Study of Women in China". *Feminist Media Studies* 7:3 (2007): 281 – 298.

UNFPA. *Gender Equality: A Cornerstone of Development,* 2009. Retrieved August 12 from www.unfpa.org/gender/

CHAPTER FOUR

Archiving Hausa Popular Entertainment through New Media Technology: An Assessment of the Recreation of *Ruwan Bagaja* into Video Movie

Asabe Kabir Usman

Abstract

The Hausa people, the largest ethnic group found in northern Nigeria, are found in Kano, Katsina, Sokoto, Zaria as well as other parts of north western and north central Nigeria. The Hausa language is one of the widely spoken languages of black Africa. The *Hausawa,* as they are called by other ethnicities, have a rich legacy of folklore which has served as a means of handing down their culture, traditions and customs from one generation to the other. The folktale, *tatsuniya* in Hausa language, is a popular genre of folklore, handed down orally and committed to memory from one generation to the other before the advent of technology. The traditional *tatsuniya* reflects the cultural and social life of the Hausa people, at the same time drawing attention to the salient aspects of Hausa culture. With the advent of writing, symbols were used to represent language and cultural norms were recorded, transcribed and shared from one place to the other. But with the arrival of the home video, Hausa people found a new means of showcasing their art-forms in the medium. It, therefore, became a useful medium for the representation of popular genres of literature, especially in the indigenous language. Folktales like *Ruwan Bagaja* have been adapted and recreated into movies. This paper, therefore, attempts an appraisal of the adaptation and recreation of a popular Hausa folktale *Ruwan Bagaja* into movie with the sole aim of preserving the genre.

Introduction

The contemporary revolution in media communication technology has had a remarkable impact in the field of popular entertainment in Hausa society. This new trend in technology has enabled a wide range of changes in the way oral literary genres are transmitted and documented to reach a larger audience. Thus, literary genres that were before now termed archaic and restricted to a small local audience are now viewed globally.

Although the Hausa video movie is a recent development in Nigeria compared to its Igbo and Yoruba counterparts, it has become an avenue through which the Hausa people sustain and preserve their various forms of folkloric traditions. The narrative/folktale has been the earliest medium through which the Hausa people, like other Africans, hand down their tradition and culture, educate their children and entertain them. The traditional narrative as a genre contains orderly creative accounts of events presented as if they actually occurred, and the fictional world that is captured by folktales seems very real. It is popular among the folk because it is created by and for the people.

From the 1990s to the present, the development and patronage of digital DVD players, and home theatre amplification systems with large LCD or plasma screens, have made it convenient for those who can, to view movies and films with great ease, and brought significant improvement in audio and visual production.

Narratives/Folktales in Hausa Society

Narratives/folktales as a genre contain orderly creative accounts of events presented as if they actually occurred. According to one critic, "They are regarded as fiction, they are not considered as dogmas or history; they may or may not have happened and they are not to be taken seriously" (Bascom 97). Folktales could, therefore, include fairy tales, animal tales, tall tales, fables, trickster tales and explanatory tales, to mention just a few of the categories. Entertainment is the first and obvious function of folktales; as tales are told, the funny ones among them make listeners roar with laughter as they are carried into the fanciful lands of talking trees and animals, a land where impossible things can happen.

The existence of narratives/folktales is quite evident in Hausaland because they are, to a great extent, "the mirror of life; they reflect what people think, how they live and have lived, their values, their joys and sorrows. They are also a means of articulating man's response to his environment, for example, his observations of nature, his speculation about life and death and his judgment upon human relation" (Bichi 10). Folktales also offer insight into the values and beliefs of the people.

This paper will follow the structural functional approach to the study of oral literature. This is a "study of folklore which lays emphasis on the social significance of folklore in the light of its contextual background" (Yahaya 19). This would clearly demonstrate the social roles of narratives/folktales as a genre of folklore in reflecting the way of life of a group of people, thereby emphasising the need to preserve it for cultural continuity. In translating the folktale into English, we employed the contextual method of translation, which allows the basic principle of creativity, taking into consideration the verbal elements and linguistic cultures of the two languages involved. It therefore "provides a translator with all the chances of rendering the meaning which is relatively equivalent to the source language" (Sarbi 96). This way, the listeners or readers can easily understand the message without distortion.

The Folktale - *Ruwan Bagaja* (River *Bagaja*)

Hausa people have good tales and storytellers, as have most past and present societies around the world which are rooted in oral cultures and traditions. They are primarily oral peoples, and their art forms have remained living traditions that continue to evolve and flourish today, even with technological advancement. One of the world's favourite folktales is the Cinderella story, which is classified as an Aarne Thompson (1966) folktale type 510A.

Cinderella is known throughout the world among different cultures under different names, but the rudiments of the story are similar. She is always a young girl persecuted by a stepmother and her daughters after the loss of her mother. The father in the story is usually absent or rather neglectful, blind to her plight and ignorant of her circumstances. The Cinderella character is always depicted as possessing all the desired qualities in a woman: selflessness, faithfulness and loyalty. She is duty-bound, honourable, meek and modest, as well as possessing physical beauty. She is the embodiment of all the morals that society has timelessly prized and valued in women. As a result, in the end, she is rewarded with great riches and happiness. Though the story has changed through the centuries, its themes remain intact and have inspired generations of storytellers.

The popular story of Cinderella continues to influence popular cultures internationally, lending plot elements and allusions to a wide variety of media. In Hausa society, one similar folktale that is well-known to embody the myth-like element of Cinderella is *Ruwan Bagaja*. Many prose fiction writers have documented different variants of the story. One such literary writer is the late Ibrahim Yaro Yahaya who also gave his story the title "*Ruwan Bagaja*" in his collection of Hausa traditional reader series, *Tatsuniyoyi da Wasanni* (1971).

The story centres on a man who had two wives, Bora and Mowa. Both wives were blessed with daughters; but Mowa was the queen of the house and Bora was made to do all the domestic chores. Though she was made to do all the cooking in the house, Bora and her daughter were only allowed the left overs. One day Mowa's daughter soiled the bedspread; but at dawn, Bora's daughter was accused and told to go and wash the bedspread at *River Bagaja,* a deadly river, which was far away from their home. Bora's daughter took the bedspread and made for the river. On the way, she met different rivers and stopped to sing at every river she got to, enquiring if they were River *Bagaja*. Each river she reached had a negative answer for her and would invite her to have a taste of what it had to offer – guinea corn, millet, soup and meat; when she refused, each river would advise, "Go along, River *Bagaja* is far ahead".

After a long walk, she finally got to River Bagaja and the river allowed her to wash her bedspread. Hardly had she begun washing that it started raining. She looked round and saw a lone hut; she rushed there, knocked and went in. She was surprised to see a dog and a human leg. The leg said, "*kn kn*"; the dog told her that the leg wanted to know what had brought her there and she narrated her story to them. The leg further asked her to go out and get a grain of rice and a single bone which she was to cook. She did as she was asked, and when it was cooked, she saw that the rice and bone had filled the pot. She was then asked to eat her fill and she did so. She stayed with them for several days and then took her leave.

When she was leaving, the leg gave her two eggs and asked her to choose one. She chose the small egg. She was asked to break the egg only if no one responded to her request of breaking the egg. She thanked them and left. She did as she was asked, emerged triumphant and was taken home on horseback with a lot of wealth and goodies. The stepmother instantly became jealous and asked her daughter to wet her bedspread. Just like her stepsister, she was asked to wash the spread at River *Bagaja;* but because she was greedy, dishonest and rude, she was punished, was rewarded with lepers, blind and disabled people of every kind on donkeys and was disgraced.

The Development of the Hausa Movie Industry

Since the early 1990s, the Nigerian movie industry, popularly called Nollywood, has released thousands of titles and brought many producers, marketers, actors and technicians into the limelight. The video movie has become a household name in contemporary Nigeria and a popular form of entertainment which replaced other forms and became instantly accepted.

The origin and development of the Hausa video movie industry, known as Kannywood, can be traced to the local theatre tradition known as the open air drama groups/clubs found in big cities in the early 1970s. Some of these drama clubs started to get involved in the production of television soap operas and in the recording of their stage performances on video (Adamu 2002). With these developments, recreational video production emerged and later evolved into what is today known as the Nigerian home video. Subsequently, towards the end of the 1980s, video movies had become a leading technological medium of transmitting popular entertainment. Haynes and Okome (1997), Adamu (2002), Behrend (2005), Furniss (2003, 2005), Johnson (1997) and Larkin (1997a, 1997b, 2003, 2004, 2005), among many others, have commented on the rise of the video movie industry in Nigeria. They have, in different ways, shown how the culture and tradition of a society affects the movies, and pointed to the various elements that aided the rise and development of the video movie industry. The first successful Hausa home video, according to Adamu, was "*Turmin Danya*, which was produced in 1990 by Ibrahim Mandawari, then president of the *Tumbin Giwa* Drama group" (206).

Just like the traditional narrative/folktale, Indian movies and western movies, Hausa popular literature, known as 'Kano Market Literature' or *littattafan soyayya*, which developed as a revival of Hausa literature in the mid-1980s and was getting more popular, especially among women readers, by the end of the 1980s (Adamu 2002), has at one time or the other formed source materials for Hausa video movies.

The video movie *Ruwan Bagaja* was produced by Sale Muhammad (Roosy) and directed by Iliyasu Abdulmumin (Tantiri). It was released sometime in 2008. It has popular Hausa movie stars like Sadiya

Muammad who acted as Ladiyo, Zainab Umar as Uwani, Shuaibu Lawan (Ilu), Baballe Hayatu (Musa), Hussaini Sule Koki (Mallam), Ali Rabiu Ali (Habu), Yahanasu Sani (Zulai), Maryam Tahir (Hamma), Ladin Cima (Gwoggo), Aminu Ari (Mallam Boka), Awwalu Marshal (Carbi), Lubabatu Madaki (Inna), Lawal M. Adams (Musa's Friend) and Adamu Umar Mujaheed (Habu's Friend).

The first scene introduces us to Mallam's house, where the differences in the status of his two wives are clearly spelt out. The first wife Zulai is seen to be the favourite and rules the home front, whereas Hamma, the second wife, plays second fiddle. Hamma is despised, made to do all the household chores and is unfairly treated by the husband and first wife. As the story unfolds, we learn that the family is childless, and upon Zulai's request, Mallam goes to a spiritualist for medication. He is given medicinal herbs which would make Zulai pregnant. Ironically, though Hamma is refused the treatment, she gets the opportunity of taking a sip from the herbal calabash and two months later both wives become pregnant, to the dismay of the husband, the first wife and Gwoggo, Mallam's mother. To show his displeasure of both wives getting pregnant, Mallam refuses to pay the spiritualist. Both wives put to bed at almost the same time, but Zulai is delivered first and we are shown how Hamma helps her during labour pains. Zulai, on the other hand, refuses to help Hamma when she is in labour. Both give birth to daughters, Zulai to Ladiyo and Hamma to Uwani.

The setting of the story takes us sixteen years later, when both daughters have grown into beautiful maidens, while the oppression and unjust handling of Hamma and her daughter still continue. They are allowed no social life but despite these maltreatments, Uwani still has close friends who stand by her and help out with the house chores. Ladiyo is allowed to visit friends, attend ceremonies, and is given the best of everything. When Ladiyo gets a suitor, Uwani's aunty Inna also asks her successful son to seek for Uwani's hand in marriage, all in a bid to ease the unfair treatment being faced by her sister and her daughter. When Ladiyo's suitor backs out from the engagement because of Zulai's bad nature and Ladiyo's indiscipline, Zulai decides to get rid of Uwani. Though she narrowly escapes death, her cousin-turned suitor takes the poisoned meal and dies.

One day, Uwani comes across the prince Musa who proposes to her. Her joy is short- lived because, not long after, she is accused of soiling the bedspread which Ladiyo had soiled. As a punishment, her father asks her to seek for River *Bagaja*, a mythical river which no one has ever seen, to wash the soiled spreads or remain forever banned from the village. Sad and disillusioned, Uwani bids her mum goodbye and goes in search of the river. On the way, she meets an old man who rewards her for her respect and polite nature. He directs her towards River *Bagaja* and disappears. Uwani comes across rivers of wheat cake, bread cake and milk but when asked to eat from the rivers, she always refuses. She finally gets to River *Bagaja* and is permitted to wash her bedspread. At the end of it all, she is given two eggs and asked to choose one; she chooses the small one and is ordered to break the egg only if no one responds to her request of breaking it. She does as she has been asked, emerges triumphant and is taken home on horseback with royal status. Her mum, dad and friends welcome her with joy.

Out of envy, Zulai also claims that her daughter has soiled the bedspread and requests the husband to allow Ladiyo go to River *Bagaja.* Against his will, he consents. Like Uwani, Ladiyo meets rivers of various delicacies but, unlike her sister, she takes time to eat everything offered her until she gets to River *Bagaja.* Then, when asked to choose an egg, she chooses the big one and her stubborn character makes her break the egg where she is asked not to. And behold! She is visited by the physically challenged who escort her on donkey back home. Her father rejects her and her mother disowns her before she runs out of the compound, raving with madness. Prince Musa formally asks for Uwani's hand in marriage and everything ends happily.

Ruwan Bagaja: An Assessment of the Adaptation and Recreation

Narratives/folktales serve as a means of cultural reflection of the society in which they are told. Hausa narratives/folktales reflect the traditional set-up of the society - friendship, family life and administrative set-up, kinship. "Both in the tales and the manner of their telling, situation after situation occurs which leads easily and naturally into discussions of what people actually do and what their belief systems are - all of which throw much light on the total culture" (Herskovits 69). In the tales, significant incidents of everyday life will appear, either incidentally or as the basis of a plot. Most of the references to the ways of life of the people are usually an accurate reflection of their habits.

Subsequently, Hausa folktales have been used as source material for their written literatures, and recently, the traditional popular Hausa *tatsuniya* has culminated in the much acclaimed popular video movie entertainment in Hausa society. Though most Hausa narratives serve as a form of entertainment, they are also used for instructing, shaping of character and preparing the young for adult roles. Today, most of the tales represent the traditional medium, which is a live interactive performance between the storyteller and the audience/listeners, while the movie represents the modern medium, an extended version of the tale which requires technology to be realised.

In the movie *Ruwan Bagaja*, the themes are developed to reflect and comment on Hausa social life. The movie clearly depicts a typical Hausa polygamous setting, with the tensions, disharmony and upheavals associated with such homes, where co-wives fight each other or even go the extra length to harm each other's children. The very first scene illustrates such a setting, where the senior wife Zulai had turned the second wife into a slave. All through the movie, scene after scene depicts the ordeals associated with polygamy. We also see the portrayal of men as unjust husbands, preferring one wife to the other and even showing preference to the children of the favoured wife. This is clearly seen in Mallam's character. His preference for Zulai is evident, and he sees nothing wrong in her maltreatment of Hamma. He even orders Hamma to obey Zulai as if she were the husband, ignoring the fact that Hamma should equally be treated as his wife.

When Hamma becomes pregnant, he does not hide his disapproval, refusing even to pay the medicine man who gave him the herb that got both wives pregnant. Surprisingly, he does not deny the pregnancy. When Uwani is born, Mallam treats her as if she is not his daughter. She is treated differently from Ladiyo, her half-sister, and when Zulai claims that it is Uwani who has soiled the bedspreads, he believes her and sends Uwani on a hopeless mission despite protests from Hamma. Ironically, Hamma and her daughter become the loved ones after Uwani's triumphant return, and Zulai and her daughter are disgraced and rejected by the husband.

The movie also depicts the evil attempt of co-wives in Hausa society who seek the help of spiritualists in order to harm each other. This is seen when Zulai visits the spiritualist, requesting for powers to harm Hamma and her daughter. Even though the intended targets are spared, a loved one, Uwani's suitor, loses his life.

Another aspect of the Hausa way of life shown in the movie concerns the characters' dressings. All the characters are wearing Hausa cultural outfits which conform to the traditional rural life in which the story is set. The artefacts seen in the movie, like mortar and pestle, thatched mud buildings, pottery and utensils, all reflect Hausa social life.

An aspect of life attached to the ruling class is also depicted in the movie. Prince Musa is portrayed, even in informal situations, in his royal regalia and royal tone of talking, thereby giving us an insight into the way of life of Hausa royalties. Showcasing the *Dandali*, the traditional Hausa playground where young boys and girls play different games during the moonlit nights, spells out a part of Hausa culture - songs with accompanying Hausa music. The moral messages explored in the movie reflect values of the Hausa society, like honesty, hard work leading to achievement, perseverance, courage, respect for elders, obedience to the society and consideration for others.

Both Hamma and Uwani are depicted as courageous and hardworking even when denied, obedient even to those they did not know. They persevere even when humiliated, and are respectful even to those beneath them. All these qualities are rewarded in their triumph at the end of the story. Zulai and her daughter, on the other hand, lose out because they have refused to abide by set Hausa societal values. Through this movie, knowledge, values and attitudes about Hausa life are conveyed and expressed indirectly and figuratively, allowing viewers to gain an insight into the system of values under which the culture functions. Indeed, the movie has made one of its greatest humanistic contributions because through it, we are able to learn moral lessons that warn people not to ignore societal norms. *Ruwan Bagaja* also respects the structure of the Hausa traditional society in general and the position of each class of people. The movie could also be said to have provided models through which people can verbalise the relationships and constitution of Hausa traditional society.

Conclusion

Today, new media in Hausaland are used to adapt, recreate and project folktales as a genre of oral literature, defined as an imaginary adventure narration with a didactic slant. They are popular because they are a participatory act that occurs between the people/listeners and the storyteller, and are created by, and for the people. This paper proves that the folktale as a category of oral literary genres in Hausa society, orally transmitted from generation to generation, is kept alive and well on the screen. The home video, a new invention in media technology, "has proliferated so much that today it is the most vibrant sector of the Nigerian media and contemporary video culture has created a distinctly new media era which interacts with older forms of the mass media and popular culture" (Larkin 110). In essence, the video movie medium in Hausaland has become an artistic outlet through which traditional oral performances are projected. The folktale *Ruwan Bagaja* and the movie it inspired depict a symbolic connection between the relics of the past and the new images of the contemporary world. The audience is then given a revitalised view of happenings around them, because it is only when past images are re-created into contemporary realities that the version becomes reality.

Works Cited

Adamu, Yusuf. "Between the Word and the Screen: A Historical Perspective on the Hausa Literary Movement and the Home Video Invasion". In *Journal of African Cultural Studies* 15 (2002): 195 – 207.

Bascom, William. *African Folktales in the New World.* Indiana: Indiana University Press, 1992.

Bichi, Abdullahi Yahaya. "Annotated Collections of Hausa Folktales from Nigeria." M.A Thesis (Unpublished). Indiana: Indiana University, 1978.

Furniss, Graham. "Hausa Popular Literature and Video Film: The Rapid Rise of Cultural Production in Times of Economic Decline". *Arbeitspapiere* No. 27, Mainz: Johannes Gutenberg Universität, 2003.

_______________. "Video and the Hausa Novella in Nigeria". *Social Identities.* 11 (2005): 89 – 112.

Johnson, Dul. "Culture and Art in Hausa Video Films". In Jonathan Haynes (ed.). *Nigerian Video Films.* Jos: Nigerian Film Corporation, 1997.

Larkin, Brian. "Indian Films and Nigerian Lovers: Media and the Creation of Parallel Modernity". *Africa* 67 (1997a): 406 – 440.

_______________. "Hausa Dramas and the Rise of the Video Culture in Nigeria". In Jonathan Haynes (ed.). *Nigerian Video Films.* Jos: Nigerian Film Corporation, 1997b.

_______________. "Itineraries of Indian Cinema: African Videos, Bollywood and Global Media". In Ella Shohat and Robert Stam (eds). *Multiculturalism, Postcoloniality, and Transnational Media.* New Brunswick: Rutgers University Press, 2003.

_____________. "Degraded Images, Distorted Sounds: Nigerian Video and the Infrastructure of Piracy". *Public Culture* 16 (2004): 289 – 314.

_____________. "Nigerian Video: Infrastructure of Piracy". *Politique Africaine* 100 (2005): 146 – 164.

Ruwan Bagaja 1-2. 2008. Directed by Sale Muhammad (Roosy).

Sale, Muhammad (Roosy). *Ruwan Bagaja* (A Hausa Movie), 2008.

Sarbi, Sulieman. *Studies in Translation.* Kano: Samarib Publishers, 2008.

Skinner, Neil. *An Anthology of Hausa Literature.* Zaria: NNPC, 1980.

Thompson, Aarne._*Motif Index of Folk-Literature.* Indiana: Indiana University Press, 1966.

Yahaya, Ibrahim. *Tatsuniyoyi da Wassani.* (6 Vols) Ibadan: Oxford University Press, 1971.

_____________. "Oral Art and the Socialization Process". Being an Unpublished PhD Thesis, Ahmadu Bello University, Zaria, 1979.

CHAPTER FIVE

Culture, Media Technology and Globalisation: The Case of Folktales in Kannywood Videos

Yusuf Baba Gar

Abstract

This paper investigates the storyline in Kannywood videos and shows that folktales can be proven to be sources of the videos, against the initial criticism that the videos are mere adaptations of Bollywood, what led to the Kannywood actors/actresses being described as the *Indiyawan Kano* (The Indians of Kano). The paper also looks at what elements are changed in the storylines under investigation, focusing on the elements that are added. The additions help in assessing African culture in general, its flexibility and the effect of globalisation on Kannywood as an industry in particular. Furthermore, the paper discusses how the inclusion of folktales in Kannywood has led to a cultural shift from orality to digital media and its subsequent preservation. To achieve this, we shall consider some selected videos such as *Ruwan Bagaja,* and *Sangaya.* At the end, the paper impresses on the filmmakers that, should they have transformed much of other Hausa genres into videos, they would not have been accused of adaptations. Addressing the critics, the paper argues that it would be better to assess thematic details of the videos and consider the fact that adaptation is a global phenomenon.

Introduction

In most cases, when people talk of globalisation, what usually comes to mind is the issue of economic globalisation. Those who think in this direction fail to relate globalisation to language and culture. Interestingly, this aspect of globalisation is frequent nowadays and it refers to the transnational circulation of popular culture. African languages and cultures are influenced by foreign languages and cultures. These linguistic and cultural assimilations enable African cultures to be flexible, which shows that language and culture are dynamic. African traditional media of entertainment and information dissemination have been affected mostly by electronic media, especially the videos, which are now a popular means of entertainment in Africa.

When the films started, discourses of enlightenment, education and the desire for national identity were some of the most striking themes selected. In addition to these issues, the first generation of African filmmakers privileged the conflict between modernity and tradition. Pioneer African filmmakers from the 1960s, like Ousmane Sembène in Senegal and Ola Balogun in Nigeria, and, a little later, Kwaw Ansah in Ghana, actively collaborated to consolidate schemes of oppositions such as tradition/modernity, countryside/city, old/new, which, in fact, translate the opposition between hero and villain, good and evil.

Colonial films and the emergence of *Littattafan Soyayya* (Love Books) written by Hausa authors set the trend for the development of Kannywood industry. As colonial films helped the natives in creating a film culture free from nudity and from the promotion of un-Islamic religious and cultural values, these films also served as a tool for presenting and inculcating colonial state ideology. On the other hand, *Littattafan Soyayya* (Love Books), which started in 1989, created a space for young urban boys and girls to adapt the style of romance interaction presented in the books. In addition, filmmakers extended the adaptation by using the plots of these love books in Kannywood videos. As a result, Kannywood videos were received with overt criticisms from ethnic Hausa, who first saw the films as pollution of their cultural values (Adamu 2011). One of the critics openly stated that

> All dances copied from Indians are a form of worship of Indian gods, depending on the signs made in the dance… In this respect, Hausa home videos are serving as agents for the spread of Indian culture of love, singing and worship of Hindi gods, in contravention of the teaching of the Prophet (SAW) that prohibits such actions. The Indians would be very pleased for this unsolicited propaganda (Ado-Kurawa 117).

In like manner, a critical remark on the intrusion of foreign values into Hausa culture through Hausa films is reflected in a letter to the editor of *Fim* (Film) *Magazine* No. 4, December 1999, 10 which reads thus:

> I want to advise Nigerian Hausa film producers that using European music in Hausa film is contrary to the portrayal of Hausa culture in

> films (videos). I am appealing to them (producers) to change their style. It is annoying to see a Hausa film with a European music soundtrack. Don't the Hausa have their own (music)? […] The Hausa have more musical instruments than any ethnic group in this country, so why can't films be produced using Hausa traditional music? (Adamu 64)

The views of the above critics show that they are ardent supporters and promoters of Hausa culture, an attitude which, according to them, Kannywood filmmakers fail to emulate. On the other hand, the critics fail to realise that artistic displays nowadays seek to go further than the issue of cultural imperialism, because the presence of technology serves as a means of cultural outreach, irrespective of culture. In like manner, ethnic Hausa too will be happy to see that, through Kannywood home videos, their culture now reaches a wider audience into all nooks and crannies of the globe. One of my informants said: "I hope that Kannywood home video has come to stay and may it progress further than our imagination, based on our culture, religion and our day to day life!"

Few viewers know that some storylines in Kannywood are based on oral tales, and this dependency demonstrates how orality is used by filmmakers as a source. This technique adopted by filmmakers incorporates modern technologies in order to best express an African genre. The strategy comes basically from oral knowledge, culture and technology. Therefore, in Kannywood, we see how technical refinement can best express oral tradition. Kannywood filmmakers were born and brought up in Africa, and were both schooled in African oral genres and engaged in theatre and/or worked with National or State Television Authorities. Through this involvement, they acquired some knowledge of cinematography and learnt how to use equipment such as cameras and recorders to their advantage, in an attempt to express Africa better.

Approach to the Study

> "Nothing is said now that has not been said before".

This quotation (see Juvan 2008) suggests that every work of art is a mention about something which has already been mentioned. Specifically, this is the central idea contained in adaptation and imitation, which are sub-themes within the main theme of intertextuality.

This paper is based on the approach to literary studies outlined in intertextuality, an idea introduced by Julia Kristeva who points to the fact that a text is a combination of quotations and / or the absorption and transformation of other texts. Within the space of a work of art, many utterances taken from other works intersect and neutralise one another in form of cross-cultural influences. By its natural linguistic logic, this means relations between texts, the interweaving of texts, the weaving of one text into another, the connectedness and interdependence of at least two related texts, the characteristic of a text of establishing a relation with another text or having another or multiple texts woven into it or interrelatedness or interaction of texts (Juvan 13).

Kristeva argues against the idea of a text as an isolated entity which operates in a self- contained manner. This assertion suggests that every text (and here we can include any cultural object: image, film, music) refers to other texts, genres and discourses. Her argument is that no text comes into being solely on its own. By implication, there is a specific type of co-extension in which part of the meaning of one particular type of thing covers part of another variety by way of overlapping - a kind of transposition of one or more events into another or a domain of transpositions of many signifying events. Although the idea behind intertextuality is connected to modern times, its use is not new. According to Juvan, Markiewicz, in his work on intertextuality, cites series of pronouncements in which writers, from ancient times to the postmodern era, show an awareness of intertextual occurrences and of the fact that every work necessarily takes into account that which was written before it (Juvan 2008).

The choice for the adoption of this approach is borne out of critics' perceptions of Kannywood videos. They sometimes consider the videos as mere adaptations and/or imitations of Bollywood films. In literary studies, adaptation and imitation depend on the reference to a pre-existent, concrete reality. Moreover, imitation is not repetition, but a highlighting in which, by reading, writing or filming, imitators express themselves while also engaging in a process of situating themselves as insiders or outsiders within a particular culture. In essence, imitation is not only a means of forging one's discourse but a consciously intertextual practice. This is possible because, by imitation, one tends to mix one's ideas with the ideas contained in the imitated material, thus leading to a hybrid product, something that consists of a mixture of two or more things.

One fact about imitation is that it has to do with materials known to the imitators, because it is logical that one cannot imitate something he or she does not know about. Interestingly, imitation of stylistic or thematic elements of older literary works into new texts, or writers' mention of their predecessors, have been a part of the art of writing, most noticeably in genres related to religious or secular traditions. For example, scriptural stories were the main source for many kinds of drama.

Imitation is to be seen, not as copying the pre-text, but as competing with it in an attempt to surpass it with inventive techniques and applying its meaning to the needs of self-speech or utterances. The pre-text is then reshaped by different means, condensing and omitting certain segments, or expanding and developing more succinct formulations in the pre-text, or changing expressions from the original. In changing the source, orators and filmmakers seek some performances or figurative space to demonstrate their mastery, inventiveness and superiority over their predecessors' eloquence.

Cultural Transformations

The so-called traditional discourses and media technology and the new cultural medium are based on the concept of convergence culture, which deals with the interaction or interweaving of basic and corporate media. According to Jenkins (2006), it is where old and new media collide and where the power of the media producer and that of the media consumer interact in unpredictable ways. This can be understood primarily as a new process bringing together many media functions within the same devices, a kind of representation of cultural shifts as stakeholders are encouraged to seek out new information and make connections among dispersed media content. It is within this perspective that Gitelman in Jenkins (2006) offers a model of media that works on two levels.

First, it is a technology that enables communication, and secondly, a medium which is a set of associated protocols or social and cultural practices that have grown up around that technology. It is evident that a medium's content is not fixed or static. Rather, it is moving, changing or developing, especially when movement or change would be good. It shifts, as in the case of storytelling and folktale media, which radio displaced before being displaced by television through the use of DVDs; and performances move from a travelling theatre - a typical local form, to stage theatre for the elite. In these cases, displacements are not necessarily elimination. As noted by Jenkins, "printed words did not kill spoken words. Cinema did not kill theatre. Television did not kill radio. Each old medium was forced to coexist with the emerging media" (14). Old media therefore did not vanish into thin air. Rather, their functions and status are shifted by the introduction of new technologies. We seem to be in an era dominated by the media. Media technologies have controlling interests across the entire entertainment industry. Today, Kannywood home videos are fully accessible via YouTube, proving that this kind of distribution fits into people's lives. Filmmakers can produce their own movies and distribute them worldwide via the internet.

In the past, many societies have succeeded in bringing about a fundamental change in the people's thinking and mentality by making acceptable and positive use of media technology. This included the use of media technology to promote literacy and bring about a change in the educational system. It included the use of modern technology such as video cassettes to promote general health care in rural areas, the use of long-range television pictures to promote modern ways of agriculture, and the use of media and communication technology to create an awareness of the need for peaceful coexistence among different ethnic groups.

Technologies generally, and media technologies in particular, do not develop in isolation from the social structures and contexts that produced them. Rather, technologies and social structures influence and shape each other. In essence, it is the social and cultural structures which necessitated technological innovation, and not the opportunity provided by the technologies. The development of media technology therefore is like an extension of cultural institutions. Technology (both as a cultural process and a vital tool in social transformation) is an essential facilitator in the process of cultural transformation in traditional societies. This crucial linkage is vital to our understanding of both the socio-cultural evolutionary trends in African film production and the changing concept of visual entertainment as transformed by these technologies in African societies.

The above assertion is relevant to the situation of Kannywood, the home video industry in northern Nigeria. In the first place, the emergence of VCR provides Hausa traditional performance with a visual and expandable communication vehicle which shifts cultural narratives to the living rooms of city dwellers in northern Nigeria. It also provides an open window through which an average Hausa urban settler comes into direct contact with other cultures. By the very nature of their format and production convention, home video technologies, particularly the VCR, allow local cultures to be packaged and delivered as popular entertainment to a multitude of audiences (both at home and in diaspora) with relative ease and at a minimum social and economic cost.

Specifically, the home video technology provides the necessary platform through which Kannywood filmmakers experiment with different narrative themes and motifs to explore the popular entertainment and educative world of folktales. In Africa and in most developing countries today, the components of culture and cultural identity are affected by technology. For example, one of my informants recalls how viewers from Ghana called him and said that "formerly our people (referring to Hausa speakers in Ghana) were watching Nollywood films, but when Kannywood started reaching us, our children started wearing Hausa dresses as seen in Kannywood. They have become attracted to their culture, and Hausa as a language became a heritage and a thing of beauty to them". In this direction, not only does technology determine the course of cultural development, it also determines the need for building social foundations. This assertion presupposes that a direct relationship exists between culture and technology and that one affects the other.

Representation of Culture in Kannywood Videos

Taylor (1970) states that culture is a complex whole, including knowledge, belief, art, morals, law, customs and other habits acquired by people as members of a society. John, in Taylor (1970), considers culture as a society's answer to a series of fundamental questions about what it values, what is worth the sacrifice and efforts necessary to pursue and possess that which is most prized. For Hall (1997), culture comprises history, identity and practice and can be regarded as a system of representation in constant change. This means that culture is in a flux, it is changing, and, with time, brings about new formations in an unpredicted manner.

Culture must also progress and incorporate new technologies, new changes. Ironically, in traditional perspective, change has been interpreted as disorder, as chaos and loss of authenticity. However, in the global mix of cultures which we are witnessing today, the authenticity of former cultures may not be lost in quite the ways we imagine them to be, as local authenticities meet and merge with urban and suburban settings. This complex process of acculturation, of meeting and merging, shows the blurring of cultural boundaries as orality adjusts to electronic media. Based on this argument, Kannywood has, to a greater degree, become involved in the process of Africa's self-reflection and identity construction by means of its cultural representations.

Kannywood is now serving as an agent of globalisation, exporting elements of other cultures without coming to the locations of such cultures, as filmmakers inculcate into their viewers some forms of local or domestic culture including music, comedy and dance involving some traditional values. Kannywood videos on the theme of comedy, for example, tend to establish the connection between humour and performance, while videos containing song scenes remind viewers of Hausa and African musical traditions. Sometimes, those songs are direct adaptations of songs from traditional performances or from a local folktale on which the video is based. Singing and dancing are already important activities during feasts. It could be right to say that Kannywood videos portray existing cultures known to the filmmakers, thus buttressing the claim that media technology helps in the preservation of culture.

Before the start of Kannywood videos in 1990 in Kano, northern Nigeria, the Hausa seemed to be satisfied with *tatsuniya* (folktales) as well as comfortable with how these were communicated by means of a storyteller (mostly old or newly married women) to young audiences. With the establishment of the Kannywood industry, the situation changed dramatically because of the need for a more effective channel which could reach people in places far and near. Despite a number of criticisms, Kannywood industry has been an example of the good rapport between media technology and culture in this era of globalisation, because of its ability to showcase a new medium which adapts cultural values that conform to the mindset of its main viewers.

Ruwan Bagaja and Its Storylines

The video *Ruwan Bagaja*, inspired by the famous Hausa folktale also called *Ruwan Bagaja* (Yahaya 1971), was directed by Iliyasu Abdulmumin. In the video, a certain man has two wives: Bora and Mowa. He loves Mowa and her daughter more than Bora and her daughter. Bora prepares food every day and is regarded as a mere cook to the detriment of her marriage. She takes up the role of a maid, while her co-wife Mowa does no domestic work. Whenever Bora prepares food, she serves Mowa, starving in the midst of plenty.

One day, Mowa's daughter passes urine while sleeping at night (bedwetting, which is regarded as a bad habit for grown up children). When they wake up in the morning, Bora's daughter is accused instead, and ordered to go and wash the *kirgi* (tanned cowhide used as bedsheet) in the river *Bagaja* which is very far and difficult to reach. She obeys the order and goes out in search of *Ruwan Bagaja* (water of bagaja). During the search, whenever she comes to a river, she asks if the water in the river is the water in river bagaja in a song, using humble and soft words along with beautiful rhythms:

Ko kai ne Ruwan Bagaja	Are you the River Bagaja
Ko ba kai ba Ruwan Bagaja	Or you are not the River Bagaja
Domin kirgi aka aiko ni	For the sake of bedsheets, I was sent
In zo in wanke a Ruwan Bagaja	To come and wash in River Bagaja

At last, she finds *Ruwan Bagaja*, washes the bedsheets, obeys the instructions and finds miraculous favour. She returns to the city and makes a triumphant entry on horse-back with escorts, drumming and musical beats befitting a princess. Now she and her mother have found honour and respect where they least expected. They continue their lives in peace and in wealth. This marks a turning point in their lives and shows a dramatic twist, because in the beginning, Bora and her daughter seemed to have been doomed, trapped in poverty with no hope of a brighter future. At the end of the movie, they turn out to be in control of expensive and beautiful possessions and riches which the daughter brought back from her travails in search of *Ruwan Bagaja.*

Having seen the honour bestowed on Bora and her daughter, Mowa instructs her daughter to bed-wet. In like manner, she is asked to go and wash the bedsheets. But because she is her parents' pet, she has been pampered and given a preferential treatment. Therefore, when she goes to wash the bedsheets, she shows disrespect to those she meets and comes back home on a donkey along with lepers as escorts. The story shows a reversal of roles: Mowa and her daughter, who seemed to be in heaven on earth, have now turned to be relegated to the background.

The Adaptation Skill in Ruwan Bagaja

In the video, bed-wetting, which is considered as a bad habit, is only imagined, unlike in the folktale[1] where bed-wetting is central - a video on this subject, called *Amalala* (a bed-wetter), was directed by Umar Jalo.

For someone who only sees the video, its source might be unclear, but someone who has trans-media experience will notice the skip. Such omission reduces the flow of content, and as a consequence, an essential piece of information is missed.

The scene of thigh (cinya) and dog (kare) in the folktale is entirely and skilfully omitted in the film, probably not because of its lack of importance, but because of the need of dealing with situations in a practical way according to what is actually possible. Therefore, the filmmaker did not incorporate actions which are better imagined than visualised, such as non-humans taking up the qualities and characteristics of humans - talking for example. Moreover, skipping the scene makes the video more realistic and suitable. Indeed, non-humans are not so easy to manipulate. On the other hand, this can be explained by Rachel's comment in Allen (2000), that every adaptation is an instance of textual infidelity.

Sangaya and Its Storylines

Sangaya was directed by Aminu Muhammad Sabo. Its source is the Hausa folktale called *Zubaina*, one of the series of folktales read by late Adbullahi Sani Makarantar Lungu and aired by Kano State Radio Corporation, Kano. The video is one of the most commercially successful Kannywood home videos. It became a household name, probably because of its song and dance scene, perfectly undertaken by the famous actor and actresses Ali Nuhu, Fati Muhammad and the late Hauwa Ali Dodo. Song and dance are part of Hausa culture - hence their inclusion in Kannywood home videos with an initial soundtrack composed with indigenous musical instruments. Yet, *Sangaya* is one of the videos that marks a turning point, for it does not only pioneer a change-over to electronic music, but also includes playback songs and choreography which indicate a revolutionising and globalising move in the Kannywood home video song.

According to Adamu (2007), trailers of the home video *Sangaya*, with the lead song being performed in the background, complete with choreography, immediately captured the imagination of Hausa urban audiences, helped along by the inclusion of a whole array of instruments such as flute, tambourine and African drums. The music, and most especially the choreography from the soundtrack, shot the video to stardom and placed it on the list of the most successful Kannywood home videos, thanks to the cross-fertilisation of influences, which results in the sending of the message that dancing and singing can sell and make meaningful impact.

The video presents a female servant called Tabawa, who, along with other female servants, works in a palace. Tabawa has a daughter known as Zubaina. Both Tabawa and Zubaina are disliked by the entire household, including the servants. Tabawa is accused of stealing sorghum flour meant to prepare pap for the king. The matter does not end as mere accusation, but it goes on with abuses, scolding, and with all sorts of maltreatment and the strong stigma attached to theft. Frustrated, Tabawa decides to seek relief and goes to sit under a tree somewhere behind the compound. A woman appears to her unexpectedly, frightening her, but tells her not to fear, adding that, despite the fact that she is not human (likely *fatalwa*, a ghost), she is a servant of God. She requests Tabawa to narrate her travails and promises to help her, asking her to come to the same place (under the tree) from time to time.

Shortly after that, Tabawa falls sick and asks for water. Her daughter Zubaina goes to other servants to request some water, but they refuse to give her even a drop and as a result, her mother dies. Before her death, Tabawa instructs Zubaida to go under the tree to meet the woman who will appear to her. "Tell the woman that I am no more. I adjure you to hold on to this woman". Tabawa then gives up the ghost. Zubaina's cry after the death of her mother attracts the attention of the servants. When they come, instead of sympathising with her, they mock Zubaina and show no concern. After this, the director takes us to a scene in which Maina (the Prince) comes back home from school in another city or country with accompanying drum beats and flutes, escorts and guards, at a time his father the king is about to leave for pilgrimage. Before he leaves, he instructs his wife the Sarauniya (Queen) to carry on with the wedding arrangements of the prince with his cousin Kilishi.

Following her late mother's instructions, Zubaina goes under the tree, the usual meeting place of her mother with the ghost. The ghost appears to her and asks her to narrate her problems. Zubaina tells her: "All the people in our household, including the prince who recently came back from school, hate me and for this reason, I prefer to die than to live". The ghost tells Zubaina that she should not worry and promises that all those who hate her will come to love her, a kind of turning point and a reversal of fate and destiny which Zubaina thinks is overdue but seems to be an impossible hurdle to cross over. However, the proverbs quoted by the ghost, such as *bayan wuya sai dadi* (after suffering comes enjoyment) and *kome na duniya yana da iyaka* (there is an end to everything on earth), comfort Zubaina and give her some assurances. The ghost then instructs Zubaina to close her eyes and recite the *Bismilla* (in the name of God) silently.

As she opens her eyes after the prayer, Zubaina discovers herself in entirely new clothes. The ghost whispers to her that any time she wants to see her, she should come under the tree. On her way back home, Zubaina meets the prince, who stops her, introduces himself to her and asks to know more about her. Zubaina says, "My name is Azumi and I am Fulani by tribe." Unknown to the prince, his new-found lover is Zubaina. They make a date to meet the next day. Zubaina goes back home where she reappears in her usual tattered clothes and stands by the entrance door. When the prince comes in and sees her there, he instructs *Jakadiya* (the chief maid) to make sure that Zubaina does not stand on his way.

Maina and Zubaina meet the next day and have the usual boyfriend-girlfriend discussion. Maina is now deeply in love with Zubaina, who also assures him of her love. For this reason, Maina changes his mind towards marrying Kilishi and tells his friend of his intention to now marry Azumi (Zubaina), his new girlfriend who is a beautiful girl that every man would like to take as wife. Maina's friends try to convince him to marry Kilishi who is also from a royal family, but he refuses and he enjoins them to consider Azumi as the girl of his choice. On seeing her, one of the friends approves of their marriage.

His proposed wife Kilishi hates Zubaina too, and says a lot of bad and negative things about her when chatting with her friends:

Kilishi: Imagine! So, there is a man who will want to marry this girl?

Friend 1: I doubt it. Any man who marries this "thing" makes a big mistake.

Friend 2: As for me, if I was a man and you give me this "thing" to marry along with 7 houses, I would not take the offer. Rather, I would say: take it to the market for another bidder.

On his next appointment, Maina takes his friend to meet Azumi. Maina's friend talks to Azumi on behalf of Maina although in his (Maina's) presence: a typical Hausa culture of courtship. Azumi agrees to marry Maina on one condition: "Can he marry me in any condition he sees me?"

This demand seems difficult for Maina's friend to answer, therefore he keeps quiet, gets back and allows Maina to move closer to talk for himself. Maina agrees to marry her, no matter the situation, and vows to eat his words by giving her his ring to seal his agreement. Azumi then promises to visit Maina's mother for introduction the following day.

Maina meets his mother along with Jakadiya, informs his mother about his intention to get married to a girl who is waiting (outside) to come and see her, and pleads with her to approve the marriage. Unfortunately for Maina, the girl who is waiting by the horse and which Jakadiya ushers in as directed, happens to be Zubaina. On seeing Zubaina, Maina asks Jakadiya the reason for bringing her, and she responds by saying that she is the girl he saw at the spot he described. Maina rejects Zubaina, but his mother says that it is not a shameful thing for him to marry Zubaina, who, despite being a servant, can be considered as a member of the household since she was born and brought up in this household and since her parents died there.

Moreover, a prince is allowed to marry a concubine. Despite his mother's explanation, Maina rejects Zubaina vehemently because, according to him, the girl he met is very beautiful. He adds that he gave her a ring as an engagement. Maina's mother asks Zubaina if this is true and Zubaina replies: "I am the girl he met and here is the ring he gave me." Maina's mother discovers that it is the ring and requests Zubaina to narrate how this romantic affair started between her and Maina. After she narrates the story in detail, Maina's mother concludes that it is the will of God for Maina and Zubaina to be a couple and decides that the marriage ceremony will be performed between Maina and Zubaina as well as between Maina and Kilishi on the same day at the same time. Maina asks Zubaina for forgiveness.

Maina's decision to marry Zubaina leaves Kilishi and her servants dumbfounded. Kilishi faces the agony of rivalry from a servant and now a co-wife, and the servants face the trouble of continuous torment of being servants to a fellow servant (now a princess) whom they despised, castigated and ridiculed. Kilishi's friends advise her to engage the assistance of a witchdoctor in order to stop the marriage.

A contest of self-expression is conducted in a performance by mainly Maina, Kilishi, Zubaina and other male and female dancers from the background. In a song, Kilishi expresses her reasons why Maina should marry her: she is of royal blood like Maina, she is his first girlfriend and everyone knows they are engaged. Zubaina, on the other hand, sings to explain why she deserves to be Maina's wife: she looks beautiful, she won the love/heart of Maina and she has no lover except Maina.

Reflections on the folktales and the clips

The folktales and their corresponding adapted videos illustrate the practice of polygamy. Here, it is not just a case of polygamy, but an instance of the marriage rites of an individual (man) to two women being performed on the same day and at the same time. In Hausa culture, it is referred to as *auren gata,* privileged marriage, as in the case of Maina to Zubaida and Kilishi. The folktales and video clips go on to explain the kind of unbalanced love and general treatment given to the wives by the husband. Such biased treatment usually extends to the offspring of the wives, which leads to intense rivalry between wives and more often than not, it is the reason for the lack of cordial relationship between stepbrothers in African societies in general.

In addition, both the folktales and the videos contain issues about child upbringing and the culture of patience, especially for a woman that is not the pet of her husband. This is seen in the proverbs *bayan wuya sai dadi, kome na duniya yana da iyaka* meaning, after suffering comes enjoyment and there is an end to everything on earth respectively. Both Bora's daughter and Zubaina suffer from maltreatment, but they endured, showed perseverance and eventually triumphed. Their situation conforms to the Hausa proverb which says that *mai hakuri yakan dafa dutse ya sha romonsa.* Literally, he who is patient can cook a stone and lick its sauce. It also means that the patient dog eats the fattest bone.

Furthermore, the folktales and the videos bring to the fore people's attitudes, opinions and feelings. For example, look at the link between tolerance and obedience, horse riding, drumming, music, escorts and scented perfume, all associated with royalty. On the other hand, leprosy, flies, insects and riding on donkey are synonymous with poverty and looked at contemptuously and negatively.

Conclusion

The storylines in Kannywood home videos have various sources. In its early years of existence, intellectuals were not the only ones to notice and criticise its adaptations of *Littattafan Soyayya* (Love Books) from *Adanin Kasuwar Kano* (Kano Market Literature), also lifted from Indian films: even ordinary citizens made this observation. In the context of northern Nigerian Muslim Hausa culture, such films are perceived as influenced by foreign cultures, accused of having a negative impact on Nigerian youths. Yet, despite the criticisms, Kannywood industry continues to spread out, with Jos and Kaduna having now joined Kano as centres of production.

Part of the reason why the industry is springing up all over northern Nigeria, even in the midst of strident demands of the Kano State Censorship Board, is found in the popularity of the language, Hausa, in which the videos are produced, and the availability of technological equipment to serve the demands of the populace in an era of mass unemployment. Observers hardly notice the second paradox of Kannywood, which is its ability to portray indigenous cultures in videos, using other conventional mass media functions such as educating, informing, entertaining and general mobilising. The two videos, *Ruwan Bagaja* and *Sangaya*, which serve as case studies here, represent an important transitional moment in the relationship between media and culture. We suggest that filmmakers should follow this up and adopt the use of other genres as sources of their films.

Works Cited

Adamu, Abdalla Uba. *Transglobal Media Flows and African Popular Culture: Revolution and Reaction in Muslim Hausa Popular Culture.* Kano, Nigeria: Visually Ethnographic Productions, 2007.

Adamu, Abdalla Uba, Adamu M. Yusuf, Jibril Umar Faruk (eds). *Hausa Home Video: Technology, Economy and Society.* Kano: Centre for Hausa Cultural Studies, 2004.

Ado-Kurawa, Ibrahim. "Hausa Films: Negotiating Social Practice" in Adamu, Abdalla, Uba, Adamu, Yusuf M, Jibril, Umar Faruk (eds).

Hausa Home Videos: Technology, Economy and Society. BUK, Kano: Centre for Hausa Cultural Studies, 2004.

Allen, Graham. *Intertextuality*. London and New York: Routledge, 2000.

Bekers, Elizabeth, Helff Sissy & Merolla Daniela (eds). *Transcultural Modernities: Narrating Africa in Europe*. Amsterdam & New York: Rodopi, 2009.

Couvares, Francis G. (ed). *Movie Censorship and American Culture*. Washington and London: Smithsonian Institution Press, 1996.

Diawara, Manthia *African Cinema: Politics & Culture*. Bloomington: Indiana University Press, 1992.

Gaws, Herbert J. *Popular Culture and High Culture*. New York: Basic Books, 1974.

Hall, Stuart. *Representation: Cultural Representations and Signifying Practices*. London: Sage Publications, 1997.

Inuwa, Umma Aminu. "Jirwayen Al'adun Indiyawa A Finafinan Hausa" in *Harsunan Nijeriya*. BUK, Kano: Centre for the Study of Nigerian Languages, 2010.

Jenkins, Henry. *Convergence Culture. Where Old and New Media Collide*. New York: New York University Press, 2006.

Jin, Dal Yong. *Global Media Convergence and Cultural Transformation; Emerging Social Patterns and Characteristics*. Hersey, PA: IGI Global, 2011.

Juvan Marko. *History and Poetics of Intertextuality*. Indiana: Purdue University Press, 2008.

Kaschula, Russell H. (ed). *African Oral Literature: Functions in Contemporary Contexts*. Cape Town: Ince (PTY) Ltd, 2001.

Kristeva, Julia. *Desire in Language: A Semiotic Approach to Literature and Art*. Columbia: Columbia University Press, 1980.

Larkin, Brian. "Indian Films and Nigerian Lovers: Media and the Creation of Parallel Modernities" in *African Popular Fiction,* Stephanie Newell (ed.) Indianapolis: Indiana University Press, 2002. 18 – 32.

Mazierska, Eva. *European Cinema and Intertextuality: History, Memory and Politics*. New York: Palgrave Macmillan, 2011.

Mazierska, Eva and Ostrowska, Elizabeth. *Women in Polish Cinema*. Oxford & New York: Berghahn Books, 2006.

McIntyre, Joseph & Reh, Mechthild (eds.) *From Oral Literature to Video: The Case of Hausa*. Köln: Rüdiger Köppe Verlag, 2001.

Mlama, Penina Muhando. *Culture and Development: The Popular Theatre Approach in Africa*. Uppsala: Nordiska Afrikainstitutet, 1991.

Taylor, Edward B. *Religion in Primitive Culture.* London: Harper & Row, Publishers, Inc, 1970.

Umar, Muhammad Balarabe. *Dangantakar Adabin Baka Da Al'adun Gargajiya.* Kano: Triumph, 1987.

Yahaya, Ibrahim Yaro. *Tatsuniyoyi Da Wasanni: Littafi Na Hudu.* Ibadan and Zaria: Oxford University Press, 1971.

Filmography

Abdulmumini, Iliyasu (Director). *Ruwan Bagaja* (The Water of Cure) Nigeria: Nagari & Sons Enterprises Nigeria Ltd, [1987], 2008.

Sabo, Auwalu Muhammad (Director). *Sangaya* Nigeria: I. U. I Production, 1999.

Note

Culturally, mothers are required to train their children by asking them to urinate before being going to bed, and, if a child persists in doing it, he is ridiculed by his peer group.

CHAPTER SIX

Mediating Countercultural Practices in Nollywood: Violence as Rebellion and Commodity in *Liquid Black Gold*

Philip Aghoghovwia

Abstract

This paper examines the cultural representation of the oil encounter in the Nollywood film, *The Liquid Black Gold* (2010) to explore, among other things, the impact of oil politics on the social and environmental structures in Nigeria. It reflects on the tropes of violence that underwrite the agitations for environmental remediation and local control of the oil resources in the Delta region, especially after the execution of the environmental activist-writer Ken Saro-Wiwa. The paper explores the dual role which violence plays in the oil politics of this region, both as a transgressive strategy and as a commoditised tool. While the disgruntled Niger Delta people, especially the youths otherwise known as resource rebels, resort to violence as a desperate move to draw attention to their plight, government officials, some oil industry captains, local representatives, and certain members within the ranks of the rebels, exploit this violence to distract the people from the actual "slow violence" (Nixon 2) taking place in the land. *The Liquid Black Gold* gives a contextual and imaginative definition to what violence in its two apparitions—physical and slow—has come to signify in Nigeria's encounter with oil exploration and all its attendant politics. Violence seems to have become a currency which circulates in exchange for the oil resource in the region. The atmosphere of agitation and rebellious mass action that the oil encounter galvanises ensures that only those who can afford this commodity of violence — either as resistance militant groups, state repressive forces, or those who flout environmental standards to maximise profit — can have access to the increasingly militarised oil wealth in the region.

Introduction

The modalities through which cultures and various discursive practices are mediated in Nollywood have been explored by a number of scholars. Ogaga Okuyade succinctly captures the strategic importance of Nollywood as a quintessential popular art medium in the representation of contemporary situations in Nigeria, when he insightfully notes that Nigerians are increasingly becoming a viewing public rather than a reading society (1). Haynes and Okome point to how Nollywood "video production has been absorbed into the realm of popular culture" in Nigeria (106). Film scholars maintain that Nollywood representations "give something like an image of the Nigerian nation [...] in the sense of reflecting the productive forces of the nation, economic and cultural" (106). Because of its wide range of subject matter and formulaic motifs drawn from contemporary national discourses, Nollywood is at the heart of the Nigerian public sphere. Adesokan puts this point more tellingly by arguing that "Nollywood films circulate as part of a welter of images in a stream of global flows, aided by the intense relationships between media and cultural imaginaries" (99).

Nollywood has a scavenger-like characteristic. With its ears close to the ground, it quickly picks its raw materials from contemporary situations in Nigeria with the speed of immediacy as they occur in society. The oil encounter and the politics of violence (resistance, warts and all) that its trajectory meets in the Niger Delta have provided sites for imaginative expression in Nollywood creativity. Eghagha opines that "The regularity with which movies are churned out yearly implies that the market is booming, [for] Nollywood enjoys great patronage among Nigerians" (71), and in fact, it is popular among 'Black' Africans in the diaspora.

As a result of its low budget production, Nollywood churns out movies with the rapidity of weekly releases. Ekwuazi observes that "Three release points of the video have since evolved. These are Lagos (Idumota Street), Onitsha (Iweka Road) and Kano" (64). He goes on to declare that "the targeted audience and, therefore, the thematic orientation of the video film determine the release points" (64). This suggests that the films are strategically circulated among targeted audience as a means of responding to, and provoking public reaction on contemporary issues in society. Hence the film *Liquid Black Gold* can be said to have been strategically produced as a means of isolating the social malaise of violence exacerbated by the oil encounter for a targeted audience's scrutiny.

There is a certain kind of local integrity and indigenous power associated with Nollywood films. This is because Nollywood's productions are sponsored by indigenous [private] producers, "who practically dictate the type of plot they want to see in the production" (Eghagha 74). Thus, what one can call an influential 'resource rebel' may well be the producer and financier of *The Liquid Black Gold*, a movie which brings to the fore an insider knowledge of the way violence is (re)appropriated from its original resistance insurgency to a currency of exploitation and distraction in the Delta.

In an auteurist film criticism on Kenneth Nnebue's creative and entrepreneurial boldness as catalyst to the Nollywood phenomenon, Haynes writes that Nnebue's creativity

> […] suffers from the faults and limitations of Nollywood as a whole […]. His great strength, which is also Nollywood's, stems from his proximity to the popular imagination. He works from what he reads in the newspapers, hears on the radio and picks up from the conversations around him […]. He converts his materials into an urban mythology of enormous reach and power (31).

The mechanical flatness and imaginative dullness identified as limitations in Nollywood movies (Haynes 31), in a rather obstinate, survivalist sense, give currency and uniqueness to Nollywood as a popular artform that has come to stay. I argue that Nollywood's technological limitations are, in a sense, over-determined, and as such, have not stunted the medium's creative ingenuity in giving narrative images, within the filmic genre, to those burning human concerns that confront the Nigerian nation.

Agatha Ukata locates Nollywood videos within the Third Cinema, where she, like previous scholars, identifies the socio-economic downturn of the late 1970s and early 1980s in Nigeria and Ghana as the most significant factors that led to the shift from celluloid to video film production (Ukata 6-9). But beyond the economic categories of low budget and lesser technical qualities that are characteristic features of Third Cinema, Nollywood is marked-off by its alternative vision and cultural aesthetics.

Nollywood films depict the lives of ordinary people in the so-called Third World in their daily struggles with postcolonial realities of poverty, ethnic clashes, cultures in transition and bad governance, to name just a few. Evaluation of a Nollywood movie as a filmic text is guided by the context, milieu and social code that underwrite its production. In the same breath, Ukata declares that Nollywood films "adhere to Nigerian standards by continually recreating the everyday lives of Nigerians within the context of their space and time" (5). This makes the medium a most popular mode of cultural expression in Nigeria and also makes the Nollywood phenomenon a significant referent in the global filmic industry (Okoye 20).

Conversely, within the context of my argument here, the above point arguably dismisses Nollywood as an art medium which produces a counter-public on the oil encounter. But in the movie under study, it seems to me that Nollywood mobilises its global circulation to a local benefit. It functions as a bridge-builder. According to Okome, Nollywood generates

> Knowledge at the local about the global that has eluded the watchful eyes of the state and corporate capital. Nollywood surely produces its own brand of knowledge in the competitive environment of the production of visual knowledge. It generates its own sense of the logic of the human condition in a postcolonial situation (4).

I share this sentiment, for the movie under study, in a rather subversive manner, refracts the concept of violence in ways that destabilise the discursive infrastructure of youth insurgency in the Delta. Here, the meta-narrative of violence in relation to the oil encounter is wrestled from the public domain and (re)appropriated to the counter-cultural domain of the Delta people (the resource rebels), where it is invested with a new grammar. This is a grammar that not only (re)negotiates the heroic struggle for the remediation of the polluted Niger Delta environment and local control of the oil resource, but also unknots the puzzling tale of militarisation and brigandage which the agitations and social protests of the people in the region have degenerated into.

What is more, at any rate, the alternative hermeneutic possibility which the movie provides in illuminating the complexity of violence validates Nollywood as fundamental to the imaginative representations of those vexing issues that attend the oil encounter in Nigeria. Throughout this paper, I argue that the new grammar of violence which the movie generates imbues violence with the status of a commodity circulating alongside the oil commodity, both of them threatening to annihilate the Delta people.

My intention in this paper, it may be stated forthrightly, is not to foray into the evolution of Nollywood as a cultural knowledge production site and formidable medium of representation in Nigeria. That subject has been adequately addressed in previous studies. Rather, I examine an aspect of its production which draws on the aesthetics of the spectacular, namely, violence that seems to attend instances of protests for environmental and social justice.

My interest resides in the modalities through which violence as a counter-cultural revolutionary tool is mediated in this movie, and the sets of epistemic categories derivable in reading this movie as representing oppositional discursive tropes and politics of the agitating people of the Niger Delta. The movie prognosticates how the agitation for environmental and social justice might be dangerously—if not already—diverted into an all-consuming violence that undermines a noble quest for justice. I argue that this (violence) might ultimately annihilate an autochthonous people who have the misfortune of being rooted in a region so richly blessed, yet cursed, with fossil fuel.

The Liquid Black Gold, directed by Ikenna Emma Aniekwe, was produced by Ossy Okeke Jnr in 2010. The movie is about an oil-producing community called Zeide, a fictional representation of the Niger Delta region. Zeide is confronted with the grim realities of oil exploration in Nigeria, that is, issues of environmental justice and sustainable development in the Niger Delta. This community is embittered about the destruction of their agrarian economy and the decimation of their socio-cultural fabric as a result of oil exploration and its attendant pollution.

The vibrant members of this community, mostly made up of the youths, march to the King's palace to demand a redress of the situation, and to have a representation in the affairs of local governance in the community. While the king, together with his council of elders, listens to the community's request, Ebipade (Sam Dede), the protagonist and the youth's de facto leader, quickly seizes this opportunity to demand a representation from among the youth to the oil company. This is where the conflict in the film is set.

More than half of the film is narrated as a series of flashbacks and documentary-style by the leader of the rebel movement to his wife. This provides the audience with the rationale and justification for the insurgency by the youth, and this includes the destruction of the fishing life, disenchantment among the youth as a result of unemployment, and the sexual abuse of women. The film also deals with the corruption and greed of the chiefs, initially elected to represent the community interests in their dealings with the oil companies, but now intent on maintaining their *nouveau riche* status. The corruption is evident at various levels of leadership and power, including in the army, and some of the youth insurgents also get co-opted into these structures.

In Nigeria's oil encounter, governance and moral reluctance in implementing people-oriented policies concerning the distribution of wealth from the oil resources are the biggest challenges to social justice and environmental remediation. These concerns, albeit fundamental in bringing lasting solutions to the Niger Delta question, have been treated with levity and hypocrisy by the government, the multinational companies and the collusive mainstream media. This is because the aspirations of the people — which are found to be in contention with the agenda of this troika — have not found a favourable alternative channel to provoke public sympathy and to embarrass the global community with what is taking place in the Delta.

Thus, this Nollywood movie seems to have stepped in to utilise its massive viewing audience in order to represent the counter-cultural narrative practices that derive from the people's defiance of the federal government, where the trajectories of the oil encounter are refracted and re-enacted for genuine public scrutiny. Okoye illuminates this point when he writes that "video film production is one such vigorous informal means by which the ordinary people productively contest their precarious social and cultural conditions" (26).

Theoretical Points of Departure

Since this paper deals primarily with the social phenomenon of violence, I shall turn briefly to what Schipper-de Leeuw has termed "socio-critical reflections" (10). Here, I look at two scholars for inspirational guidance and theoretical insights on the discourse(s) of violence: Frantz Fanon and Rob Nixon. Expressed exactly half a century apart, in 1961 (Fanon) and in 2011 (Nixon), both scholars' interests in the concept of violence intersect with the argument that animates this article. Fanon's idea of violence gestures to a libertarian weapon of defiance against forms of oppression, especially colonialism and its patrimonies of neo-liberal imperialism. Fanon's pronouncements on violent resistance enable us to understand the debates inaugurated by the twin issues of environmental degradation and of social injustice in the Delta.

The issues are framed as a new form of colonialism and the intervention deployed to resist it invokes an anti-colonial temper. Nixon's concept of slow violence signals a manifestation (though not visible) of the amoral practices of capitalism, evident in the oil extraction industry, which has polluted the environment and impoverished the autochthonous peoples of the Niger Delta. Both forms of violence have come to clash on the landscape of the Niger Delta. Attempts to make the slow violence visible through the human agency of insubordination and insurgency have resulted in a spiral of violence that threatens the continued existence of the Delta people.

In *The Wretched of the Earth,* Frantz Fanon advocates a kind of violence which serves as a revolutionary tool for rebellion against oppressive colonialism. Although Fanon's interest is in a resistance movement that is national in spirit, his avowals loom in the sub-national ethos that drives the resource-control agitators in the Delta. Their grievances, just like the anti-colonial movements, seek to challenge the environmental and political economic hegemon rooted in a historical, political, and eventually, economic trajectory that sprang from the colonial encounter and all those hegemonic philosophies that enabled colonialism to succeed. The trajectory of what appears to be the oppression of the Delta people, and the exploitation of the oil wealth the region bears by the Nigerian state, are framed as a kind of colonialism. Decolonisation, Fanon argues, is a struggle "between two protagonists" (28), so that the agency/catalyst - in this case: violence - with which that process is undertaken becomes the villain.

In the Delta's oil encounter, violence manifests as a double bind agency: a rebellious tool and a commodity in the hands of both the Delta resistance groups and their perceived villains. Violence seems to have become a currency which circulates in exchange for the oil resource in the region. The atmosphere of agitation, and the rebellious mass action that the oil encounter galvanises, ensure that only those who can afford this commodity of violence can have access to the wealth that the 'crude' oil generates. I shall return to this presently.

The insurgency of the resource rebels becomes the new enemy on the block. It insulates the main issues of social and environmental justice from public scrutiny, and usurps the rebellion it was deployed to bring about. After such insurrection, there seems to always be "the searing bullets and blood-stained knives which emanate from it" as reminders of the victims, mostly as collateral damages (Fanon 28). In the movie under study, the youth's eventual resort to violence re-echoes Jean-Paul Sartre's dictum in the preface to Fanon's *Wretched of the Earth* that "no gentleness can efface the marks of violence [slow violence]; only violence [sabotage] itself can destroy them [marks of violence]"(18).

Sartre notes that for Fanon, irrepressible violence is neither man's degeneracy to savagery, nor a misguided resentment of constituted authority; it is his resolve to re-create himself in the face of oppression (18). In the movie, I read violence, not as a tool for decolonisation in a strict Fanonian anti-colonial temper, but as a form of resisting vestiges of (neo-) colonial patrimony evident in the oil trajectory in Nigeria.

If, in the Fanonian paradigm, social protest and subversion are the uses to which violence is put in this movie, violence also serves as a commodity and as a tool of distraction. Nixon's *Slow Violence and Environmentalism of the Poor* provides insight for environmental pollution and the inequitable distribution of a country's resources to be seen as another form of violence: a non-physical violence. This idea has important resonance in this study, for it is environmental pollution and the destruction of the people's agrarian and fishing economy that exacerbate the agitation which results in physical violence in the Delta. Nixon's *Slow Violence* enables us to explore alternative ways of conceiving environmental degradation as a form of violence inflicted on the landscape and its inhabitants, 'the natives'—to use Fanon's term. This violence is insulated by the popular media's veneration of the spectacular violence engendered by the insurgency.

The primary concerns and grievances of the Zeide Community in the movie centre on environmental and social injustice. This is what Nixon calls "Slow Violence": an "environmentally embedded violence that is often difficult to source, oppose [...] and reverse" (7). Environmental pollution can be seen as an exemplar of what Nixon describes as the "unspectacular...slow violence" which stands as the most attritional violence (Nixon 2). Attempts at challenging this pillage are met with physical violence, bringing as much destruction and death as the environmental pollution itself.

I read this movie as a modest answer to Nixon's call for representational intervention in the oil encounter. He is of the view that artists—literary and visual—should be actively creative in drawing public attention to catastrophic acts that are low in instant spectacle but high in long term effects. Let me indulge myself by proposing that the movie, however, is unable to adequately draw public attention to this non-physical violence of environmental degradation. I will show that the action is quickly overtaken by physical violence and insurgency. But it succeeds in drawing attention to the increasing uselessness of structures meant to uphold order, in the face of changing dynamics motivated by self-interest on the parts of the chiefs and military leaders.

The king is portrayed as useless and ignorant, and easily swayed by the crooked chiefs' opinions. He is isolated in his palace and relies on the lies the chiefs feed him. This, in a sense, signals the ascendancy of political and economic power over cultural power in African modernity. Monarchs, supposedly the custodians of cultural values and societal cohesion, are rendered powerless, if not useless, in the socio-political economy of power structures — such as that which the oil politics underwrites — in postcolonial Nigeria.

Interesting parallels can be drawn between colonialism (motivated by economic exploitation) on the one hand, and oil exploitation and the politics of violence it galvanises on the other. Both can be apprehended within the context of colonial patrimonialism in the Niger Delta. During colonialism, natural resources such as palm oil, cocoa, cotton and groundnuts were imperially exported (expropriated, actually) to feed industrial Europe and to fund the continent's colonial project of imperialist expansionism. So too is the crude oil resource from the Delta siphoned to feed international demands for fossil fuel, and the wealth accrued is misappropriated by the Nigerian federal government. Both employ the force of violence in achieving their goals. Little wonder then that violence seems to be the most formidable tool in the hands of the 'natives' for challenging the oppressive order.

The Niger Delta dissidents invest their struggle with the grammar of colonial violent resistance by locating their agitation in the context of Nigeria's socio-political and economic history, which was bequeathed to the country by its British colonial masters. According to Fanon, in oppressive systems, the peasants are the actual revolutionaries. They embrace violence without the luxury of an option. Once they have access to weapons and the use of force, there is no going back for them until their goals are achieved. They believe that either way the pendulum swings, "they have nothing to lose and everything to gain" (Fanon 47). They believe that only violence pays, because, for the first time, they are able to express their grievances and call attention to themselves. That the authority is paying attention to their demands — either by pacification, by reprisal attacks or by negotiation — makes them sometimes overstretch the struggle, even if that means degenerating into brazen criminality, until their long-repressed anger is sated.

Representing Violence as Strategic Resistance and Strategic Commodity

No doubt, oppressive regimes in most of Africa — of which Nigeria is a case in point — are a matter of politics and of economics. The exploitation of the Delta and its people has always been, first, of an economic, and then, of a political nature, in order to maintain the status quo of the former. In *Liquid Black Gold*, Ebipade understands the importance of political power in having one's voice heard. He knows that change and development can only come when someone with the peoples' interest at heart sits at the discussion table where deliberations with the oil corporations are made. With this in mind, he demands youth representation when the dialogue between the community and the oil corporation will be in place. In the presence of the entire community and council chiefs, he addresses the king:

> *Ebipade*:
>
> One more thing your majesty: the youths of this community have decided that we want to sit and discuss with the White man [referring to the oil corporation]. Face to face [*this rouses applause from his followers*]. We do not want any more representatives. And we want to be part of the sharing and distribution process. No more representations.

This pitches him against the crooked chiefs who represent the community. The elite chiefs understand that if the youths are allowed to deliberate with the oil companies, their greed and betrayal of the community will be exposed. They connive among themselves to destabilise the brewing resistance and turn the social protest against itself:

Chief Zeide:

I know that boy will rubbish our effort. That boy has always struck me as a devil. I knew that boy alone would mess up our game.

Chief Paul (cuts in):

But I won't let him; I cannot allow that, that…oh I must do something.

Chief Ebi:

Indeed we must do something. We just have to do something…

These chiefs quickly identify a few youths in the community who have benefited from their corrupt practices and select them to become their stooges and oppose the 'authentic' youth leadership. These youths are paid and supplied with guns to cause disunity among the youth group: from here, violence is let loose between factions. Frustrated by this distracting opposition, Ebipade and his youth followership take to violence to make their voices heard. The youths continue to take the path of dialogue as the best option to seek to be heard, but the chiefs are bent on destabilising that pursuit for their own benefit. Their decision to employ violence is only vindicated when they are attacked, even while still deliberating on the available peaceful means to address the situation. The fighting that ensues distracts them from the real problem they had set out to address in the first place. The youth's frenetic display of energy and indignant exuberance are identified and turned into a commodity as a distractive strategy by the chiefs.

Other interest groups who benefit from the restiveness in the region swoop in to exploit the resistance movement to their parochial benefit. Two national leaders, Ogbuefi and Alhaji who call themselves "elders representing federal military interest", invite Ebipade to their house and offer to support him only if he decides to take to violence:

Ogbuefi:

So my dear young man, you need to fight, not just to fight but to fight hard. That your so-called chiefs and representatives are ripping you and your entire community off […]

Alhaji:

You need to fight with all seriousness. We have promised to supply you with guns and ammunition […] you need to fight them down and make them respond to the cries of your people.

Ogbuefi:

> All we need is our commission; (chuckles mischievously), just our commission and we'll give you plenty of ammunition to fight.

As the violent resistance degenerates into hostage-taking between the youth factions, the quest to find solutions to the environmental and the social problems is jettisoned. When Mr Aswani, an expatriate oil company official, shows reluctance to sponsor the insurgency, having been approached by Ebipade to help them get arms and ammunitions, an emissary from his oil-bunkering partners is sent to convince him to let the youths fight while their 'black-market' business goes on. The emissary assures Aswani that while the government tries to douse the tensions occasioned by the youth insurgency, their oil-bunkering business will go on undetected. The people are thus totally distracted from the actual violence of environmental pollution and pauperisation of their people on account of the oil encounter.

The idea of violence, both epistemologically and materially, can be read in this film as a pervasive capitalist tool, especially in the sense in which Terry Eagleton defines capitalism, as a leveller of status which does not care whom it enriches or impoverishes. Eagleton declares that "capitalism is an impeccably inclusive creed: it really doesn't care who it exploits. It is admirably egalitarian in its readiness to do down just about anyone. It is prepared to rub shoulders with any old victim, however unappetising" (19).

Violence is depicted in the movie in this same sense, as an enabler, both for the perceived villains and for the ostensibly genuine militant insurgents. A resonance can also be drawn from Wole Soyinka's conjecture on violence in a different context: the University of Ibadan student violence of 1980. Although the scholar's interest is with "the language of alienation" (as he calls it) with which such a social phenomenon is articulated by a "class of the bourgeois intelligentsia [...who engage in] the act of appropriating a harsh reality to a *langue* of scholarship" (135), he declares: "Nothing can be more proletariat than violence. [...Violence is] one of the few universal commodities" which "cannot be placed under license" (134).

The movie under study refracts questions of violence as a subversive tool which transcends the discursive. The movie dramatises how violence has become an intractable creed and the only language available to the contending formations that have emerged in the Delta over the years, especially after the execution of Ken Saro-Wiwa and the Ogoni Eight in 1995. The movie gives "an imaginative definition to the occluded relationships that result from slow violence and from the geographies of concealment in a neoliberal age" (Nixon 47). The movie seems to suggest that these relationships — of rebellious violence and commoditised violence — mobilise a discourse of resistance that is articulated in the grammar of physical violence as the environmentalism of the discounted poor.

Focalisation, Storytelling, and Mediation of Violence in *Liquid Black Gold*

In what appears to be technological deficiency in giving filmic representations to "slow violence", the movie deploys narrative characteristics of dialogue, storytelling and narrative-embedding to inaugurate the discourse of violence in the Delta. What the film lacks in cinematic techniques, such as giving visual images of the oil pollution of the Delta rivers, gas flaring or even violent confrontations between insurgent factions, it makes up for in dialogue; it imbues Ebipade with the art and act of telling — not showing — as would a griot in an oral performance. And this speaks to an earlier point of Nollywood's speed of immediacy in responding to, and drawing materials from contemporary situations in Nigeria.

Ebipade is strategically placed as the subjective focaliser to articulate the film's discursive schema in a way that signals the immediacy of a direct, if not live, conversation with his audience, although this takes place in a dialogue with his wife, Ihuoma. This, then, makes Mieke Bal's observation resonant when she notes that "The concept of focalisation pertains to narrative as a discursive genre but also yields insights into discourse itself as a semiotic system" (Figurations 1290). Thus, Ebipade's artistry in focalising instances of violence is negotiated by the film's oppositional discursive agenda for representing tropes of violence occasioned by the oil encounter in the Delta.

Ebipade has just returned from an insurgent expedition and his wife is uncomfortable with the spiral of violence in which the resistance is embroiled. She reprimands Ebipade for turning against his own people whom he [Ebipade] deems as traitors who have colluded with the government and the oil multinationals to exploit their community. Ihuoma charges Ebipade:

> Ihuoma:
>
> You so stoutly justify and defend the actions of you and your boys, Ebipade? Even when you fight and kill your own brothers and sisters? People who you should be within this so-called struggle?
>
> Ebipade:
>
> Yes, because those brothers and sisters who should be with us in this noble struggle have turned around to kick our backs [...]

In the film, Ihuoma represents a voice of alternative advocacy and the one who offers Ebipade the medium to rationalise the insurgency. Ukata interrogates ways in which women have been represented in Nigerian (Nollywood) films. She argues that such representations derive from, and reinforce stereotypical notions about women that inhere in patriarchal African societies such as Nigeria (6). Such stereotypical gender dichotomy is at play in this film, for Ihuoma is portrayed as the listening subject to Ebipade. But she seems to be playing an equally important role in the movie: she is the one who stimulates him to enter into a monologue (through subjective focalisation) in which the actions of the film are recounted.

Ebipade is positioned here as the focaliser, the one who mediates between the telling and the showing of the tropes of violence in the movie as a means of mitigating the deficiency in giving filmic realisation to instances of violence in the movie. Ebipade's monologue is interspersed with the camera movement, which pans out in a montage sequence to show how the people live in squalor even as their land produces much wealth for the Nigerian nation. The rest of his argument is acted out, through his stream of consciousness account of the incidents of violence that unfold in the film. At this point, only images — not action — backed with Ebipade's focalisation, could portray the thrust of the people's concerns. The mutual intersection of Ebipade's telling and of the intervention of the camera in refracting tropes of violence in the film resonates with Lawrence Bowling's submission on the use of stream of consciousness technique in fiction, where he notes that

> Although it is not easy to determine the exact point at which the mind drops below the level of language usage and functions by means of pure images and sensations, we do know that there is always in the consciousness a vast amount of mental activity which our minds never translate into language, and any attempt on the part of a writer [or director] to make a character think this non-language material into language form (that is, into interior monologue) sounds awkward and unreal (337).

Thus, the break in Ebipade's monologue by the camera montage does not suggest that he lacks the vocabulary to articulate the ideology of their resistance, but that Nollywood production, while taking cognisance of its technological limitation in giving artistic realisation to instances of violence, deploys modes of oral performance in the griotic artistry of Ebipade to complement its visual representation. The film's medium of portraying violence can be termed 'oraltronics': a blend of oral rendition and filmic mediation in the moving picture. For Ebipade does not act as though it is a film; he faces the camera and addresses his audience as in a live performance. Where the film is unable to show spectacles of violence or give filmic realisation to slow violence, Ebipade's monologue, in the form of monologist commentary, interjects to give expression to that which the movie refracts.

In discussing storytelling as a mode of representing violence in *Liquid Black Gold,* I shall align myself with Walter Benjamin's postulations on the art of storytelling. In his reflection on the fictional works of the nineteenth century Russian novelist Nicolai Leskov, Benjamin discusses the writer's artistry in capturing the essence of "Experience" through uncommon craftsmanship in telling stories (81). Benjamin notes that "The storyteller takes what he tells from experience — his own or that reported by others. And he in turn makes it the experience of those who are listening to his talk" (83). The centrality of storytelling as a veritable art in representing lived experiences of the oil encounter narratives in the Delta, which, sometimes elude mediation, has never been more aptly captured as by this scholar (Benjamin) when he draws a distinction between the storyteller and the one who merely informs. Benjamin declares that

> […] it is half the art of storytelling to keep a story free from explanation as one reproduces it […] The most extraordinary things, marvellous things, are related with the greatest accuracy, but the psychological

> connection of the events is not forced on the reader. It is left up to him to interpret things the way he understands them, and thus the narrative achieves an amplitude that information lacks. The value of information does not survive the moment in which it was new. It lives only at that moment; it has to surrender to it completely and explain itself to it without losing any time. A story is different. It does not expend itself. It preserves and concentrates its strength and is capable of releasing it even after a long time (85-86).

Confronted with the technological challenge of making a graphic statement in the film about the environmental and the social injustice in Zeide, the Nollywood film imbues Ebipade with uncommon craftsmanship in chronicling the oil encounter in Zeide Community, "For storytelling is always the art of repeating stories, and this art is lost when the stories are no longer retained. It is lost because there is no more weaving and spinning to go on while they are being listened to" (Benjamin 87). The inability of Nollywood to graphically capture the slow violence in the Delta is compensated by Ebipade's craftsmanship in relating the narrative. He makes his role in the struggle marginal while maintaining the importance of the agitation which is cardinal to the realisation of the twinned justice of the environmental and the social in the Delta. Thus, the meaning of his life and his experience with the oil encounter (that is, the agitation and the brazen violence) is revealed only in the struggle he throws his life into.

According to Benjamin, a storyteller does not tell us what we do not already know, but does it with such craftsmanship that

> The storytelling that thrives for a long time in the circle of work—the rural, the maritime, and the urban—is itself an artisan form of communication, as it were. It does not aim to convey the pure essence of the thing, like information or a report. It sinks the thing into the life of the storyteller, in order to bring it out of him again. Thus the traces of the storyteller cling to the story the way the handprints of the potter cling to the clay vessel. Storytellers tend to begin their story with a presentation of the circumstances in which they themselves have learned what is to follow, unless they simply pass it off as their own experience (87).

The above lines illuminate how Ebipade narrates the story of Zeide community within the context of the oil encounter. The struggle becomes a struggle for his own life; he does not tell us what we do not already know. Ebipade weaves and spins the story through his own involvement in the resistance, so that the Niger Delta struggle becomes a fresh tale of the oil encounter. Through his storytelling, one is able to establish how violence is paradoxically deployed to become a commodity as well as a rebellious tool in the hands of the agitating youths and in the hands of the oppressive order they set out to resist in the first instance.

Through this technique of narration, the oil encounter is re-enacted experientially in the action that unfolds in the movie to make bare the banality of violence. Benjamin contends that "All great storytellers have in common the freedom with which they move up and down the rungs of their experience as on a ladder" (95). He argues further that a great storyteller embodies "the image for a collective experience to which even the deepest shock of every individual experience, death, constitutes no impediment or barrier" in producing sets of epistemic categories for understanding complex encounters such as that invoked by the oil trajectory in the Delta (95).

Transgression as a subversive strategy against authoritarian order is not a static phenomenon, it is constantly shifting positions. And so, the dissidents involved have multiple subjectivities, which are sometimes conflicting. The characters embody the paradoxes that attend the oil encounter in the Niger Delta — of heroism and villainy, integrity and compromise, wealth and poverty, morality and amorality, husbands and insurgents — all at the same time. Hence, Tejumola Olaniyan argues in another context that, "Even so, whether ankle-or neck-deep in complicity, there is always complicity, for the ground of resistance is veritably impure…" (51).

This ground of complicity, as far as I can extrapolate in the above observation, is cogent in understanding the seemingly contradictory roles Ebipade plays in the film, for he embodies the contradictions and inconsistencies inherent in the oil encounter. Much as Ebipade is the leader of the dissident youth and the "supreme commander" of the foot soldiers in the Delta creeks, his humanity and moral standing are in no way brought into question. That his wife reprimands him at home suggests that he considers her as an equal partner in the domestic sphere, because it seems important to him that she understands the driving force behind their insurgency. So, he does not impose himself and his beliefs on her, but makes it a point of duty to explain the complexity of violence(s) in the community. And this, in a sense, illustrates that dichotomy of husband and insurgent in Ebipade's character.

Although Ebipade is ideologically motivated and morally upright, he is by no means perfect. He is not a flat character. He is perceptive, for he understands the enormity of the task he is faced with. As such, he is able to demand youth representation and seek social justice throughout the insurgency. For instance, Ebipade's decision to avenge the betrayal and murder of his friend and "sergeant-at-arms", Layefah, pushes him to restrategise. He compromises as a means of sustaining the resistance only when such a move ensures his continuous strength against his assailants, and this means that he is able to hold a firm stance to its conclusive end.

When the "elders who represent powerful interest from above" decide to stop financing their struggle, he plays a hand from his numerous aces, which will only ensure the continuous flow of arms and ammunition for their insurgency. Firstly, he seeks a youth representation among the community delegation to the oil company to deliberate and negotiate without violence as a peaceful means of remedying the effects of oil exploration on the community. When that is scuttled by the elite chiefs, he agrees to be supplied with ammunition by the two elders, Alhaji and Ogbuefi as a desperate move to make the youth's voices heard and bring attention to their concerns.

He strikes a deal with an official of the oil multinational, Mr Aswani, a 'white' man seen as one of those in connivance with some local elites to bunker oil in the region. Ebipade agrees to turn a blind eye in return for arms and ammunition to sustain the rebellion. At this stage, the movie creates a context for the insurgency in the region and serves as a subtext to the dubious role which violence plays in perpetuating an atmosphere of restiveness which makes meaningful development in the region impossible. But even as the youth resistance turns inward in a current of brigandage, Ebipade does not degenerate into acts of greed or parochial interests; his actions become acts of strategic sabotage as a means of pushing forth his community's demands.

Even while he is detained without trial — after being deceived out of the creeks by the cunning chiefs — his young followers remain loyal to him. His boys frame Ebipade's unlawful detention as a strategic game of war. They too deploy their own tactics of kidnapping and hostage-taking, but this time, they kidnap the expatriate officials of the oil multinationals, who had, hitherto, been left out in the insurgency. The youths see the violent confrontations between factions and the dubious Chiefs as a sort of witty game; thus, they deploy metaphors of sport contest to articulate their resistance.

When the second-in-command, Biokpor, is approached to cease hostility by Chief Teride, the new government-appointed negotiator, he [Biokpor] tells of his readiness to "play the game [of war] when the whistle is blown", that there is "no game [of peace] unless Ebipade is released". This seems to suggest that since Ebipade is the initiator of the insurgency demanding environmental and social justice, he is also seen as pivotal to the resolution of the conflicts and key figure in the entrenchment of true justice and meaningful development in his community.

Conclusion

The Liquid Black Gold can be read as an allegory of the contemporary socio-political situation in the Nigeria. But the film, just like most movies typical of Nollywood productions, heads for narrative closure, where every conflict is resolved and the people live happily ever after. I think that a narrative such as the oil encounter which resides in the discursive atmosphere of the irresolvable incoherencies, contradictions and paradoxes should eschew closures in order to prompt varied and alternative means of apprehending the crises occasioned by the oil politics in the Niger Delta. We need to know that narratives of the oil encounter in the Nigerian context are on-going historical processes with chains of events — contradictory and paradoxical mostly — which co-occur, not in a linear process, but in a cyclical discursive process. Noel Carroll writes that:

> Closure then transpires when all of the questions that have been saliently posed by the narrative get answered […]. The impression of completeness that makes for closure derives from our estimation, albeit usually tacit, that all our pressing questions regarding the storyworld have been answered (4-5).

This point holds only to the extent that the said narrative is meant to entertain and destabilise the foundations of our received wisdom. But when a narrative is also meant to serve an agenda, a narrative of discursive resistance, it ought to arrive at an open-ended conclusion. From the very beginning, the film sets out to apprehend the issues of social and environmental justice, seen as slow violence, but gets intercepted by physical violence. This physical violence was meant to be deployed as agency of resistance and bring to the fore the unspectacular, slow violence in the region; but it gets hijacked by the perceived villains and turned against the agitating youths whereby all get drowned in an abyss of physical violence. However, *The Liquid Black Gold* seems to be giving a moral definition to the subject of violence in the region: that, beyond the display of frenetic energy by the youth resource-rebels, there lies a desperate longing for an amicable and permanent solution to the Niger Delta crises. More than anything else, the people appear to be weary of the restiveness and the long-drawn confrontations with the government and the oil majors. Thus, the movie seems to suggest that the Delta people long for a day where all will sit and draw up a master-plan for a logical solution to the problems exacerbated by the oil encounter.

Note

For a comprehensive study of the evolution and practices of the Nigerian film industry known as Nollywood, see Hyginus Ekwuazi's *Film in Nigeria* Jos: Nigerian Film Corporation, 1991, and his essay: 'Nollywood: Historical as Economic Determinism or as an Accident in Evolutionary Trends/Creative Process', In *International Journal of Multidisciplinary Scholarship* Vol.3, No.5, Motion Picture in Nigeria (2008): 135-142. Other suggested readings include Agatha Ukata's 'Images of Women in Nigerian (Nollywood) Videos'. Unpublished PhD Thesis: University of the Witwatersrand, 2010; Akin Adesokan's 'Anticipating Nollywood: Lagos circa 1996' *Social Dynamics: A Journal of African Studies,* Vol.37, No.1 (2011): 96-110.

Works Cited

Adesokan, Akin. "Anticipating Nollywood: Lagos circa 1996." *Social Dynamics: A Journal of African studies* 37.1 (2011): 96-110.

Bal, Mieke. "Figurations." *PMLA* 119.5 (2004): 1289-1292.

Benjamin, Walter. "The Story-Teller: Reflections on the Works of Nicolai Leskov." *Chicago Review* 16.1 (Spring, 1963): 80-101. 18 March 2012.

Bowling, Lawrence Edward. "What is the Stream of Consciousness Technique?" *PMLA* LXV. 4 (June, 1950): 333-342.

Carroll, Noel. "Narrative closure." *Philos Stud* 135 (2007): 1-15.

Eagleton, Terry. *After Theory*. London: Penguin Books, 2004.

Eghagha, Hope. "Magical Realism and the 'Power' of Nollywood Home Video Films." *Film International* 5.4.28 African Video Film (2007): 71-76.

Ekwuazi, Hyginus. "The Hausa Video Film: The Call of the Muezzin." *Film International* 5.4.28 African Video Film (2007): 64-70.

Fanon, Frantz. *The Wretched of the Earth*. London: Penguin Books, [1961] 1967.

Haynes, Jonathan and Onookome Okome. "Evolving Popular Media: Nigerian Video Films." *Research in African Literatures* 29.3 (1998): 106-128.

Haynes, Jonathan. "Nnebue: The Anatomy of Power." *Film International* 5.4.28 African Video Film (2007): 30-37.

Nixon, Rob. *Slow Violence and the Environmentalism of the Poor*. Cambridge, Massachusetts: Harvard University Press, 2011.

Okome, Onookome. "Nollywood: Africa at the Movies." *Film International* 5.4.28 African Video Film (2007): 4-9.

Okoye, Chukwuma. "Looking at Ourselves in our Mirror: Agency, Counter-Discourse, and the Nigerian Video Film." *Film International* 5.4.28 African Video Film (2007): 20-29.

Okuyade, Ogaga. "Women and Evangelical Merchandising in the Nigerian Filmic Enterprise." *KEMANUSIAAN* 18.1 (2011): 1-14.

Olaniyan, Tejumola. "Narrativizing Postcoloniality: Responsibilities." *Public Culture* 5.1 (Fall 1992): 47-55.

Schipper-de Leeuw, Mineke. "Introduction." *African Perspectives* 1.1 Text and Context: Methodological Explorations in the Field of African Literature (1977): 7-10

Soyinka, Wole. "The Critic and Society: Barthes, Leftocracy, and Other Mythologies." *Black American Literature Forum* 15.4. Black Textual Strategies (1981): 133-146.

The Liquid Black Gold. Dir. Ikenna Emma Aniekwe. Perf. Justus Esiri, Enebeli Elebuwa Sam Dede. Ossy Affasson Limited, 2010.

Ukata, Agatha. "Images of Women in Nigerian (Nollywood) Videos." Unpublished PhD Thesis, University of the Witwatersrand, 2010. 1-33.

CHAPTER SEVEN

Nollywood Unbound: Benin Language Video Films as Paradigm[1]

Osakue Stevenson Omoera

Abstract

Apart from the usual Nigerian video films done in English language, Nollywood films are often addressed within the animated spectra of Hausa, Yoruba and Igbo language film studies. However, new frontiers of the glocalised order such as Benin, Nupe, Afemai and Ibibio language films have yet to receive critical attention in popular culture discourse in Nigeria and elsewhere. Employing historical analysis, interviews and document observation techniques, this study reviews existing literature on indigenous language movies in Nigeria and signposts the Benin video film as one of the vibrant new frontiers. The paper further examines the Benin video film against the backdrop of the Benin worldview that sets the subsection apart from other Nigerian film cultures. It concludes by asserting that, in terms of output, the film culture is representational and consequential, considering that close to 400 movies have been made in its visual existence, and canvasses for support for the culture both from the academic and professional circles so that it may realise its fullest potentialities in a glocalising Nollywood.

Introduction

In the first ever academic foray into the Benin video film culture, Omoera (*Benin Visual Literature*...234) provided a filmographic corpus of over 200 Benin language films, but today, close to 400 Benin movies have been made. This is a considerable output which ought to be given attention as a redoubtable corpus of indigenous film production. Yet the Benin language film is very much neglected, with little or no attention given to it in the academic as well as other learned arenas, hence the significance of a study of this nature which is aimed at asserting the Benin video film as a vibrant and viable Nollywood film culture beside those of the Hausa, Yoruba and Igbo/English.

Aside from the known film schools or acknowledged Nigerian film cultures of Yoruba, Igbo/English and Hausa (Zajc 67; Ekwuazi 4; Ogunsuyi 25; Idachaba 17), there are massive cultural productions in Nupe, Ebira, Afemai, Tiv, Efik, Ibibio, Itsekiri, Ijaw and Benin subsections of indigenous language films in Nigeria. These forms of media productions appear to have raised the ante of the 'glocalising order' in Nollywood because of the increasingly diverse and powerful cultural and linguistic energies they throw up. Onuzulike (233) seems to have made this point when he affirms that, in many ways, video film itself stands as an example of technology that can be used for cultural explorations and representations, mostly for the individuals or groups who cannot afford celluloid.

In fact, for over two decades now, Nollywood has experienced a tremendous mutation and growth in both the professional and academic arenas. This is likely to continue for a number of reasons. First, there are now many indigenous language film productions sites across the country, apart from the dominant ones. Secondly, a considerable number of academic journals, books, conferences, professorial chairs and academic centres have been/are being dedicated to Nollywood studies in and outside Nigeria. The efforts of the Nollywood Studies Centre, Pan-Atlantic University, Lagos, Nigeria; *Film International*, an esteemed journal on the stables of Intellect Books, London, United Kingdom; *Postcolonial Text*, a Canada-based humanistic journal of international clout; *Ijota: Ibadan Journal of Theatre Arts*, a highly rated University of Ibadan-based specialised journal of international standing - all deserve commendation in this respect.

It is from the foregoing perspective that this study argues that Nollywood is unbound, that it has gone beyond the 1980s and 1990s geographical and linguistic categorisations and interpretations to include a lot more in a 'glocalising order', which, at present, appears not to be receiving attention from film critics, film scholars and film theorists.

Nollywood Films and the Glocalising Order

As a concept, glocalisation relatively recently crept into film as a form of media production in Africa. Glocalisation is a word that was invented in order to stress that the globalisation of a product (for instance, film as a cultural and *edutainment* product) is more likely to succeed when the product or service is adapted specifically to each locality or culture it is marketed in. The term combines the word globalisation with localisation – an earlier term for globalisation in terms of product preparedness for international marketing is internationalisation. The expression first appeared in the late 1980s in articles by Japanese economists in the *Harvard Business Review.*

According to Roland Robertson, who is credited with popularising the term, glocalisation describes the tempering effects of local conditions on global pressures. He specifically argues that glocalisation "means the simultaneity – the co-presence – of both universalising and particularising tendencies" (12). For instance, the increasing presence of Nollywood films worldwide is an example of globalisation. On the other hand, the variegated outlook of Nollywood movies as expressed in Yoruba, Hausa, Igbo/English and Benin, among other ethno-linguistic lines, is another example. This outlook comes with different language tropes, customs, artefacts, distributive channels, deployment of technologies, exhibition agencies and market mixes in an attempt to appeal to local audiences in parts of Nigeria, Congo, Ghana, Sierra Leone, Gambia, South Africa, Kenya and Tanzania.

Glocalisation serves as a means of combining the idea of globalisation with that of local considerations. Thus, initially developing an understanding of globalisation offers a great deal of assistance in beginning to understand the function and meaning of glocalisation. Philip Hong and In Han Song explain that

> Globalisation corresponds to the integration of local markets into world capitalism. Manifested by global changes in structures of the economy, globalisation entails a restructuring of the world economy and a spatial reorganisation of production and consumption processes across political states. (658)

Relying on Beck's interpretation of glocalisation as "internalised globalisation," Roudometof further develops the foregoing definition primarily by solidifying its roles within and relationship to transnationalism and cosmopolitanism. Roudometof insists on the need of clearly defining these terms to more fully understand glocalisation, with which they are interrelated (113). In a larger context, he explains that the emerging reality of social life under the conditions of glocalisation provides the preconditions necessary for transnational social spaces, and that this process of glocalisation may lead ultimately to a cosmopolitan society (118). Agreeing with Roudometof but with a specific reference to the Nigerian film, Okome (3) asserts that

> While the wholesale adoption of video technology by practitioners in Nollywood has been an unqualified local success, it is the spirit to defy the economic malaise of the cinema industry in Nigeria that led to the adoption of this 'new' technology. What this success signifies is the will to overcome the problems occasioned by economic and political hiccups in the 1980s with the slump in the local currency. Perhaps even more important is the desire expressed by video filmmakers to keep local stories in the narrative programme of this local visual culture. By appropriating the terms of video technology the way that Nollywood has done… this local cinema has demonstrated to its audience and to the cinema world at large (transnationalism) that it has not despaired of making some kind of sense out of its own hieroglyphics. In the same vein, it has invested in its playful narratives of the social and cultural life (cosmopolitanism) of the Nigerian post-colony a nuanced essence of parody… (Parentheses mine).

Again, while stressing that cosmopolitanism and transnationalism are, without a doubt, unique concepts, Roudometof presents the insight that the two conditions often have a very close correlation to one another, a source of confusion repeatedly uncovered during many attempts to describe interconnected global processes. However, based on his extensive research, Roudometof (130) offers an understanding of transnationalism as the connectivity and motion of everything from immigrants to the practices of capitalism, religion, or activism across state borders.

Indeed, one could consider globalisation as an economic form of transnationalism, since the social movement described by transnationalism entails a reduction in the significance of boundaries to all forms of activity globally, from political to cultural or economic processes. While the relationship is not linear or automatic, many forms of transnationalism may nevertheless serve as indicators of developing cosmopolitanism within a state (Roudometof 131). Yet again, cosmopolitanism, which to Roudometof (130) signals a preexisting blending of global and local considerations in real life through glocalisation, can be conceptualised as a moral and ethical standpoint or quality of openness manifested in people's attitudes and orientations toward others. As he notes, cosmopolitans (for instance, *Lagosians* in

Nigeria) living in a transnational world are known to adopt a more open, encompassing attitude toward peoples and regions distinct from their own (131).

Thus, as boundaries fade in importance due to transnational motion, the integration of global and local forces defined by glocalisation makes transnational social spaces, in which those people and processes that have crossed borders interact, a reality. Ultimately, this process of glocalisation may provide societal encouragement for the more culturally open mindset of cosmopolitanism. The foregoing interesting and intersecting scenarios seem to be unfolding with the emergence of Nollywood in the transnational film ecologies of Nigeria, continental Africa, African diaspora and indeed the Western world.

For instance, the multiple award-winning Benin language/Nollywood filmmaker, Lancelot Oduwa Imasuen's *Adesuwa*, which premiered in the Odeon Cinema in the United Kingdom in 2012, the world tour of *The Figurine* by Kunle Afolayan, the exhibition of Tunde Kelani's *Thunderbolt* in different festivals and cinemas in Africa and indeed across the world, among many other Nollywood movies, indicate the transnational potentialities of Nollywood films in an increasing glocalising world. It is important that Nigerian film scholars and researchers begin to interrogate aspects of these extended readings of the Nigerian film with a view to deepening global as well as local understanding of the highly diversified nature of Nollywood for the socio-economic, socio-cultural and socio-political imports and even impacts it has made and is still making.

Theoretically and practically, therefore, the aesthetic and economic possibilities of an emergent glocalising order in Nollywood are yet to be fully explored and exploited by development agents in both the academic and professional circles of the cultural and entertainment industries in Nigeria. According to Eregare and Afolabi (145), the cultural and entertainment industries are vehicles for social and cultural relations. These industries, whether they are news, drama, music or film, are responsible for the 'manufacturing' of meanings.

Glocalising the meanings and symbols produced by these industries through effective and pragmatic platforms such as Nollywood can benefit those interested in discussing or exploring the phenomena of translocal cultures, global linkages and transnational networks that impact and shape identities, cultural heritages and relationships among and between Nigerians and other Africans, Africans and the people of African descent and other peoples worldwide.

However, this discourse is more interested in how the Benin video film, by virtue of the Benin *weltanschauung*, can be distinguished and become accepted as a viable aspect of Nollywood, and in the need for film scholars, film critics and theorists, among other stakeholders in the academic and professional circles, to give the required support for the film culture to realise its fullest potentialities in a glocalising Nollywood. Before delving into this, it may be useful for this discourse to briefly reflect on the dominant Nollywood cultures in relation to some of the new ones, which the Benin film emblematises.

Dominant Nollywood Film Cultures vis-a-vis the New Ones

Nollywood is arguably the most diversified film ecology on the African continent, with distinct production points of releases and the exploration of diverse subject matters. Haynes and Okome observe that

> Nowhere else in Africa has a domestic market been captured so successfully. The video films are produced on a number of distinct bases, and have a variety of forms, styles, and themes, as well as a language of expression. Taken together, they give us something like an image of the Nigerian nation – not necessarily in the sense of delivering a full, accurate and analytical description of social reality, but in the sense of reflecting the productive forces of the nation, economic and cultural (106).

In an attempt to examine these 'productive forces', Ogunsuyi (*The Aesthetics of Traditional*…32; *African Theatre Aesthetics*…21) contends that three popular approaches to the epistemology of films earlier agreed upon by Yearwood (65) and Ekwuazi (*Film in Nigeria* 133) could be applied to a purposeful reading of the traditional African theatre films in Nigeria. According to Ekwuazi in Ogunsuyi (*African Theatre Aesthetics*…21),

> The first of these approaches is the iconic criterion. This is said to assert the identity and meaning of the film image… The second is the indexical criterion. It asserts the socio-cultural background of the filmmaker and applies this as an index to conceptualising the film. The third and the last is the intentional criterion. This is where the very

basis of evaluating the film is based on the intention per se of the filmmaker.

These approaches are referential because they serve aesthetic inquiries. It is germane to note too that these approaches direct our attention to contemporary studies associated with conceptual instruments of linguistic and semiotic science traceable to post-modernist culture. Exploring the foregoing along with the economic practice within society that clearly discerns the place of film, Ogunsuyi posits that there are three schools of film in Nigeria. These are the Yoruba School of Film, The Hausa School of Film and The Igbo School of Film (Ogunsuyi, *The Aesthetics of Traditional*…36-53; *African Theatre Aesthetics*…25-35). Idachaba (17) and Zajc (67) agree with this classification of the existing schools of film in Nigeria.

As earlier noted, these identified schools have received and continue to receive scholarly attention from many disciplinary backgrounds, nationally and internationally. Larkin (232), Johnson (203), Ekwuazi (*The Hausa Video film*… 66) and Adamu (77) agree that Hausa video films have close engagements with the styles of love present in Indian films as well as certain preachings which emphasise the Islamic worldview. Ekwuazi (*The Igbo Video film*…147), Ugor (76) and Enem (29-30) affirm that there is an undeniable thread which runs through the Igbo video film: the inherent drive for individual success, which has made the Igbo personality to be seen as a victim of egotism and crass materialism. The Yoruba video film, on the other hand, is to a great extent influenced by the animated cosmos of the Yoruba people. Life to the Yoruba mind is cyclical, involving the worlds of the living, the dead and the unborn. Therefore the Yoruba film is steeped in mysticism, belief in reincarnation and rites (Ogundele 100; Asobele-Timothy 4; Eghagha 73). This, perhaps, explains why Okome argues that the Nigerian video film has an unchallengeable *presence*, which has called attention to itself from the world on its own terms (*Nollywood: Africa*…6).

Some other critical inquirers into the Hausa video film include Mohammed Bala (1992), Yusuf Adamu (2004), Mathias Krings (2004), Hyginus Ekwuazi (1997), and Abdalla Adamu (2007; 2009; 2010; 2011). For the Igbo video film, some of those who have inquired into its nature also include Anyanwu Boniface (1995), Hyginus Ekwuazi (1997), Nwachukwu-Agbada (1997), Chukwuma Okoye (2007), Nnamdi Malife (2008) and Stefan Sereda (2010). Again, Onokoome Okome (1991;

1993), Hyginus Ekwuazi (1994), Durotoye Adeleke (1995; 2005; 2007; 2009), Wole Ogundele (1997), Afolabi Adesanya (1997), Obododimma Oha (2002), Daniel Seiffert (2004), Olufadekemi Adagbada (2005; 2008), Adewale Rafiu (2007) and Saheed Aderinto (2012) are some of the Nigerian film scholars and critics who have done incisive scholarly studies in the area of the Yoruba video film.

Issuing from the foregoing, it is no surprise to observe that Nollywood, for a very long time, was structured along the lines defined in colonial times, with three main regions: the Northern region with Kano, the South-eastern region with Onitsha and the South-western region with Lagos. This is why it is part of the burden of this study to dispel this notion by arguing that a considerable amount of filmmaking activities is taking place among other micro-national film cultures in Nollywood which remains generally underexplored and under-theorised and yet can be demonstrated to be representational and consequential in terms of production output, audience reception and opportunities for contending views and voices as well as the cultural display of difference.

This, perhaps, best explains why new frontiers, beyond the generally known Hausa, Igbo and Yoruba Nigerian video movies, have emerged in the cultural firmament of the country. In fact, some film scholars, film producers and film aficionados are now working on various film projects that explore their cultural and tribal affiliations. For instance, Mabel Evwierhioma is working on Urhobo video films (Mabel Evwierhioma in an interview with this researcher in 2008). Prolens Movies Limited has produced *Ukpebuluku* (2009), an Urhobo film. Supreme Movies Limited has produced another Urhobo video film, *Urhieuvwe* (2010).

Similarly, Steve Amedu is already producing films in Esan language (Steve Amedu in an interview in 2008). Tony Boye produced *Inaghomi* (2008), an Itsekiri video film; Alex Eyengho also made *Oma tsen-tsen* and *Suara La* in Itsekiri language. Uncle City has produced *Igbabo-Eva* (2009), *Ifiogbodon Se Eraman* (2010), *Emo Isagbo* (2010), *Okpor-Ogie* (2010), among others, in Afemai language. Emem Isong premiered an Ibibio language movie, *Mfina Ibagha* in 2006; and many others have been produced in other Nigerian languages such as Fulfulde, Kanuri, Tiv, Efik, Ijaw and, of course, Benin, which is the fulcrum of discussion in this study.

Benin Videography: Early Beginnings, Production Sites and Audiences

Historically speaking, Ozin Oziengbe, aka Erhietio Sole, a man widely believed to be the doyen of Benin video drama (in an interview with this researcher in 2009) contended that the Benin have produced video dramas long before the commonly acknowledged ones. To buttress his point, he cited video works such as *Ikioya* (1988), *Ewemade* (1989), *Ehizomwanogie* (1990) and others which he made in technical collaboration with the Nigerian Television Authority (NTA), Benin Centre. His position appears to enjoy the support of Ogunsuyi (*African Theatre Aesthetics*…66) who also remarks that, as at 1987, he had produced *Erhi Ifueko* (*Ifueko's Father*), a folk drama for the screen at the NTA, Benin Centre. However, Baba Cliff Igbinovia, a prolific Benin movie-maker and actor (in an interview with this researcher in 2009), pointed out that the first commonly acknowledged Benin video drama appeared in 1992 with the Uyiedo Theatre Troupe's *Udefiagbon*.

Although *Udefiagbon* treats the contemporary social issue of child abandonment, Peddie Okao (in an interview with this researcher in 2009) noted that it is *Evbakoe*, subtitled in English as *Reap what you Sow* and released by Soul 2 Soul Nigeria Limited in 1998, which many people regard as the first video drama of Benin language expression. Regardless of when, where and how video filmmaking in Benin commenced, Ibagere (in an interview with this researcher in 2011) observed that Benin video films, which numerically rank fourth, after Hausa, Igbo and Yoruba film cultures, have not yet been granted as much academic attention as the others.

Benin is the present-day capital of Edo State in South-Southern Nigeria. The term 'Benin' is vested with several meanings and connotations, the earliest of which date back to between 900 - 1200 AD, when it started enjoying the status of a kingdom ruled by the Ogiso (Egharevba 1). Benin is also interchangeably used with the term 'Edo' (Agheyisi 39; Omoregie 10-11; Lawal-Osula 2). Aside from being a geographical entity, the word 'Benin' is also used to describe the people and the language spoken in this area. With the current geopolitical arrangement, the Benin-speaking people are mainly found in the southern part of Edo State (Edo south), which comprises seven (7) local government areas (LGAs), namely Oredo, Egor, Ikpoba-Okha, Orhiomwon, Uhunmwonde, Ovia South-West and Ovia North-East.

The inhabitants of these LGAs are, for the most part, native speakers of the Benin language and the primary market target of all the Benin video film producers/videographers who produce Benin movies.

Benin filmmakers operate from two distinctive points, Benin and Lagos, with several production sites. While Lancewealth Images Nigeria Limited is a clear Benin film producer from the Lagos end, Prolens Movies Nigeria Limited, Pictures Communications Nigerian Limited, Osagie Mega Plaza Nigeria Limited, Triple 'O' Resources Nigeria Limited and 99 Entertainment Nigeria Limited, to mention a few, constitute and animate the creative and productive mitochondrion of filmmaking at the Benin end.

The non-native residents of the Benin-speaking areas, as well as the general viewing public, including audiences in other parts of Nigeria, Africa, the Diaspora and the Western world, constitute the other markets for the Benin language film. Perhaps, this speaks to the potentialities of the Benin video film in a glocalising Nollywood, which are largely untapped at the moment. Some of the outstanding names in the Benin video culture are John Bull Eghianruwa (Sir Love), Eunice Omoregie (Queen of Benin movies), Omo-Osagie Uteteneghiabe (the unmistakable voice of Benin movies), Loveth OKH Azugbene (Emama no kasedo/Ovbesa kpooo), Osagie Legemah, Osaretin Igbinomwanhia (Akpaka 99), Prince Ayomi-Young Emiko, Onions Edionwe, Osarodion Enogieru, Monday Osagie, Lancelot Oduwa Imasuen, Davidson Esekeigbe, Baba Cliff Igbinovia, Osasuyi West, Ogbeide (Ukeke), Andrew Osawaru, Wendy Imasuen, and Omodele Uwagboe.

These have featured as actors/actresses or producers/ directors in movies such as *Ikoka* (2003), *Ikuemitin* (2007), *Emotan* (2003), *Ekuase* (2004), *Agbawu* (2007), *Yasin* (2008), *Olidara* (2008), *Ebuwa* (2009), *Ovbimwen Osemwen* (2011), *Okpaniya* (2006), *Okagbe N'ogbeti* (2011)and *Adesuwa* (2012), among many other great Benin films. In a bid to draw attention to the Benin subsection of Nollywood, Omoera asserts that most of these films are linked with the Benin Oba or royalty, but generally explore mundane and contemporary issues as well as matters from previous epochs, using Benin language, proverbs, folklores, costumes, artefacts, songs and adages, among other icono-cultural paraphernalia as distinctive means of communication, which are steadily carving a niche for Benin movies in the pantheon of indigenous films in Nigeria (*A Taxonomic Analysis…*52; *An Assessment of the Economics…*forthcoming). Having briefly looked at aspects of the history, production and audiences of the Benin film, this study elects to examine the Benin worldview in the Benin video film as a way of concretising what really makes the Benin film 'tick' in a glocalising Nollywood.

The Benin Worldview: An Infrastructural Base for the Benin Video Culture

Generally, worldview denotes a comprehensive and usually personal conception or view of humanity, the world or life. In relation to African arts and worldview, Trowell (19) argues that

> In reality, the essentials of art study are more fundamental and necessitate a thorough understanding of man's nature, physical and spiritual; of his modes of expression, visual and otherwise; of his reactions to surrounding; of his relationships with the world, in each and all of its various aspects; and of the progress of all these factors through time.

Trowell's profound assertion still holds true today about traditional African arts, their practitioners and the society where they live. The traditional Benin society is steeped in customary observances which allow for the devolution of authority from the Oba down to the ordinary citizen. Ezra (3) asserts that the Benin Oba is the central figure in the kingdom, combining vast spiritual powers that result from his divine ancestry with enormous political clout.

According to the Edo Arts and Cultural Heritage Institute (EACHI), Benin is one of the oldest traditional kingdoms in West Africa, which still exist today. Much of what is known about Benin today is its rich arts and crafts that adorn many museums around the world. During the colonial era, Europeans looted a lot of the sacred and popular arts of the Benin people (Osahon 48), and efforts to retrieve some of these art works are still on-going (Igbinovia 13). Meanwhile, another popular art form is emerging: the Benin video film, a performance art purveyed to large audiences, both Benin-speaking and non-Benin speaking, through the use of videographic gadgets such as cameras, video compact disks and digital video disks, among other modern media technologies.

Omoregie (in an interview with this researcher in 2009) remarked that it appears that the rich history, artistic and cultural heritage of the Benin are now being transmitted through the agency of the video film as a form of modern media production. Of course, this is what impels this investigation of the Benin-speaking audience's reception of the Benin video film. Ezra (3-4) and Erhahon (123) opine that almost all the folklores, popular beliefs, customs, stories, music, dance, legends, festivals, oral history, proverbs, aphorisms, sculpture, weaving, sports and games of the Benin people are either derived from the Benin royalty or associated with it in one way or the other. Hence, the Benin have popular songs such as the 'Eguae ruese' folksong which goes thus:

Text in Benin	**English Translation**
Kponmweoba me	Thank the Oba for me
Kponmwen ekhimwen oba me	Thank his chiefs for me
Iwina ne eguae ye vbe Edo oyemwen	The work the palace is doing in Benin pleases me

Chorus

Eeee Eguae ruese   Thanks go to the palace for everything

The above and many more traditional components of the Benin worldview appear to have found their way into the Benin video art (Omoregie in an interview with this researcher in 2009). At any rate, the traditional observances within the Benin culture space may be categorised into cultural, socio-religious and economic bases.

Culturally, Igbe (*The Okaegbee*…59) points out that the male folk are generally regarded as the head because the traditional Benin home and community are built around patrilineal or patriarchal 'edifices' such as the 'Omodion' (eldest son) inheriting the estate of a deceased person. Traditionally, a man who has many wives is said to have many 'urho' or 'doors'. That is, if he has three wives, he has three 'urho' or 'doors' (Eweka1; Ehiemua 3). The traditional Benin sees the number of 'doors' in a man's house as an indicator of whether he is a man of substance or not in society. Thus, any Benin man who is unable to cater for his family is despised and considered as belonging to the dregs of society. The women are traditionally expected to bear children, see to the needs of their husbands and generally manage the home front. Hence, in their kinship and lineage organisation, there is a marked patrilineal bias and emphasis upon primogeniture (Eweka 1-2).

A critical look at *Adaze* (2003), a video drama produced by Ama Films, shows this patrilineal bias of the Benin society, where women tend to be relegated to the background in the decision-making process in family affairs. Ukata (*The Images(s) of Women* …1; *Conflicting Framings*…65) has roundly condemned this seemingly unfair representation of women in the Nigerian society as well as in Nollywood films. She contends that Nollywood videos such as *I was Wrong* (2004), *More than a Woman* 1 and 2 (2005), *Omata Women* (2003) and *Glamour Girls* (1997), among others, typified women in very outrageous ways that tried to feed on the stereotypes of women in Nigeria and by extension in African societies, as if women had nothing good to contribute to the society other than destroying moral values.

In the socio-religious domain, Izevbigie (78), Obanor (1), Ebohon (20) and Lawal-Osula (7) assert that the traditional Benin person leads a sedentary lifestyle and believes in the existence of a supreme God/being (Osanobua) whom he/she worships and communicates with through intermediaries such as the ancestors, Ehi (guardian angel) and other smaller deities such as Olokun or Ogun, among others. Obanor (20) further posits that the average Benin man believes in reincarnation and that a man/woman reincarnates fourteen times to complete a full circle of his/her existence. Substantiating Obanor's view, Ebohon (*Cultural Heritage* …7; *Ebohon and his Centre*...20) argues that the Benin believe that calamity or evil can be avoided or averted through appropriate propitiation rites at ancestral shrines such as Aro-Era (Father's shrine), Aro-Iye (Mother's Shrine), Aro-Osun (Osun's shrine) or Aro-Ogun (Ogun's shrine), among others. Perhaps, it is such a belief that informs the 'Ugieewere' ceremony which gives every Benin man or woman the opportunity of warding off evil from the land and requesting good fortune yearly (Omoruyi 12-13; Osemwengie-Ero 4).

On the economic front, the Benin are very industrious people who specialise in industries such as bronze casting, farming, coral bead-making, and general merchandising. Osawaru and Eghafona (82) contend that the present day bronze casters in the Igun quarters of Benin City are reminders of the high sense of craftsmanship and industry of the Benin in the past. Technologically, Osagie (64-65) states that the early Benin local technology developed in about ten base areas, including metal, wood, ivory, bone, shell, fibre, leather, clay, mud and stone. However, there seems to be a gradual but consistent shift from this pristine Benin worldview to the one which is constantly being assailed from many angles. This trend is perhaps due to the advent of time, modernity, urbanisation, foreign religion, globalisation, foreign languages and other contemporary challenges. This discourse will reflect on some more values that the Benin people hold dear, using the postulation of Ekwunife (70) as described in his 'Quinquagram of Igbo traditional religious values' before examining some of the contemporary challenges in the Benin people's worldview.

Although Ekwunife uses the Igbo traditional society as a reference point, the issues canvassed are illustrative of the values that are central to the worldview of traditional Africans, including the Benin people. Ekwunife (70) identifies five pillars on which many of the traditional African values are built by drawing on the Latin word *quinqua* meaning five. Putting *quinqua* in perspective, Ekwunife contends that "Life, Offspring, Wealth, Peace and Love" are the cardinal values around which other traditional African values cluster (72). Scruton (483) had earlier noted that the term 'value' is often applied to all those objects thought to be worthy of human pursuit on moral, aesthetic or religious grounds. This position dovetails with Shorter's (111-112) observation that

> ...value is the worth which we ascribe to choice – choice of an object, an opinion, a course of action, a relationship, a role, an experience. In a choice, one alternative is preferred to the other (or another) and a worth is conferred upon it...Values are expressed as a repeated and consistent leitmotif. In any number of contexts, through any number of images or symbols, they become a regularity or pattern in the thought of people or culture...

The point being made here is that there can be no value if man has not got the potentialities of choosing from many alternatives. These alternatives may be objectively good or bad, moral or immoral, just or unjust, praiseworthy or blameworthy. When a person is faced with these alternatives, he/she evaluates them, making choices which may later on be discovered to be either detrimental or beneficial to his/her general welfare and that of the society where he/she lives. It is in this context that this discourse gets clearer by looking at the Benin worldview vis-à-vis the five cardinal traditional African values as put forward by Ekwunife.

For the traditional Benin of southern Nigeria, life is the supreme gift of God to man. It is a supreme value (Igbe Okaegbee 54; Obazee 50) meant to be cherished and preserved at all costs. No other human value should be preferred to this supreme value: it is sacred, belongs to God and is given to man on trust. Hence, no Benin ever toys with his/her life or with another person's life. Emovon (28) affirms that the Benin express this belief in their prayers, sacrifices and offerings, songs and music, dances, video arts, in the names given to children, proverbs, pithy sayings, betrothals and marriage ceremonies, myths and folklores, in their social and political interactions, in their economic ventures and organisation.

Igbe (*Izomo…*53) further states that the value of human life as a supreme gift from God is commonly expressed among the Benin in the names given to their children, such as Osayande (God owns the day), Orobosa (everything is in God's hands), Osayaentin (God owns the might of life), among others. Other names and maxims expressive of this sentiment are Agbondimwin (life is deep), Agbonze (life is of great value) and N'agbonrhienrhien ze iro dan (the person who is enjoying life does not harbour evil thoughts). If, therefore, as scholars like Awolalu and Dopamu (28-29), Ikenga-Metuh (250) and Ekwunife (74) rightly point out, African names are pregnant with meanings, it is because these names not only express personalities but also rich African values. For the Benin, the greatest human value is life. Perhaps, this thought is better captured in the Benin folk saying/song which reads:

Text in Benin	**English Translation**
Ede agbon mwen	My life
Rhie obosa ne akpama	Is in the able hands of God
Afianma gie fiannmwen	Fear is far from me
Udu gie khuemwen	My heart will never fail me
Rhunwunda tegha muso vbe nerho	Because I must realise my dreams
Vbe agbon nerhie	In this life.

Second in the Benin hierarchy of values is the offspring. Osayande and Abolagba (3) state that the Benin people place a very high premium on biological fruitfulness. This, in the view of Igbe (*Izomo…*53), is reflected in such names as Omorowa (a child is the house), Omosede (a child is of greater worth than wealth), Omorose (a child is beautiful), Omorotiomwan (a child is one's family or lineage), Omoruikhuomwan (a child is one's inheritor), Omorunomwan (a child performs one's transitional rites) and so on. Indeed, having many offspring - usually from polygamous marriages - is greatly valued in Benin traditional culture, not only to supply the needed manpower for economic purposes, but also to continue the cherished ancestral lineage (Erhahon

151). Mere (93) substantiates the point being made when he observes that

> Traditionally children are highly valued. They have to continue the ancestral line in order to retain the family's ownership of whatever property that belongs to it. The reality of family extinction cannot be ducked where children are not forthcoming. Such a situation is socially abominable.

It is therefore no surprise that the average Benin parent believes that having children wards off the anxiety of growing old and the fear of loss of property to undeserving fellows. This is consistent with Obazee's (43) argument that the high premium the Benin people place on their offspring impels them to go to great lengths in ensuring continuity of family lineages. One of such socio-cultural mechanisms, according to Omoregie, in an interview with this researcher in 2009, is the levirate system of remarrying within a particular family as a result of the death of the person's spouse. This practice, which is still prevalent today, requires a man to marry his brother's widow for procreation purposes.

The meaning of wealth in Benin custom is better described than defined in the strict sense of the word. Wealth, in the traditional Benin thought system and practice, does not necessarily mean abundance of material goods as modern Africans may conceive it, nor does it exclude some measures of affluence. Agheyisi (39) posits that wealth, for the traditional Benin person, is a comprehensive term which includes in its purview some landed properties, numerous children, relations and dependants, human skills and other endowments of nature through which a man or woman can make a living. Indeed, one may say that for the Benin person, there are two major ways of acquiring wealth, namely by ascription or inheritance and by achievement or through one's skills and labour. With respect to the former, the Benin would say Efe-Erha (wealth of the father) or Efe-Iye (wealth of the mother), while they call the latter Efe-Obomwan (wealth of one's hand or labour) which is further amplified in the inimitable Benin proverb, "A ma mie eson a i mie uwa" meaning "one does not experience prosperity or wealth without labour" (Erhahon 2).

Fourth in the pecking order of Benin traditional values is love. Love and peace are interrelated. However, for explanatory purposes, we will treat them separately. 'Awe-emwen-omwan' which can be literally translated as "good neighbourliness among human beings", is perhaps, the best word in Benin to describe love. To the Benin mind however, Erhahon (68) opines that it is a dynamic quality expressed in multiple human actions whose principal functions are to promote, cement and enhance human interactions in three vital areas – ontological, socio-political and religious/spiritual.

Omoregie (in an interview with this researcher in 2009) argued that if love (awe-emwen-omwan) exists between two people or communities, they will strive to uphold or support one another. Everyone will endeavour to conform to family and social etiquette of not breaking known taboos of both the land divinity and other popular divinities of the community or of the ancestors such as suicide, incest, adultery, stealing, to mention a few. Husbands will support their wives and vice versa, children will respect their elders and leaders, and the family, clan and community will lead responsibly if love is shared among them.

The opposite could spell doom for the individual, clan or community. For instance, for a husband to kick his wife in the belly during pregnancy for any reason whatsoever is a serious offence against 'awe-emwen-omwan' (love). The reason is obvious. In doing so, the man is manifesting his hatred for the sanctity of human life (the wife and the child in her womb) and by extension hatred for the society in need of continuity and perpetuity. He is equally offending the ancestors of the family, the clan and community, morality and ultimately God the author of human life. In a sense, all moral offences in the traditional Benin society are offences against love (awe-emwen-omwan). This is probably why love in Benin thinking expresses itself in concrete actions which are meant to promote social ties, communal bonds and religio-cultural advancement (Omoregie in an interview with this researcher in 2009).

Like 'awe-emwen-omwan' (love), the idea of peace (ofunmwengbe) is not apprehended in abstract terms in the traditional Benin society. Rather, it is viewed in terms of social relations, social justice and religious interactions. 'Ofunmwengbe' (peace) as the traditional Benin perceive it is to be gauged in terms of social relationships: family relationships, clan relationships, village relationships or community relationships. Borrowing from Buddha's "Noble eight-fold path" (Parrinder 78), one may say that Benin social relationships which engender peace are characterised by three of these paths. These are: "Right Speech, Right Action and Right Livelihood." 'Right speech' in Benin cultural context implies the choices and expressions of words that always cement social relationships. A common Benin maxim to this effect is 'Ota ne khuerhe o mua ekhoe rhie oto' meaning 'It is a pleasant speech that puts the mind at rest'. And, of course, it is the mind at rest that can contribute to the peace of the home and community.

With regard to 'right action' in social relationships, the Benin custom expects all strata of its citizens to be acquainted with the social norms and taboos of each sub-cultural area and observe them meticulously. Through the process of socialisation, children and youths are inducted into these various norms and taboos of society, either in their various families or by acquaintance with age grades, peer groups or through instructions by accredited leaders of society. For example, children and youths are expected to greet their elders and relinquish their seats for them in a gathering. Failure to observe this will earn sharp reprimands from parents, guardians and responsible elders. Hence, the Benin place a high premium on the notion of 'Ima omo emwin', which means 'a child must be taught something to live by' (Erhahon 19).

Besides, every Benin clan/lineage has its lineage greeting and people/youths from each clan are expected to greet others/elders in the morning, using their clan salutation/greeting. This gives everyone in the traditional Benin society an instant mark of identity in terms of the family he/she belongs to (Egharevba 79). Hence, the Oba lineage greets with 'Lamogun', the Iyase of Benin family greets with 'Lavbieze', the Ezomo clan salutes with 'Lagiesan', the Oliha lineage greets with 'Laogele' and the Ero family salutes with 'Lamosun', among many other morning family greetings. Incidentally, Benin Kingdom is reputed to be the only place where such lineage salutation is practiced in Africa.

At the level of 'right livelihood', every member of the Benin society is expected to be trained in one skill or the other to be useful to his/her immediate family, extended family and society at large and to have a meaning for living. It is such thinking that informed the Oba's setting up of different guilds where youths can learn various arts and crafts in addition to the usual farming skills. Dark (5) observes that a strong tradition in Benin is that of bronze casting, which was learned during the time of Oba Oguola. By this arrangement, every youth in the traditional Benin society grew up knowing that the society would make allowance for his/her training and subsequent employment. This also helped in maintaining fairness and social justice in the land.

As an all embracing phenomenon, peace (ofunmwengbe) encompasses in its purview the ideas of social relations, social justice and religious interactions. It is the 'fruit' of 'awe-emwen-omwan' (love), the end term value in the hierarchy of values of traditional African culture as postulated by Ekwunife. In any case, the Benin Oba has consistently been emblematised in all Benin art forms, whether old or new, including the Benin video film. Ezra (4) affirms that art forms such as sculpture, bronze casting and carving, as practiced in Beninland, constitute a royal art which has the Oba as its centre piece.

Some Implications and Conclusion

Undoubtedly, the media presents a vital sphere where glocalisation is made evident. A powerful means of making connections on an international scale, the media is nonetheless a tool also capable of having an impact at a more local stage. Hampton (1112) offers a meaningful example of this reality through his study of Internet use by local communities of urban underclass citizens. Developing a naturalistic experiment that examined the use of the Internet for communication at the neighbourhood level, Hampton was able to identify the role of the media in encouraging local social cohesion and community engagement. Examining a topic of interest in which studies are presently quite limited, Hampton (1131) was able to determine that connection across distance may not be the only affordance of Internet-based communication. Rather, according to his studies, when a critical mass of individuals within a shared local environment adopts the Internet for communication, they cultivate an increased awareness that this tool affords communication locally as much as it does across distant space. In this light, use of the Internet for communication at the local level offers a strong example of the phenomenon of glocalisation.

Drawing on the foregoing, this discourse holds that the Benin worldview as a firm infrastructural base for the Benin video film is capable of vitalising greater video works, beyond the heights reached by *Ikoka* and *Adesuwa*, thereby boosting the presence of the Benin video film in a glocalising Nollywood. To fully aggregate the gains of the Benin worldview which teems with great stories, folklores, artefacts, icons and images of universal appeal, this study proposes a small but dialectically relevant paradigm which it tags 'homefrontism'. As a concept, it calls for a more painstaking aesthetic inward-looking attitude of Benin filmmakers into their social cultural milieu in making video films. It posits that a conscious scouring up of iconic cultural resources such as proverbs, myths, folklore, heroic exploits, Benin Obaship rites and pithy adages, among other linguistic tropes, which are in abundance and currently largely untapped, can widen the entertainment and cultural relevance of Benin films in Nollywood and beyond.

For instance, if culturally germane stories are given aesthetic twists and depths via videographic nuances, among other digital-enabled processes, the created contents are likely to stand the Benin film out as embodying unique communicative figurations amidst other mediatised cultures. Apart from the fact that the foregoing proposition enjoys a considerable support from a sampled audience of Benin speakers (Omoera *Audience Reception*...131), its intellectual resourcefulness is underscored by Okezie's (204) assertion that

> The languages and customs of Africa define and identify the people at their local settings. They guide their behaviour and determine the outcome of their efforts. It means that without their languages and customs, the continent has no identification and thus cannot be defined, cannot think, nor act constructively and independently, which are necessary elements for development.

Therefore, Benin video film practitioners, scholars, critics, enthusiasts and theorists should embrace and possibly adopt the rather deconstructive dialectics of 'homefrontism' to theoretically benchmark the output of the teeming Benin video culture in a glocalising Nollywood.

A diachronic review of the different forms of artistic/media production in Beninland would show that landmarks, myths and folklores linked with the Oba have been a major source/repertoire from which indigenous artistes – dramatists, novelists, poets, bards, musicians and dancers - have continued to draw inspiration. For instance, a careful examination of the creative works (stage plays, poems, carvings, sculptures and music) of O.S.B. Omoregie, High Priest Osemwingie Ebohon, Ambassador Osayomore Joseph, Sir Victor Uwaifo, Akaba Man, Chief Arala Osula, Evbinma Ogie and other Benin performing artists attest to this fact. The Benin video film, being a cultural and edutainment product of the latest technologies available and accessible to the Benin people, appears to have become the trendiest audio-visual purveyor to aggregate the advantages of other art forms/forms of media productions it met, in order to assert itself, gain credibility and acceptance of the Benin populace and indeed other micro and macro national populations.

The foregoing development has a theoretical mooring in media studies. McLuhan (65) asserts that when a new medium supplants older forms, it borrows the nuances, paraphernalia and other materials from the older forms to gain credibility and acceptance from the people (users). Indeed, this is what the video film as a form of media production has done to other art forms in the Benin culture area, with a view to asserting itself in a glocalising Nollywood.

Furthermore, we noted that change triggered by a number of factors such as urbanisation, globalisation, foreign religion, modernity, technology and foreign language seems to have swept through the Benin culture area in the last few decades, leaving in its tracks weighty changes that are worth reflecting on in relation to the Benin worldview. This is probably the point Masagbor and Idemudia make in their allusion to Benin City when they observe that

> …there is ongoing writing and rewriting. The physical transformation particularly with the current beautification and modernisation of the city, the realignment of roads and so on, there is reflexivity in the palimpsest. This has its heartaches and hurt as well as the benign… (17).

In a way, a majority of the Benin people, especially the youths, are now 'itinerant' persons. Leaving their erstwhile sedentary way of living, the Benin people now travel around the world seeking the Golden Fleece. There is nothing wrong with this but there is this negative colouration to the fact that hundreds of thousands of Benin girls engage in 'igbiragia'- literally meaning prostitution - and other indecent acts in many European cities in Spain, Italy and Germany and even in the Americas (Ehiemua 1). This trend has given Beninland a negative image at home and abroad.

Besides, in a bid to travel abroad, boys now sell their fathers' houses. This act has brought hardship on both the male youths and their parents. A local artiste, Don Ziggy (2010), laments over this negative development in his musical video 'Libya Story'. Many of these boys die in the deserts of Libya while attempting to illegally cross to Spain or other European nations. A number of their parents also die of heart attack when they suddenly realise that their boys have sold their houses under their nose. Another video work entitled *Amaekpavbeowa* vividly explores the precariousness of Benin youths' travelling. Again, Mamudu (83), in *Blind Search*, aptly captures the sorry Benin scenario: landlords (parents) are under siege from adventurous sons and the only handy remedy is to inscribe on the walls: 'This house is not for sale'.

Even this precautionary measure has been beaten time and again by the collusion of desperate sons, hard-nosed estate agents and money bags who believe they can buy anything or anybody with money. Perhaps, it is this kind of problem that made Odunsi (27) to lament, though in a slightly different context, that

> The varieties of pleasurable display that life offers are contrasted with ejections of its dynamic complexity so that a lifetime is punctuated here and there, now and then, with various problems. Like logical constants and music refrains, problems have become a regular pattern of human life, constitutive, as it were, of our 'conditio humana' as far as we remain wayfarers. They are there in the private and family lives, in the social, economic, political and religious lives as well.

Worst are the problems of cybercrime commonly referred to as 'Yahoo Yahoo', armed robbery and kidnapping for ransom - perhaps the latest challenge assailing the Benin people. Although these has been attributed to scathing poverty, youth unemployment and general sense of despondency in the land, it stands to reason that life is more than the pursuit of crass materialism. All kinds of persons have been kidnapped: children, adults, the poor, the rich, medical doctors, teachers, politicians and many others have either died or been humiliated to the extent of parting with huge sums of money to stay alive. In fact, it now appears that what binds the Benin people together is falling apart and not even the police, the welfare department or the youth and culture ministries have been able to do much to salvage the situation. It is this whole gamut of transitory tendencies and trends in the Benin worldview that seems to have been factored into the creative combustion of the Benin video film as a contemporary performance art.

In spite of the regrettable negative developments noted above, the Benin video film has emerged as a viable variant of Nollywood, owing to a large Benin-speaking audience and a considerable output of video works. Indeed, the mediating role of the video film as a form of media production has, to a large extent, helped in rejuvenating the people's interest in some of the traditional beliefs, pristine ethos and cherished mores of the Benin in the face of raging globalisation, especially as the Oba of Benin as an institution appears to be the epicentre of many of the Benin language movies. In the words of Oha (64), the Benin video films, as "visual media, are thus to be considered central in the project of cultural re-orientation and education in Africa, given the ways they assist in constructing and reshaping perceptions of the link between the present and the past."

As a popular art, the Benin video film should be used to revive the interest of Benin speakers and other Nigerians/non-Nigerians, especially the youths, in the seemingly dying Benin language. It should be used to propagate the socio-cultural practices of the Benin, which are capable of standing out in an increasingly glocalised Nigerian (African) society. Development agents such as community based organisations (CBOs), non-governmental organisations (NGOs), and even governmental organisations (GOs) in the Benin area and in the Diaspora, should make conscious efforts to see that the Benin language film is allotted a channel on DSTV's African Magic bouquet, a mileage that the dominant Nollywood film cultures enjoy at the moment. Such a proactive step will further authenticate the unbound character of Nollywood and expand the visibility which Benin videos currently have in a glocalised Nigerian film environment. In order to improve the audience of the Benin video film, filmmakers should take advantage of the current development in film production by making cartoons. Making animated movies of Benin orientation will aid Benin videographers to buy into the children's niche market where cartoons are an irresistible attraction.

The multiplier effects of reframing the Benin language film along the above artistic and economic lines can well redound to the development of human and material resources in the Benin video subsection of Nollywood and indeed the larger Nigerian society. However, this is against the current grain of thought, as many a Benin youth is jobless, hapless, crime-prone, and lacks marketable skills. This damning trend needs to be redressed urgently. In this regard, Omoera (*Bridging the Gap*…forthcoming) notes that

> There is so much talk about youth empowerment and development without commensurate action to actually provide templates for the youths to unlock their creative abilities. For this reason, the level of unemployment among the Benin youth remains considerable. A

majority of youths in the area under study do not have the financial means to acquire formal education; they lack marketable skills and are chronically poor. Furthermore, there are few socioeconomic structures to support or empower the youth to fend for themselves and this contributes to the underdevelopment of Benin and indeed Nigeria. In view of the situation on the ground in the Benin locality, where a large number of the youths do not have any form of formal education or marketable skill and do not hope to have any in the near future due to their social-economic handicaps, it can be argued that hands-on education in the various crafts or enterprises in filmmaking will be a good starting point.

As Nollywood is unbound, the need for frontiers such as the Benin, Ebira, Fulfulde, Ijaw and Urhobo, among other indigenous language movies to be studied and considered as both a reflection of and an influence on cultural issues, is becoming more crucial in order to better understand and navigate an increasingly glocalised Nigerian film ecology. It is hoped that this study will further vitalise academic interest in the Benin video film by film scholars, critics and theorists within and outside Nollywood.

Works Cited

Adagbada, Olufadekemi. Womenfolk in Yoruba Video Film Industry. Unpublished Thesis. Linguistics and African Studies, Arts, University of Ibadan, 2005.

___ "Yoruba Texts on Screen." *Africa through the Eye of the Video Camera.* Ed. Foluke Ogunleye. Manzini, Swaziland: Academic Publishers, 2008.208-224.

Adamu, Abdalla U. "Istanci," "Imamamanci" and "Bollywoodanci": Media and Adaptation in Hausa Popular Culture. *Hausa Home Videos: Technology, Economy and Society.* Eds. Abdalla U. Adamu, Yusuf M. Adamu and Umar F. Jibril. Kano: Centre for Hausa Cultural Studies/Adamu Joji Publishers, 2004.83-99.

____"Currying Favour: Eastern Media Influences and the Hausa Video Film." *Film International* 5.4 (2007):77-89.

___2009. Media Parenting and the Construction of Media Identities in Northern Nigerian Muslim Hausa Video Films." *Media and Identity in Africa.* Eds. Kimani Njogu and John Middleton. Bloomington, IN: Indiana University Press, 2009.171-84.

___"The Muse's Journey: Transcultural Translators and the Domestication of Hindi Music in Hausa Popular Culture." *Journal of African Cultural Studies* 22.1(2010):41-56.

___"Transnational Flows and Local Identities in Muslim Northern Nigerian Films." *Popular Media, Democracy, and Development in Africa.* Eds. Herman Wasserman. New York: Routledge, 2011. 223-235.

Adamu, Yusuf M. "Bulungudu: Space and Coinage in the Hausa Home Video Industry." *Hausa Home Videos: Technology, Economy and Society.* Eds. Abdalla U. Adamu, Yusuf M. Adamu and Umar F. Jibril. Kano: Centre for Hausa Cultural Studies/Adamu Joji Publishers, 2004. 221-231.

Adeleke, Durotoye A. Audience Reception of Yoruba Films: Ibadan as a Case Study. Unpublished Thesis. Linguistics and African Studies, Arts, University of Ibadan, 1995.

___ "Culture, Art and Film in an African Society: An Evaluation." *Nordic Journal of African Studies* 12.1(2003): 49-56.

___"The Social and National Integration Phenomena in Yoruba Video Films." *Yoruba: Journal of the Yoruba Studies Association of Nigeria* 3.1 (2005):21-33.

___"Communication in the Yoruba Court: Reflections from Yoruba Video Films." *Africa: Revista do Centro de Estudos Africanos* 27-28 (2007):115-133.

___"Reconfiguration of Sango on the Screen. *Sango in Africa and the African Diaspora.* Eds. Joel E. Tishken, Toyin Falola, and Akíntúndé Akínyẹmí. Bloomington: Indiana University Press, 2009.135-156.

Ademiju-Bepo, M.K.A. Themes and Trends in the Drama of the Post-Osofisan Generation on Stage and Screen. Unpublished Thesis, Theatre Arts, Arts, University of Ibadan, 2005.

___"Towards the Nationalisation of Nollywood: Looking Back and Looking Forward – A Reading of the Thematic and Economic Trends. *Ijota: Ibadan Journal of Theatre Arts* 2-4 (2008): 148-161.

Adeoti, Gbemisola. "Home Video Films and the Democratic Imperative in Contemporary Nigeria." *Journal of African Cinemas* 1.1 (2009):35-56.

Aderinto, Saheed. "Representing "Tradition," Confusing "Modernity": Love and Mental Illness in Yoruba (Nigerian) Video Films." *Mental Illness in Popular Media: Essays on the Representation of Disorder.* Ed. L. Rubin. Jefferson, NC: Macfarland, 2012. 256- 269.

Adesanya, Afolayan. "From Film to Video". *Nigerian Video Films.* Nigerian edition. Ed. Jonathan Haynes. Jos: Nigerian Film Corporation 1997. 13-20.

___ "From Film to Video." *Nigerian Video Films.* Revised and expanded edition. Ed. Jonathan Haynes. Athens, Ohio: Ohio University Centre for International Studies, 2000.37-50.

___"Human, Technical & Financial Resources Management in Motion Picture Production. *Making the Transition from Video to Celluloid.* Eds. Hyginus Ekwuazi, Mabel Sokomba and Onyero Mgbejume. Jos: National Film Institute, 2001.47- 74.

Agheyisi, Rebecca N. *An Edo-English Dictionary.* Benin City: Ethiope Publishing Corporation, 1986. Print.

Aimiuwu, Leonard E. 2007. Benin Culture: Towards the Next Level. *A Compendium of Speeches /Lectures at the Symposium on Igue Festival: The Religious and Socio-Cultural Relevance in Modern Society.* Benin City: Benin Traditional Dance Foundation, 2007.4 -7. Print.

Asobele-Timothy, S.J. *Yoruba Cinema of Nigeria.* Lagos: Upper Standard Publication, 2003.

Awolalu, Omosade J. and Dapomu, Adelumo P. *West African Traditional Religion.* Ibadan: Onibonoje Press and Book Industries (Nig) Ltd., 1979. Print.

Bala, Mohammad A. "The Hausa Film: A Study of Slow Growth, Problems and Prospects". *Operative Principles of the Film Industry: Towards a Film Policy for Nigeria.* Eds. Hyginus Ekwuazi and Yakubu Nasidi. Jos: Nigerian Film Corporation, 1992:179-204.

Dark, P. J. *An Introduction to Benin Art and Technology.* Oxford: Oxford University Press, 1973. Print.

Ebohon, Osemwengie. *Cultural Heritage of Benin.* Benin City: Mid-West Newspaper Corporation, 1972. Print.

_*Ebohon and his Centre: A Life.* Benin City: Ebohon Centre Publications, 1996. Print. Edo Arts and Cultural Heritage Institute. "Edo Arts and Culture." Web. 21 May 2009.

Eghagha, Hope. "Magical Realism and the 'Power' of Nollywood Home Video Films." *Film International* 5.4 (2007):71-76.

Egharevba, Jacob U. *A Short History of Benin.* Benin City: Fortune and Temperance Publishing Company, 2005. Print.

Ehiemua, Gladys F. A. "Edo Culture and the Prevalence of International Sex Trade among the Edo Women: A Gender Perspective." *Paper*

Presented in a Seminar in the Department of Religious Management and Cultural Studies, Ambrose Alli University, Ekpoma, 15 June, 2009.

Ekwuazi, Hyginus O. *Film in Nigeria.* 2nd edition. Jos: Nigerian Film Corporation, 1991. Print.

_"Perspectives on the Nigerian Motion Picture Industry. *Making the Transition from Video to Celluloid.* Eds. Hyginus Ekwuazi, Mabel Sokomba and Onyero Mgbejume. Jos: National Film Institute, 2001. 3- 11.

_____"The Igbo Video Film: A Glimpse into the Cult of the Individual. *Nigerian Video Films.* Revised and expanded edition. Ed. Jonathan Haynes. Athens, Ohio: Ohio University Centre for International Studies, 2000.131-147.

_"The Hausa Video Film: The Call of the Muezzin. *Film International* 5.4 (2007): 64-70.

Ekwunife, Anthony. Quinquagram of Igbo Traditional Religious Values: An Essay in Interpretation. *Nsukka Journal of the Humanities* 8 (2007): 69-97.

Emovon, E. "Edo Customary Marriage." *Edo Cultural Voyage.* Ed. O. Uwaifo. Lagos: Hanon Pub. Ltd., 2006. 27-41.

Enem, Benjamin E. Content and Context of the Igbo Film. Unpublished Dissertation, Theatre Arts Department, University of Ibadan, 2008.

Eregare, Emmanuel A. and Afolabi, Olukayode A. "The Effects of Globalisation and Deregulation on Nigerian Culture Industries." *Journal of Social Sciences* 21.2 (2009): 145-151.

Erhahon, I.E. *Edo Proverbs and Figures of Speech.* Benin City: Uniben Press, 1998. Print.

Eweka, Basimi E. Evolution of Benin Chieftaincy Titles. Benin City: Uniben Press, 1992. Print.

Ezra, K. *Royal Art of Benin.* New York: The Metropolitan Museum of Art, 1992. Print.

Hampton, Keith N. "Internet Use and the Concentration of Disadvantage: Glocalisation and the Urban Underclass." *American Behavioural Scientist* 53.8 (2010): 1111–1132.

Haynes, Jonathan and Okome, Onokoome. "Evolving Popular Media: Nigerian Video Films." *Research in African Literatures* 29.3 (1998):106-128.

Hong, Phillip Y.P. and Song, In Han. "Glocalisation of Social Work Practice: Global and Local Responses to Globalisation." *International Social Work* 53.5 (2010): 656–670.

Idachaba, Armstrong A. "Elements of Traditional African Drama in Contemporary Nigerian Video Film." *The Performer: Ilorin Journal of the Performing Arts* 10 (2008):17-24.

Igbe, Sam O.U. "The Okaegbee." *Edo Cultural Voyage*. Ed. O. Uwaifo. Lagos: Hanon Pub. Ltd., 2006. 59-64.

_"Izomo: Naming the Child in Edoland." *Edo Cultural Voyage*. Ed. O. Uwaifo. Lagos: Hanon Pub. Ltd., 2006. 53-58.

Igbinovia, Patrick E. *The Future of the Benins in the Future Nigeria: Looking Backwards and Looking Forward*. Benin City: Ethiope Publishing Corporation, 2010. Print.

Izevbigie, Omokaro. Olokun: A Focal Symbol of Religion and Art in Benin. Unpublished Thesis, Arts, University of Washington, 1978.

Ikenga-Metuh, Emefie. *Comparative Studies of African Traditional Religions*. Onitsha: IMICO Publishers, 1987. Print.

Johnson, Dul. "Culture and Art in Hausa Video Films." *Nigerian Video Films*. Revised and expanded edition. Ed. Jonathan Haynes. Athens: Ohio University Centre for International Studies, 2000. 200-208.

Krings, Mathias. "From Possession Rituals to Video Dramas: Some Observations of Dramatis Personae in Hausa Performing Arts. *Hausa Home Videos: Technology, Economy and Society*. Eds. Abdalla U. Adamu, Yusuf M. Adamu and U. F. Jubril. Kano: Centre for Hausa Cultural Studies/Adamu Joji Publishers, 2004.162-170.

Larkin, Brian. "Hausa Dramas and the Rise of Video Culture in Nigeria." *Nigerian Video Films*. Revised and expanded edition. Ed. Jonathan Haynes. Athens, Ohio: Ohio University Centre for International Studies, 2000. 209-241.

Lawal-Osula, O.S.B. 2005. *Edo-Benin Grassroots Voice*. Benin City: Arala Osula Press. Print Malife, Nnamdi S. Igbo Literature and the Emergence of Igbo Screen Art. Unpublished Dissertation. Theatre Arts, Arts, University of Ibadan, 2008.

Mamudu, Adekunle. *Blind Search*. Benin City: Headmark Publishers Limited, 1997.

Masagbor, Richard A. and Idemudia R.U. "Patterns of Iconicity in the Benin City Palimpsest." *Journal of the Nigeria Association for Semiotic Studies* 2(2011):8-18.

McLuhan, Marshall. *Understanding the Media: The Extensions of Man*. London: Routledge and Kegan Paul Ltd., 1973.

Mere, Ada A. "Social Values Heritage of the Igbo." *Ikenga: Journal of African Studies* 11(1973):1-16.

Nwachukwu-Agada, J.O.J. "Women in Igbo Language Video Films: The Virtuous and Villains. *Matatu* 19(1997): 67-80.

Obanor, Maria N. Traditional Religion of the Benins – Olokun Ritual Experience in Printmaking. Unpublished Dissertation, Fine and Applied Arts, Arts, University of Benin, 1994.

Obazee, G.O. "Edo Methods in Ante and Postnatal Care." *Edo Cultural Voyage*. Ed. O. Uwaifo. Lagos: Hanon Pub. Ltd., 2006. 43-52.

Odunsi, D. "Authority as the most Veritable Source of Knowledge: An Essay in Transcendental Existentialism." *Enwisdomization Journal: An International Journal for Learning and Teaching Wisdom* 4.3 (2010): 27-46.

Ogundele, Wole. "From Folk Opera to Soap Opera: Improvisations and Transformations in Yoruba Popular Theatre." *Nigerian Video Films*. Revised and expanded edition. Ed. Jonathan Haynes. Athens, Ohio: Ohio University Centre for International Studies, 2000. 89-130.

Ogunsuyi, Stephen A. The Aesthetics of Traditional African Theatre: A Gestalt for Television Drama Production. Unpublished Thesis, Theatre Arts, Arts, University of Ibadan, 1999.

_ *African Theatre Aesthetics and Television Drama in Nigeria*. Abuja: Root Books & Journal Limited, 2007.

Oha, Obododimma. *Abstracts of Papers Presented at the International Conference on Teaching and Propagating African History and Culture to the Diaspora and Teaching Diaspora History and Culture to Africa* Organised by the Centre for Black and African Arts and Civilization (CBAAC), November 11-13, 2008, State University of Rio de Janeiro, Brazil.

Okezie, G.N. "Theory on Development, Language and Custom for Africa [DLC Theory]. *Journal of Black and African Arts and Civilization* 4.1(2010):203-218.

Okome, Onokoome. "Nollywood: Spectatorship, Audience and the Sites of Consumption." *Postcolonial Text* 3.2 (2007):1-21.

_ "Nollywood: Africa at the Movies." *Film International* 5.4 (2007): 4-8.

Okoye, Chukwuma. "History and Nation Imagination: Igbo and the Videos of Nationalism. *Postcolonial Text* 3.2 (2007):1-10.

Omoera, Osakue S. "Benin Visual Literature and the Frontiers of Nollywood." *International Journal of Multi-Disciplinary Scholarship (Special Issue- Motion Picture in Nigeria)* 3-5(2008):234-248.

_ "A Taxonomic Analysis of the Benin Video Film." *Ijota: Ibadan Journal of Theatre Arts* 2-4(2008):39-55.

_ "An Assessment of the Economics of the Benin Language Film in Nigeria." *Quarterly Review of Film and Video* 31.5 (forthcoming).

_"Bridging the Gap: Answering the Questions of Crime, Youth Unemployment and Poverty through Film Training in Benin, Nigeria." The Education of the Filmmaker in Africa, the Middle East and the Americas. Ed. Mette Hjort. New York: Palgrave Macmillan, (forthcoming).

__Audience Reception of the Benin Video film. Unpublished Thesis, Department of Theatre Arts, University of Ibadan, 1999.

Omoregie, Osarenren S.B. "Forty Q&A on Ubiniology." *Great Benin: A Handbook on Ubiniology*. Ed. Osarenren S.B. Omoregie. Benin City: Noreso Publishers Limited, 2000. 10-35.

Omoruyi, Aghama. *Benin Anthology*. Benin City: Cultural Publications, 1981. Print.

Onuzulike, Uchenna. "Nollywood: The Influence of the Nigerian Movie Industry on African Culture. *Human Communication: A Publication of the Pacific and Asian Communication Association* 10.3 (2007):231-242.

Osagie, A.U. Art and Technology in the Civilization of Edo People." *Great Benin: A Handbook on Ubiniology*. Ed. Osarenren S.B. Omoregie. Benin City: Noreso Publishers Limited, 2000.63-70.

Osahon, Naiwu. 2006. "The Correct History of Edo." Web. 11 July 2007.

Osawaru, Rex I. and Eghafona, K.A. "An Assessment of the Benin Guild of Bronze Casters for Tourism Potentials in Nigeria." *South-South Journal of Culture and Development* 6.2 (2004):81-104.

Osayande, R.I. and Abolagba, J.A. 2006. Music as a Tool of Cruelty: An Appraisal of Music Denigrating the Childless Among the Benins of Southern Nigeria. *EJOTMAS: Ekpoma Journal of Theatre and Media Arts* 1.2:1-11.

Osemwengie-Ero, O. *The History of Benin: Ogiso Dynasties 40BC-1200AD*. Benin City: Nosa Computers, 2004.

Parrinder, Geoffrey. *The World's Living Religions*. London: Pan Books Ltd., 1964. Print.

Rafiu, Adewale K. "Stemming the Tide of Yoruba Language Endangerment through Home Video Production." *The Performer: Ilorin Journal of the Performing Arts* 9: (2007):176-182.

Robertson, Roland. Glocalisation: Time-Space and Homogeneity-Heterogeneity. New York: Sage Publications Ltd., 1995.

Roudometof, Victor. "Transnationalism, Cosmopolitanism, and Glocalisation." *Current Sociology* 53.1 (2005): 113-135.

Scruton, Roger. *A Dictionary of Political Thought*. London: Hill and Wing, 1984. Print.

Seiffert, Daniel. *Nollywood: Von den Volksopern des Klassischen Yoruba Wander Theaters zu den Seifenopern der Nigerianischen Videofilmindustrie.* Norderstedt: Grin, 2004. Print.

Sereda, Stefan. "Curses, Nightmares, and Realities: Cautionary Pedagogy in Fespaco Films and Igbo Videos". *Viewing African Cinema in the Twenty-First Century: Art Films and the Nollywood Video Revolution.* Eds. Mahir Saul and Ralph A. Austen. Athens: Ohio University Press, 2010. 194-208.

Shorter, Aylward. *African Christian Theology*. London: Geoffrey Chapman, 1975.Print.

Trowell, M. *Classical African Sculpture*. London: Faber and Faber Limited, 1970. Print.

Ugor, Paul. "Folklore, History, Identity and Social Critique: Classifying Popular Indigenous Igbo Video Films." *Theatre Studies Review* 4.1 (2004):64 -78.

Ukata, Agatha. "The Images(s) of Women in Nigerian (Nollywood) Videos". Published Thesis, University of Witwatersrand, South Africa, 2010.

__"Conflicting Framings of Women in Nollywood Videos." *Journal of African Nebula* 1 (2010): 65-75.

Yearwood, G. L. *Black Cinema Aesthetics: Issues in Independent Black Filmmaking*. Athens, Ohio: Ohio Centre for Afro-American Studies, 1982. Print.

Zajc, Melita. "Nigerian Video Film Cultures. *Anthropological Notebooks* 15.1 (2009):65–85.

Note:

An earlier version of this paper, with the same title, was published in *Africa Update Newsletter* vol. XX (1), winter 2013, http://web.ccsu.edu/afstudy/upd20-1.html

CHAPTER EIGHT

The Remediation of Religion in a Visual Culture: Understanding the Interaction of Media, New Religious Experience and Globalisation[1]

Damian Amana

Abstract

This paper assumes a paradoxical stance concerning religion and its place in modern society. While some scholars, from Charles Taylor in his *Secular Age* to Pope Benedict XVI, evoke the growing secularisation of the pillars of society, others, from Derrida to Meyer, argue for the resurgence of religion. The paper, while taking a middle stand, argues rather for a change in the way we experience religion in modern society. As such, the new onus of argumentation is not about the decrease or increase of the belief culture but about the changing ground of its experience and remediation by the new and prevailing media. The paper postulates that in an ever-increasing visual culture, representations of religion assume the language of the visual culture, thereby creating a fecund ground for the promotion of the very spectacular aspects of religious practices, and silencing, through minimal coverage, aspects of religion that do not flow with the visual logic. In the same line of thought, the paper postulates that representations of religion within this evolving visual culture in the ambit of the predominance of visual media may follow the logic, language and profit of show-business globally.

Introduction

Sociological projections on the trajectory of religion in modern society have assumed a dual albeit contrary stance: the *requiem* and the *resurrectio*. Many scholars from diverse fields of learning, informed by a certain analysis of the data and processes of culture, have predicted the ineluctable requiem of religion, defined in the effacement of religion from the public space and in its relegation as a guide in the private fora.

To this effect, the emergence of the public space in Habermas is relative to the decline of religion, which becomes nothing more than just one among the many opinions in the public space subject to the rule of rational discourse (Habermas 4). In his *Secular Age,* Charles Taylor defined the requiem of religion in a three strand secularity. In secularity one, the public space is defined as been emptied of God. Secularity two consists of the "falling off of religious belief and practice, in people turning away from God and no longer going to church." Most incisive is secularity three, articulated in the changed 'conditions of believing' summed in a cultural propensity where the belief in God is "no longer axiomatic" or in "conditions of experience" that no longer necessarily encourage a default option for a theistic response to the human question (Taylor 1-22).

For theologians, the anticipated crisis of religion is articulated in religious indifference, atheism and religious apathy. John Sobrino and Felix Wilfred described this crisis of religion with reference to Christianity in the form of indifference, apathy and outright disenchantment with Christianity (Sobrino and Wilfred, 2005). While defining the contingent dignity of man relative to his communion with God, *Gaudium et Spes* delineates the crisis of the church in atheism. According to the document, "many of our contemporaries have never recognised this intimate and vital link with God, or have explicitly rejected it." Thus atheism must be counted among the most serious problems of this age (*Gaudium et Spes* No. 19).

The religious crisis manifests not just as a question of a particular religious body but of a crisis of God. People no longer believe in God. However, other branches of contemporary research manned equally by veritable scholars are singing the vibrant tones of a "resurrectio" of religion (Derrida, 2006, Greeley, 1972, Castells, 1996). Derrida recognises the "return or resurgence of religion", not in terms of a religion that did disappear, but as a *re-apparition* of the one that has been repressed by multifarious forces in the society. Meyer emphatically concludes: "clearly, it is inadequate to dismiss the public presence of religion. The marked articulation of religion in the public realm destabilises the narrative of modernity as defined by the decline of the public role of religion" (Meyer 6).

While attributing the dismissal of religion in public space to scholars' ideological bias, Meyer does disagree with Manuel Castells's[1] ascription of

---

the resurgence of religion as a fundamentalist reaction to an unattainable modernisation and with Derrida's definition of the resurgence as a return of the repressed (Meyer 2006). For Derrida, "[T]here is, because of the repression [of religion due to diverse forces in society], an accumulation of force, a heightening of potential, an explosion of conviction, an overflowing of extraordinary power" (Derrida, qtd in De Vries & Weber 673).

Recognising the salience of Meyer's 'ideological bias', this paper opines that most of the analyses decrying the decrease of religion thus suffer from the problem of limited horizon of analysis or of concern circumscribed by 'ecclesiocentrism' of particular religious bodies. In this regard, the analysis of the state of the religious tempo is delimited by the fervour of religious attitude in a particular religious institution like the Catholic Church, and subsequently ascribed and generalised to all religious life in the world. This analysis can equally be influenced by 'traditio-centrism'- where the rhythm of the religious atmosphere and its tempo are measured in resemblance to, in resonance with, in deviation from, or in continuation of a particular and past religious manifestation, to the detriment of new nuances of a dynamic belief-culture in an ever-changing world.

The religious situation in Africa and Nigeria, in particular, apparently adheres closer to the flourishing of religion than to its effacement, both in the private and public domains. As an American journalist and Vatican observer noted of one of the numerous religions in Nigeria,

> In the 20th century, Africa went from a Catholic population of 1.9 million in 1900 to 130 million in 2000, a staggering growth rate of 6,708 percent. Half of all adult baptisms in the world, the surest sign of missionary expansion, are in Africa. Inexorably, pastoral and intellectual energy in the church will follow population, and this means that African leaders are destined to play an increasingly important role. Nigeria will have 47 million Catholics by 2050, and has the human capital and ecclesiastical infrastructure to become an African 'voice' in the global church (Allen 96).

This bloom and blossom of the African Catholic Church is not limited to an exponential population growth. Liturgy in African Catholic churches is "not a staid moral duty performed amid pomp and rigid ritual beneath the stained glass of one of Europe's cavernous and magnificent cathedrals" but a lively worship and an exuberance of pastoral activities

(Leonard 2005). John Allen further adds that "Seminaries here are full, and vocations to the religious life are booming, parishes are very strong. Catholic spirituality here is very devotional, with lots of pious leagues and societies (Allen 2007). This Church is truly the hope of the future of the Church (Onyalla 160). The question, though, might still remain on the nature and veracity of such numbers.

Wider analyses rooted in the consideration of a multiplicity of variables are beginning to demonstrate the return of the religious and religion in the public and private fora. This return of religious culture is related to the evolution of modern media of communication.

Ihejirike Walter (2006), like David Martin (2002), appraised the role of the mass media in the flourishing of different religious practices in modern times, especially Charismatic and Pentecostal practices. For Eickelman and Anderson (1999), a greater Muslim public has been created with the use of the media so that "Religion finds technology". Bierdorjer and Meyer call this resurrection of religion within the diffusion of mass media as the "entanglement of religion and media" (4). Derrida tags this collaborative relationship between the media and the resurgence of religion as "the mediatic manifestation of religion" (61). This return of the religious in modern *sit im leben,* "reintroduces a new sort of transcendental fiduciary" (63).

The correlation of religion and media brings to the fore the ancient and often unacknowledged "irreducible bond between religion and media."[2] Religion and media interact and intermingle on many fronts. However, an overt characteristic of the two is in the act of mediation. Religion can be understood as an experience of mediation between the sacred and the secular, the transcendent and the human. Likewise, media usage is an exercise in mediation. And all religious experiences are mediated experiences, though not necessarily mass-mediated. What then happens when these two modes of mediation meet?

Within the web of a growing interfacing between mass media and religion in a globalised and multicultural intermingling, there is an imminent need for an interrelational, interdisciplinary study of the phenomena outside the limited scope of a purely disciplinary fidelity to the study of media or religion (Plate 15). Within the same matrix of enlarged multicultural scenery divesting outside the frontiers of the

Christian-Euro-America scenario, the analysis of the interaction of media and religion must assume multiple variables.

From such interactivity between media and religion in contemporary society, the two therefore exert an influence on each other. Of the religion birthed out of this unusual amalgam, it has been observed that "we are heirs to religions that are designed precisely to cooperate with science and technology" (Derrida 61). The recognition of the influence of the media on the resurgence of religion and of the form of this religious resurgence is once again validating the utility of some of the views inherent in the nexus of Marshall McLuhan's media conjectures. This is what is today transmuted and popularised as the theory of 'remediation' and its double logic of 'immediacy and hypermediation'.

In McLuhan, the media extend the senses of man, so that when a new medium is introduced within a culture, a new sense ratio is orchestrated (McLuhan 7). "The content of any medium is always another medium. It is as a result of this that existing processes are amplified or accelerated" (8). However, McLuhan presumes a passive or docile cultural submission to the technology of media and seems to undermine the content of the various media. The theory of media as a remediation, therefore, gives a more ample field for an understanding of the rapport of media and culture within the wider gamut of historico-cultural dynamics.

According to the theory of remediation with its double logic of immediacy and hypermedia, modern media promise to deliver reality unmediated, with a promise of absolute transparency. It therefore seeks to efface its media. To carry out this act of immediacy, media must however assume within their grammar multiple ranges of other media technologies, which, in the long run, short-change their immediacy. Media must remediate because "The logic of immediacy dictates that the medium itself should disappear and leave in the presence of the thing represented" (Bolter & Grusin 5). However, "immediacy depends on hypermediacy" (Bolter & Grusin 5). The push for immediacy impels borrowing from other media and at times repurposing and refashioning the old media. For example, an internet page like CNN would need to borrow the technology of video to show its clips. Through the act of 'remediation', old and new media are refashioned, accentuating different arts and appealing to different senses. This therefore influences the act of experiencing through the remediation.

It is no fallacy to assume that modern people see themselves through the optics of their media. "We understand ourselves as the reconstituted station point of the artist or the photographer. When we watch a film or a television broadcast, we become the changing point of view of the camera" (Bolter & Grusin 231). This does not imply an inescapable technological determinism but that "we employ media as vehicles for defining both personal and cultural identity. New media offer new opportunities for self-definition" (Bolter & Grusin 231). As new media are installed within the equilibrium of a culture, representational modes are affected and different media appeal to different senses and extend different senses. When religion is remediated, it is also refashioned. New media are potent with the potential for a new mode of representation and experience, subject to reception according to cultural heritage and personality dispositions.

The Question

If a new medium, therefore, remediates older media in its striving for immediacy, creating a forum for a different form of repurposing, refashioning and experiencing, how then does the presence of the Nigerian video films (New Media) repurpose an older culture of religion in Nigeria? Cognisant of the importance of the images of God in people's *weltanschauung*, how do the modes of the manifestation of the transcendental in the popular video films affect the religious imagination of the viewers of the films?

As Christian Hearth and Paul Luff asserted, "it has long been recognised that video, and before that, film, provide the social sciences with an unprecedented opportunity to analyse human culture and social organisation" (Hearth & Luff 2008). It is the hope of this paper, therefore, that an interrelational analysis of the media and religion in Nigeria can grant us a greater understanding of the Nigerian socio-cultural environment.

A New Media in Nigeria

Nollywood, the Nigerian video film industry, has become a magnificent surprise to many who took it for granted as a joke, as Nollywood has established itself as a major source of entertainment in Nigeria and beyond. Given the visual character of the video, what is the nature of religious epiphany in Nigerian video films? How does Nollywood negotiate with the popular religious worldview in Nigeria? Considering that the religious content is wide and that this forum is limited in space, this paper has chosen to focus on what is central to most religions and particularly fundamental to African religions: the relationship with, and anticipation of, the transcendent.

The Nigerian video film represents basically most of the issues that affect African life in general and Nigerian culture in particular. However, it is worth noting that, while Nigerian films remediate almost every aspect of the Nigerian life, Ukah emphasises the fact that "religion has come to occupy a disproportionately high place" (Ukah 204). To him, Nollywood can be conceived as a forest of religious symbolism. In other words, while Nollywood touches on almost all aspects of Nigerian life, religion features prominently in many films.

Ukah (203-208) still emphasises the political economy of religious representation in Nigerian video films. The plethora of religious representations in Nollywood follows the line of religious affiliation and marketing: Pentecostal film producers insist on tenets of Pentecostalism, while in films made by Muslims, Islamic faith has the upper hand. This also holds true for Catholicism and other religious affiliations.

One of the most scholarly responses to the question of religion in the African home video films comes from the Amsterdam Professor of religious research Birgit Meyer, who describes the remediation of religion in Nigerian video films as the resurgence of a Pentecostal spirituality. "Video film producers in Ghana and Nigeria have framed their movies in line with Pentecostal concerns, while at the same time the encounter with film and television has transformed Christianity and drawn it into the sphere of entertainment"(Meyer 2). According to the scholar, "This image economy, I contend, plays a crucial role in designing a new public sphere replete with Pentecostal Christianity" (Meyer 186). With regard to the remediation of the divine in the home video films, she rightly notes that "The remediation of the divine through the instrument of the video gives 'room to a new form of spectatorship' and techno-reality" (290).

Meyer buttresses her stand on the Pentecostal prevalence in the interface with video films mainly on the grounds of the demonisation of traditional religion, a subject she researched for her doctoral thesis. While this is true in many films, it cannot be attributed to the emergence of Christianity alone, on the grounds that the dualistic framework within which Pentecostalism seems to thrive now has long been present in traditional Africa. African religions were very much aware of the negative power of the influence of witches and wizards and the counter-power of positive sacrifices to good spirits long before Christianity set foot on the continent. This war paradigm among traditional religions finds expression in some modern African films where the battle between the good and the evil spiritual forces is by no means relegated to the drama between a Pentecostal good God and traditional bad African demons, but within forces prevalent in Africa without recourse to Pentecostal spirituality.

The preeminence of Pentecostal spirituality in the African public space has also compelled the African church, in Meyer's view, to accept and promote the Catholic charismatic renewal. Here, the acceptance of Pentecostalism in West African Catholic churches was contingent on the fear of losing their members to Pentecostals. According to her, "Even some mission churches have incorporated pentecostally-oriented prayer groups in order to prevent their members from leaving the church" (Meyer 1995). In the footnote, she mentions Catholicism precisely. Here too lies the tying of variables to a theoretical whole, variables that have no relationship to the assumed theoretical corpus. For Catholics precisely, the emergence of charismatic spirituality in the Church despite the struggle between the Orthodox Church and the charismatic movement has deeper roots than the emergence of Pentecostalism in Africa. It was a phenomenon that was by no means peculiar to West Africa but a whole Catholic phenomenon, beginning in America and spreading through Europe to Africa.

The new wave of video film production in Africa has not come of a particular guided school of thought: Pentecostal, but the assumption of styles that was more prevalent in the people's culture so that the assumption of a 'root culture paradigm' holds better promise of plausibility than the Pentecostal attribution assumed by Meyer. As Meyer herself wrote, "the accessibility of video technology enabled not only Pentecostal-charismatic cultures which embraced these new opportunities… but also enabled initially untrained film lovers to produce and market their own feature films" (Meyer 157).

My contention and difference of stance, gleaned from the film analyses, is articulated on the return of a character that was long prevalent in the African religio-cultural *weltanschauung*: a pragmatic hierophany.[3] In

William James, pragmatism is defined in practical significance. According to him,

> To attain perfect clearness in our thoughts of an object, then we need only consider what conceivable effects of a practical kind the object may involve -what sensations we are to expect from it, and what reactions we must prepare. Our conceptions of these effects, whether immediate or remote, are then for us the whole of our conception of the object, so far as that conception has positive significance at all (James 18).

Sequence to his pragmatic principle, his *varieties of religious experience* can be viewed reducibly, albeit as exemplification of his theory, to show some pragmatic effects of religious experiences (James, 47). Amidst the varieties of religious experiences he enunciated, one cord seems to tie them all, the pragmatic consequence of such an experience.

This pragmatic tendency in African traditional religions and as used in this paper to describe one of the modes of the manifestation of the transcendent in Nigerian video films, can be understood on two counts. One is the anticipation of the divine in pragmatic-utilitarian notions. This is present in situations where the divine is sought to meet the day-to-day concrete needs like food, drink, healing, protection, success and deliverance from evil. Related to the first pragmatic utilitarian anticipation of the intervention of, and relationship with the sacred, necessarily follows the second defined in visible signs. By necessary consequence of verification, the pragmatic utilitarian relationship assumes the form of a pragmatic-empirical, sensational, tactile manifestation.[45]

By commonality of such a denominator in Africa, the plethora of film and video makers, though of diverse origins, assume basically a similarity of pattern. From a pilot study of the hierophany in Nigerian films, this paper conjectures the fact that the mode of the manifestation of the transcendental in Nigerian video films is as multiple and variant as are the films. However, in these many modes of representing the manifestation/perception of the transcendental in the Nigerian video films, the multiplicity of particular styles seems to buy into a prevailing mode of representation: the techno-visualisation of spiritual forces.

In the video language of 'modern' Nollywood, the pragmatic manifestation is remediated in 'voyeuristic' terms, creating, as has been earlier attested, a 'spectatorship of the spirit' through the utility of techno-and video special effects. The pragmatic manifestation of the divine is articulated in the intervention of the divine, in such a way that it bears semblance to the concept of *deus ex machina* and at once departs from it. The concept of *deus ex machina* does not define the reality of the hierophany in Nigerian video films, because the divine intervention falls very much within the logic of the African worldview, not as a transcendent being breaking into the natural realms to salvage it but as a transcendent/immanent reality. According to Mbiti, "Because traditional religions permeate all the departments of life, there is no formal distinction between the sacred and the secular, between the religious and non-religious, between the spiritual and the material areas of life; wherever the African is, there is religion" (Mbiti 2). In the African concept, the distinction, between a transcendent and an immanent divinity does not hold water, as divinity is at once immanent and transcendent in most African religions and in the Nigerian religious experience in particular.

It is the conviction of the paper that the remediation of 'pragmatic hierophany' is a major key to understand the current religious affiliation in Nigerian and in most African countries. It is through the prism of the remediation of pragmatic hierophany that we can understand the coexistence of corruption and religion, political insanity and deep religious reliance in Nigeria. The Pentecostal/charismatic spirituality, because it re-echoes the pragmatic hierophany, a cultural heritage that seems to have been embedded in the religious unconscious of the African, does flourish naturally in Africa. But pragmatism underscores functionalism and functionalism must show in a visual ambience.

Patterns of Remediation in Nollywood Films

An analysis of a few films depicts this modality of the representation of the holy or the intervention of the gods in the drama of humanity. Such patterns of representation of the intervention of the gods are prevalent in films like *Power Change Hands, Light and Darkness, Total Destruction* and *Sin of the Father.* Because of the visual logic of these films as a medium, the artists and producers represent the intervention of the gods in overtly 'voyeuristic' terms, creating a spectatorship of the spirit. In some of these films, the intervention of the gods is displayed in the context of war (when traditional medicine men confront one another, or confront a different deity) when the pragmatic efficacy is manifested as fire shooting out of the staff of one priest against the other, or thunder striking one at the desire of another. Most of the time, the intervention and efficacy of the gods on behalf of men are shown in very visible and visual contests. In the matrix of the representation of the invisible in the visible medium, common in Nollywood, the invisible is made visible through fire, water, wind, earth or strange signs orchestrated through special effects. This mode and manner of representation of the gods in Nollywood falls in what has been described as a visual culture.

The Global Recognition of the Visual Culture by Scholars

From Harold Innis, Walter Ong, Marshal McLuhan and Neil Postman to the new trends in media ecology, the conception that the media's impact is contingent on the content permissible through a given medium has continued to be debunked in the realisation that the 'medium is the message'. This awakening to the impact of the media as technology on the prevailing cultural tenets has widened the horizon of media analysis beyond the Lasswellian parameters of source, content, audience and channel analysis. According to Graham Mcphee (2002), modern society is a visual society.

Visual culture studies recognise the predominance of visual forms of media, communication and information in the postmodern world. Thus, visual culture celebrates the centrality of image flows occasioned by the predominance of visual technologies in both public and private arenas. According to the American National Education Association, "Western civilisation has become more dependent than ever on visual culture, visual artefacts and visual communication as a mode of discourse and a means of developing a social and cultural identity" (NEAA 2011). This visual characterisation of modern society affects both the so-called low cultures and the high cultures.

Guy Debord may have gleaned this succinctly when he noted in his *Society of Spectacles* that "The whole life of those societies in which modern conditions of production prevail presents itself as an immense accumulation of spectacles" (2008). Apaslan endorses the definition of modern society as an image society when he argues that "We face a shift from text-based communication to image saturation today. This shift is also dramatically reflected in the field of art education today" (Alpaslan 1).

The thesis of the visual culture does not in any way negate the other senses. This is because the visual works with the other senses too. Bal argues that the notion of visual culture does not imply an exclusively visual experience but visual experience is itself synaesthetic, involving other sense-laden and sense-based activities such as listening, reading, movement and touch (Bal 9).

Debord wrote that "The spectacle is not a collection of images; rather, it is a social relationship between people that is mediated by images" (4). While visual culture is society's strategy of how we perceive and interpret reality, it is worth noting that the visible is naturally not just self-evident "but arises out of a set of social and cultural exigencies that create the conditions for *seeing* a particular phenomenon or artefact" (Becker 2008).

Conclusion

In the visual ambience of modern cultural scenarios, visibility is accentuated. Whether one buys into the logic of the visual as social relations or as an effect of the predominance of visual technologies, a common denominator is that modern society privileges the visual and reinforces this through the multiplex of technologies that promote it. From print images and graphic design, TV and cable TV, film and video in all interfaces and playback/display technologies, computer interfaces and software design, Internet/Web as a visual platform, digital multimedia, advertising in all media (a true cross-media institution), fine art and photography, fashion, to architecture, design, and urban design, modern technologies promote the visual.

Further to this, in the midst of an ever-increasing visual culture, representations of religion assume the language of the visual culture, thereby creating a fecund ground for the promotion of the very spectacular aspects of religious practices, and silencing, through minimal coverage, aspects of religion that do not flow with the visual logic. Within the same cultural matrix that privileges the visual and the logic of an improved aesthetical representation, when religion is remediated, it naturally buys into the logic of visibility orchestrated by prevailing technologies and culture. In the throes of the visual culture, religious experiences shift from the context of just the heart to the display screen where the impact and effect must be represented. This imposes a frame of representation on religion and poses a challenge to religious representation. If religion is functional – and it is, it should be seen. Can this visual ground hone the pattern of religious experience? Our middle ground answer is in the affirmative: the ground demands a religious representation that must show, as long as the visual culture has become a prevailing global culture.

Notes

[1] Meyer thus responds to the roots of religious resurgence as found in Manuel Castells' *The Information Age* (Oxford: Blackwell, 1996). Castells did ascribe the rise of fundamentalist Islam to the failed attempt by Muslims to attain an admirable modernisation, which leads them to exhibit a reaction against such modernistic traits they could not attain, the evil globalisation. Similarly, he attributes the rise of Christian fundamentalism to the reaction against the uncontrollable forces of globalisation. For Meyer, the rise of these religions is far more explainable by their adoption and use of the modern media than by a reactive reaction.

[2] Religion, in whatever form it has ever existed, has in one way or the other availed itself of the service of mediation. In whatever religious context one may choose to evaluate, there is, enshrined within the fabric of the religious life, the attempt to mediate between the visible and the invisible, between the supernatural and the natural. Mediated religious experiences however have to be carried over from one generation to the next. This act of transmission of religion from one epoch to another and from one generation to another entails strongly the act of mediation to the employment of different forms of media, from ancient hagiographies and sacred stories to the modern mass-mediated religion (De Vries 2001, Derrida and Vatimo 1998, Meyer and Moor 2006, Plate, 6).

[3] Hierophany is assumed here simply as "a manifestation of the divine" (Mircea Eliade, *Patterns in Comparative Religion,* New York: Sheed and Ward, 1958, 7). This paper chose to focus on the manifestation of the divine in African films because it is central and common to most African religious thought. As Mbiti rightly observes, African religious beliefs are totally concerned with belief in God, belief in Spirits… (J. S. Mbiti, *An Introduction to African Religions.* London: Heinemann, 1975).

[4] Pragmatism, according to William James, "represent a perfectly familiar attitude in philosophy, the empiricist attitude, but it represents it, as it seems to me, both in a more radical and in a less objectionable form than it has ever yet assumed…pragmatist turns …towards concreteness and adequacy, towards facts, towards action and towards power (ibid 20).

Works Cited

Allen, John, *Two Parallels for Understanding the 'Powerhouse' Church in Nigeria.* http://ncrcafe.org/node/ (2007). 96

Alpaslan, Ucar. "Aesthetic Understanding through Visual Culture" Proceedings of the International Congress of Aesthetics entitled: "Aesthetics Bridging Cultures", Turkey, 2007.

Bal, Mieke. "Visual Essentialism" *Journal of Visual Culture* 2 (1) 2003: 5-32.

Becker, Karin. *Where is Visual Culture in Contemporary Theories of Media and Communication?* PDF Books, 2008.

Bierdorjer, F. in Meyer, Birgit. *Religion, Media and the Public Sphere.* Bloomington: Indiana University Press, 2006.

Bolter, J. D. and Grusin, R. *Remediation, Understanding New Media.* Cambridge: MIT Press, 2000.

Castells, Manuel. *The Information Age.* Oxford: Blackwell, 1996.

Debord, Guy. (2008) *Society of Spectacles.* Soft copy.

Derrida, Jacques. "Above All, No Journalists" in H. De Vries and S. Weber. *Religion and Media.* California: Stanford University Press, 2001.

Derrida, Jacques in B. Meyer. *Religion, Media and Public the Sphere.* Bloomington: Indiana University Press, 2006.

Gaudium et Spes No. 19

Greeley, Andrew. *Unsecular Man: The Persistence of Religion.* New York: Schocken Books, 1972.

Habermas, Jürgen. In Birgit Meyer. *Religion, Media and the Public Sphere.* Bloomington: Indiana University Press, 2006.

Hearth, C. and Luff, P. "Video and the Analysis of Work and Interaction". In Pertti Alasuutare, Leonard Bickman and Julia Brannnen. *The Sage Handbook of Social Science Research Methods.* Los Angeles: Sage publication, 2008.

Ihejirike, W. *From Catholicism to Pentecostalism, role of Nigerian televangelists in religious conversion.* Port Harcourt: University of Port Harcourt Press, 2006.

James, William. *Pragmatism.* New York: Dover Publications, 1983.

______________. *Varieties of Religious Experience.* New York: Mentor,

Leonard, Terry. *African Catholic Church Growing Rapidly,* 2005 http://www.freerepublic.com/focus/f-news/1384382/post

Macphee, Gaham. *The Architecture of the Visible.* New York: Continuum, 2002.

Martin, David. *Pentecostalism: The World their Parish.* Oxford: Malden Press, 2002.

Mbiti, J. S. *African Religions and Philosophy.* London: Heinemann, 1969.

McLuhan, Marshall. *Understanding Media, the Extensions of Man.* New York: McGraw Hill Books, 1964.

Meyer, Birgit. "Delivered from the Power of Darkness". In *Africa 65* (2), 1995.

_____________. "Religious Remediations: Pentecostal Views in Ghanaian Video-movies". In *Postscript 157,* 1996.

NEAA 2001 "Thriving in Academe: A rationale for visual communication" National education association advocate online December, 2001.

Onyalla, D. B. O. "Tribalism in Religious communities in Africa" in *African Ecclesiastical Review.* 2005

Plate, S. B. "Introduction: Film, Myth-making, Culture making," in *Representing Religion in World Cinema,* ed. S. Brent Plate. New York: Palgrave Macmillan, 2003.

Postman, Neil. *Amusing Ourselves to Death.* New York: Pearson, 1996.

Sobrino, Jon and Wilfred, Felix. *Concilium: International Journal for Theology,* 2005.

Taylor, C. *A Secular Age.* Cambridge: Harvard University Press, 2007.

Ukah Asonzeh. "Advertising God: Nigerian Christian Video Films and the Power of Consumer Culture". In *Journal of Religion in Africa* 33(2) pp.203-231, 2003

Note

An earlier version of this chapter was published as "The resurgence and Remediation of Religion in a Visual Culture" in the *Global Journal of Arts Humanities and Social Sciences* Vol.2, No.9, pp. 22-31, November 2014.

CHAPTER NINE

Realism in Nollywood Video Films: The Materiality of Lagos and the Nigerian Video Film Industry

Alessandro Jedlowski

Abstract

The specificity of Lagos, its architecture, its infrastructure, its noisy atmosphere, the special conception of time that organizes the life of most Lagosians, and the violence of the diffused criminality that used to oblige them to stay in their homes as soon as the sun sets, are elements that forged the attributes of Nollywood economic and social organisation as well as its aesthetic specificities during the first few years of the video phenomenon (in the early 1990s). At the same time, over the same period, Nollywood videos came to represent a sort of mirror of Lagos. They reflected (and to a large extent still reflect) in original and meaningful ways Lagos' life, as well as the aspirations, the dreams and the fears of its inhabitants. Some Nollywood scholars analysed this relationship, proposing an interpretation of the way the city and the experience of Nigerian city-dwellers are represented in Nollywood videos. In this paper I intend to contribute to this debate by focusing my analysis on two different but interrelated topics. On the one hand, in order to highlight the links between Nollywood films to the city of Lagos, I will look at the interaction between the materiality of the city and that of the videos' modes of production and dissemination. On the other hand, I will analyse the interactions between the videos' contents and the reality of Lagos life, in order to interpret the particular form of narrative realism which Nollywood videos have created.

Introduction

The Nigerian video film industry emerged as one of the largest film industries in the world (UNESCO 2013) and its success is today well known around Africa and in the international arena. The industry is characterised by a high level of internal differentiation and regional fragmentation, with sections of it producing films in different languages and reflecting the life and reality of different regions of Nigeria.

However, the section of the industry which gained the largest international visibility is undoubtedly the one producing video films in English and Pidgin, generally labelled "Nollywood" by both local and international critics and scholars (cf. Jedlowski 2011). The centre of Nollywood's growth and success is Lagos, the economic and commercial capital of Nigeria, a megacity which has often attracted the imagination of African and foreign scholars because of its complex and original modes of organisation (Gandy 2005; Koolhaas 2002).

My interest toward the material dimension of the Nigerian video film industry and its connections with the material and infrastructural attributes of the city of Lagos has been driven by the work of Daniel Miller. As he pointed out:

> [...] Objects are important, not because they are evident and physically constrain or enable, but often precisely because we do not "see" them. The less we are aware of them, the more powerfully they can determine our expectations by setting the scene and ensuring normative behaviour, without being open to challenge (5).

Following this perspective, in the first section of the text, I propose an analysis of the way in which Lagos, and its specific materiality as a megacity, have shaped Nollywood and its modes of operation as a film industry. In the second section, then, I try to invert the terms of the discourse to turn my attention toward the way in which Nollywood reflects and shapes Lagos through its contents and aesthetics, helping us to understand the way the megacity works, feels and dreams. The metaphor of the mirror has been often used in film theory to describe and analyse the relationship between the image and the object represented. The image reflected is always something different and autonomous from the original, and even realistic representations cannot be but fictional.

The relationship existing between the object and its representation is always a complex one, and this complexity is nicely caught by the Italian novelist Italo Calvino's words in the novel *The Invisible City*:

> [...] At times the mirror increases a thing's value, at times denies it. Not everything that seems valuable above the mirror maintains its force when mirrored. The twin cities are not equal, because nothing that exists or happens in [the city of] Valdrada is symmetrical: every face and gesture is answered, from the mirror, by a face and a gesture

> inverted, point by point. The two Valdradas live for each other, their eyes interlocked; but there is no love between them (Calvino 54).

Calvino's idea of mirror is intriguing. It allows us to point toward the ambiguity of Nollywood's representation of Lagos and its complementarities with the visible materiality of the city. To better structure the analysis that follows, I decided to limit it to the early period of Nollywood existence, roughly to the first five to six years of the industry. Nollywood has in fact experienced a very rapid growth and its aesthetics, contents and narratives, as well as its modes of operation have evolved very quickly (Jedlowski 2013a). In this sense, even if a significant continuity can be observed in the history of the development of the Nigerian video film industry, generalisation should be done carefully.

The Materiality of Lagos and the Generation of Nollywood

Lagos is a megacity. It is one of the largest urban areas in Africa and, if it continues to grow as it did over the past two decades, it is destined to become one of the largest cities in the world in the years to come. As geographers, urbanists and anthropologists have underlined, its economic and social organisation is largely based on the informal sector and on the myriad of "spectral" practices (Simone 2002) which allow people to make a living in a post-structural adjustment era. The complex economic and social interactions that originate in such a context shape the city and the way its inhabitants live. In Nigeria, as in many other African countries, the introduction of the Structural Adjustment Program (SAP) dictated by the International Monetary Fund and the World Bank at the beginning of the 1980s marked the end of state-controlled investments and inaugurated a period of progressive collapse of national infrastructure. As far back as in 1984, Chinua Achebe wrote in a book significantly titled *The Trouble with Nigeria*:

> Look at our collapsing public utilities, our inefficient and wasteful parastatals and state-owned companies. If you want electricity, you buy your own generator; if you want water, you sink your own bore-hole; if you want to travel, you set up your own airline. One day soon, said a friend of mine, you will have to build your own post office to send your letter! (Achebe 20)

The situation did not improve in the following years and Lagosians have been inevitably forced to adapt to the situation. Throughout the 1980s and 1990s, because of the application of the SAP policies, the efficiency of most of public infrastructures progressively worsened, with the collapse of the system of electric power supply being probably the most dramatic example of this trend (Olukoju 2004). People started to organise themselves in what Biodun Jeyifo defined as "micro-municipalities", informal micro-associations, often not even larger than the population of a compound, whose members share expenses (the price of a generator, the fuel to make it work, the expenses to build a water pipe and to guarantee security) to provide essential services. The collapsing condition of most of state-owned infrastructures is the issue of constant debates in Nigeria, but as Jeyifo points out:

> [W]hat are not much known, what are barely talked about, are the "hidden", unquantifiable and epiphenomenal costs of the emergence and proliferation of these private mini-municipalities in the contemporary urban setting [...] One is the extreme fragmentation and privatisation of processes, activities and imaginaries that are normally social, public and collective (Jeyifo 83).

As many accounts of the development of the Nigerian video film industry have shown (Barrot 2005; Haynes 2000), Nollywood originated within the social, economic and political context generated by the application of the Structural Adjustment Programme, a context of crisis in which cinema-going culture and the long-standing tradition of Yoruba travelling theatre had begun to die out. The national television no longer had the money to produce local series, and violence was spreading all over the country, making it difficult for people to participate in outdoor entertainment activities. The environment of Lagos social and economic life shaped the new form of entertainment that was slowly coming to life. Little and informal production companies emerged and started to produce low-cost films to be released straight into the market in VHS format. These production companies could be seen as working on the same principle of the above-mentioned micro-municipalities. In fact, they originated from the collapse of cinema and television infrastructure, and imported into the entertainment business a system of privatisation similar to the one described by Jeyifo.

The industry that started to develop in this environment became the agent of what Ravi Sundaram has labelled "recycled modernity" (1999). In fact, as the result of the very material condition of perpetual crisis in which the city of Lagos was plunged, this industry had to recycle and pirate technologies and contents to create original and appealing commercial products out of a situation of general scarcity and emergency. As AbduMaliq Simone interestingly points out,

> If production possibilities are limited in African cities, then existent materials of all kinds are to be appropriated – sometimes through theft and looting; sometimes through the "heretical" uses made of infrastructures, languages, objects, and spaces; sometimes through social practices that ensure that available materials pass through many hands. The key here is to multiply the uses that can be made of documents, automobiles, houses, wood, or whatever, and this means the ability to put together different kinds of combinations of people with different skills, perspectives, linkages, identities, and aspirations. This multiplicity of social organisation constitutes a kind of perceptual system, a way of seeing that then engages the urban environment in such a way that single items, objects, and experiences are put to many otherwise unanticipated uses (Simone 214).

Nollywood itself can be seen as the result of a creative way of dealing with the harshness of the post-structural adjustment Lagos: it gave new uses and values to existing materials and structures. As the experience of Kenneth Nnebue, one of the most influential figures in early Nollywood (Haynes 2007b), shows, the straight-to-video distribution strategy, which is one of the most important elements of Nigerian videos' commercial success, originated from this kind of process. In fact, according to the almost legendary tale about the birth of the industry, Nnebue recycled unsold VHS blank tapes to commercialise locally-produced video films, thereby reaching the audience directly into their homes.

The infrastructural environment of the city and the economic networks which grounded its life participated in generating the success of early Nollywood videos. As a matter of fact, the "infrastructures of media piracy", which were already in place because of the well-established business of distributing foreign pirated products, shaped the modes of distribution and consumption of Nollywood videos (Okoye [aka Gaboski] 2014; cf. also Larkin 2004). Furthermore, the materiality of piracy influenced Nigerian videos' perceived quality through the interferences and breakdowns accumulated during the reproduction process (Adejunmobi 2007; Larkin 2004), and can (at least partly) be held accountable for the bad reputation of early Nollywood videos' sound and image quality.

If early Nigerian videos were characterised by an extensive use of music and sound effects (often badly deformed and transformed by the distortion caused by pirated production and distribution processes), the omnipresence of sounds and noises cannot be seen as devoid of meaning. In fact, as James Ferguson emphasised, "the semiotically unintelligible (noise) and semiotically sensible (signal) may be equally intelligible in terms of a social logic of practice" (211). Noise inhabits the everyday life of Lagos' streets, courtyards, markets and buses. All-day-long churches and shops' faulty speakers loudly project songs and sermons in the atmosphere of the city, and video and music shops turn the volume of their sound sets to attract new customers. Silence is rare and in most cases it represents something fearful.

In early (as in many more recent) video films, one can observe something similar. Silence is practically absent, while dialogues, music and background noises crowd the films' auditory atmosphere. It is as if the noise that characterises Lagos everyday life had somehow found its way into Nollywood video films, both consciously, through the directors' choice of an extensive use of sound effects, and unconsciously, as the material result of specific modes of production and distribution which left their marks on the skin of the video films. As Jahman Anikulapo, a Lagos-based journalist and artist, reported to me in an interview,

> [...] The role that sound plays in your culture [in Europe] is different from the one it plays in ours. Does your wife wake up in the morning and sing while she is cooking? Here, it's part of the environment. If you are a child, your mother will wake you up with songs... you are surrounded by noises and it's part of you, and if you don't hear them, you think that something is missing... when I'm in the West, the most painful thing for me is silence. When I wake up and I don't hear that noise, and the weather is cold and dark, and there is no music and you are supposed to talk to somebody forever, it kills me... (Anikulapo 2010).

The materiality of Lagos life also shaped the way in which videos were (and partly still are) consumed, and somehow guided the development of the industry, creating the spaces and the times for

Nollywood films to fit in. As mentioned above, the economic transformations due to the application of the SAP policies deeply impacted on the Nigerian economy, influencing, among other things, the way in which most people's time was organised. In their essay about the history of leisure in sub-Saharan Africa, Emmanuel Akyeampong and Charles Ambler highlight the fact that the large majority of unemployed African urban youngsters have huge amounts of "empty time" at their disposal, a kind of time in which, in many ways, Nollywood has found the room for its popular success. As they underline,

> […] The burgeoning scale of unemployed youth in African cities is perhaps making redundant the division between "work" and "leisure" time. This is a class with time on their hands. Can they be seen as "leisured class"? Leisure time is time consciously set aside for social and recreational activities or even for "rest". Unoccupied time due to unemployment is imposed "empty time", not leisure time purposely set aside for recreation and pleasure. Unemployment puts those without work on a time schedule different from others in the community (Akyeampong and Ambler 15 – 16).

It is often in this imposed "empty time" that largely characterised Lagos life in the early 1990s that Nollywood videos were watched. This empty time was not only caused by high rate of unemployment, but also by a number of other factors, such as the long wait for public transport at street corners, where video shops often positioned their screens for the promotion of new releases (cf. Okome 2007), or by delays in public offices, banks and fast-food restaurants, where a television post was (and is) always on to entertain both customers and employees during long queues and waits.

As a matter of fact, the city's infrastructures, their failure as well as their specific way of functioning, and the way of using time and space that the city imposed on its inhabitants largely influenced the development of the Nigerian video industry. In turn, the videos became a sort of mirror of Lagos, which absorbed its life and reflected it to its inhabitants in multiple ways.

Lagos Life and the Peculiar Realism of Nollywood Video Films

As underlined in the previous section, the Nigerian video industry has been generated by the peculiar material and economic conditions of Lagos, and Lagos is omnipresent in early Nollywood videos, even if often through implicit references more than through explicit visual representations. Most of the early films were shot on location, because low budgets did not allow for the construction of artificial settings. Locations were in most cases indoor (wealthy living rooms, offices, restaurants and bars) because of the challenges of shooting in the public space (lack of official authorisations, traffic jams, thieves and other racketeers).

As Jonathan Haynes underlines, "The fact that public space is incoherent and artistically unmanageable encourages retreat into the family compound and the genre of domestic melodrama, the dominant mode of Nollywood film" (2007a: 144). Within this context, the city landscape was often almost absent, and eventually represented only through a number of establishing shoots that "seem to be emulating the look of Hollywood films" and that "often occur in romantic films or at romantic moments to provide an image of a desired good life in a normal city" (Haynes 2007a: 142).

The familiar reality of poverty and collapse of urban infrastructures, which is "irresistible to foreign documentary filmmakers" (Haynes 2007a: 143), was rarely visually shown, but at the same time it profoundly informed the dominant feelings of most early videos. As Onokoome Okome (2002) emphasised, anxiety was the key structuring feeling of early Nollywood films, a feeling which characterised (and perhaps still characterises) the life of many Lagosians and, more generally, Lagos as a postcolonial city: anxiety due to the desire of a better living, of a better job, of a social freedom from the ties imposed, even within the city, by family, gender and religious obligations. In early Nollywood films, this anxiety was expressed through a focus on the intimate dimension of the family. It is within the family, in fact, that, in early videos, the deepest insecurity was manifested, and that the conflicts that dominate the urban landscape were internalised.

As Brian Larkin has observed, "In Nigerian films, the family is often the source of the deepest treachery, and family members are represented as corrupt, cheating people of money and betraying them as well as offering love and support" (171). However, the retreat into the intimate sphere of the family is probably a key narrative element of melodrama as a genre, an element often used to represent wider social and political transformations. As Ravi Vasudevan underlines while discussing the melodramatic attributes of Indian popular cinema,

> There is a case for considering the way melodrama, its public/private architecture, and its backward-looking temporality, is mobilised to drive epically-scaled works that stage an engagement with the reconfiguration of national imaginaries. […] These emerge at critical moments in the transformation of social, cultural, and political circumstances, and are bodied forth in key works which place the home, interpretable as a zone of primary affective attachment, at the critical intersection of the narrative relationship between community, public life, and political structure (58).

In early Nollywood films such as, for instance, *Living in Bondage* (1992), *Mortal Inheritance* (1996) and *Died Wretched* (1998), stories of betrayals, treachery and murder are common. They depict the anxiety and instability of urban life but they do it through a transposition within the sphere of the intimate. As Achille Mbembe (2001) has evidenced, the postcolonial ruling class and the regimes it produces are characterised by the open manifestation of excess and exaggeration, something close to what Mikhail Bakhtin (1984) has defined as the grotesque. But, as Brian Larkin has pointed out, Nollywood films take this grotesque dimension "away from the figure of the postcolonial dictator and place it back into the family […] There the grotesque plays out within and between family members and the dense political field Mbembe identifies is sublimated into personal relationships" (184).

Through this process, the hardship, the violence and the excesses of urban life, rather than being explicitly represented, are emotionally internalised and become the ground for what Brian Larkin defined as the "aesthetic of outrage" typical of Nollywood films, an aesthetic that uses "spectacular transgression, luridly depicted, to work on the body, generating physical revulsion" (2008: 186). The representation of the city and of the urban life that comes out of this process of re-elaboration is both realistic and hallucinatory. It constantly takes inspiration from the reality of the city life, but at the same time avoids fully visualising this experience and the way it is lived through by common people.

It thus tends to draw on dreams and urban legends rather than on images of common people's everyday life. In this sense, the Lagos of early Nollywood video films is probably not the Lagos you would see when walking around the megacity, but it is the Lagos of the invisible fears and dreams, horrors and miracles that inhabit the imagination of Lagos city-dwellers, an emotional reality suddenly made visible and palpable by the video technology.

However, beyond the hallucinatory representation of Lagos that early Nollywood films propose through their melodramatic narrative structure, it is possible to identify also another way in which videos connect to the city, something that has to do with their peculiar form of narrative realism. Nigerian videos have often been described as a purely melodramatic genre, based on moral polarisation and aesthetic excesses (Haynes 2000; Larkin 2008; Adejunmobi 2010), and their narrative structure has been defined as the result of the incorporation of both transnational narrative models and local forms of popular culture. However, if, among scholars, the use of the term melodrama to define the Nollywood film genre is almost uncontested, it "is virtually never used" by Nollywood professionals and members of the audience (Haynes 22).

On the contrary, people tend to define Nollywood as a purely realistic narrative form. In fact, while somehow adopting some of the key elements of what scholars define as the "melodramatic imagination" (cf. Brooks 1976), Nigerian video films are also implicitly and explicitly the result of a strong concern for the sincere and naturalistic representations of reality. This aspect transpires evidently from interviews with video-makers and producers. For many of them, realism is *the* key aspect of film language in Nollywood videos. For instance, according to Lancelot Imasuen, one of the most successful Nollywood directors,

> We [Nigerians] surpass every other film industry in our realism […]. People need to be able to relate with the movie, the crowd wants to be committed with the story. This is one aspect of Nollywood that you cannot take away! Every time you don't use it, then it's not Nollywood. We cannot lose our realism! That is the beginning of our cinema, which is the end of it! (2010)

This particular concern with realism manifests itself both through explicit narrative and aesthetic choices and through contingent technical aspects that make the reality "interfere" with the construction of the film narrative. In this sense, we can talk of both an "explicit" and a "contingent" realism in Nigerian video films.

The explicit realism can be identified as a direct consequence of the specific concern for "real-life stories" that Imasuen's statement summarises. It is connected to Nigerian directors and producers' widespread preference for plots inspired by newspapers articles and street rumours, and it tends to reinforce what many defined as the educational role of Nigerian videos. Like many forms of popular culture in Africa, in fact, Nigerian videos tend to have a didactic orientation, which takes inspiration from everyday life episodes (cf. Obiechina 1971; Barber 2000).

As numerous directors have underlined in the interviews I conducted during my fieldwork, Nollywood films focus on what preoccupies Nigerian people in their everyday existence, that is, family issues (infertility, infidelity, jealousy, widowhood and polygamy), political problems (corruption, political violence, injustice, ethnic tensions and illicit money-making practices), and the challenges related to the daily survival in the city (how to make money, how to get a job, how to get a woman/a man, etc). While the representation of these issues is in most cases informed by the melodramatic imagination inherited from both international and local forms of popular culture, and thus metamorphosed by it, the original concern for these real, actual, everyday problems makes Nigerian video-makers claim that their films are purely and simply about reality.

As Nelly, an assistant director interviewed in the documentary *Nollywood Babylon* (2008), says toward the end of the film,

> You can never tell the story of Nigeria by propaganda […]. You can never say [it] by sending a communication minister to go and talk on CNN. The world is not stupid […]. They know politicians can say anything, but they want to see it from the people who are feeling the pain. And that's what Nollywood does, that's what is unique about us, *we tell it the way it is.* Even though people come out and say they don't like this, they don't like that, *we tell it the way it is.*

This statement is confirmed by what many members of the Nigerian audience feel. During fieldwork, I conducted numerous informal conversations with Nigerian videos' habitual viewers, and most of them were almost literally repeating Nelly's words: "Nollywood videos tell it (the reality) the way it is, and this is the main reason why we watch them".

The nature of this realistic representation, however, is somehow unconventional, and it has something "contingent" to it. Because of the restricted production budgets and the limited availability of high quality technical infrastructures, many Nigerian videos (and those produced in the early years in particular) are defined by the use of natural or minimal lighting, digital handy cameras and nonprofessional extras. Natural sounds, when not covered by heavy digitally recorded soundtracks, emerge strongly, and often in ways not directly related to the plot (car horns in the background, the sound of the power generator, the noise of people chatting in the vicinity, church bells and mosques' calls to prayer).

Camera movements and shooting angles, when not directly inspired by the classic soap-opera-style (highly dramatic close ups and quick frame alternation), tend to reproduce the basic technique used in the early years of Nigerian television to film local programmes and theatre shows (cf. Esan 90). This technique privileged long take sequences in order to simplify the editing process and reduce the post-production time and budget, thus involuntarily subscribing to one of the key features of neorealist film language, that is, long-take shots and uncut sequence time *durée* (cf. Bazin 1971). Furthermore, in early videos, the special effects and make-up tended to be handcrafted and, when not overstated, they participated in creating a sense of crude naturalism.

Intuitively, one would be pushed to think that the combination of the above-listed elements would make the film look more artificial, because of the absence of the specific craft (in what concerns special effects, extras' acting skills, sound and light tuning, camera technique) that makes the technicality of filmmaking, its "artificiality", almost invisible. But, surprisingly, the result is, at least in my view, exactly the opposite. The evident artificiality of some scenes, the fact that the reality behind the camera continuously re-emerges and interferes with what is being filmed, give the videos a particularly realist flavour, contingent but significantly effective.

An instance of this contingent realism is given by two of the best known scenes in *Living in Bondage* (1992). The first represents one of the numerous occult rituals in which Andy, the protagonist of the film, participates throughout the film. In the particular scene that I have in mind, which happens toward the end of the film, a goat is decapitated right on Andy's head. The bare naturalism of this scene is related to the fact that there is no technical mediation to it. The relatively artisanal special effects added to further dramatise the action (an un-naturalistic neon-like green light and an unsettling electronic soundtrack), while creating an almost hallucinatory atmosphere, do not filter the violence of the scene.

Again, paradoxically, instead of reducing the images' verisimilitude, the imperfection of the special effects ends up, at least in my view, accentuating it. The goat is physically killed in front of the camera and the scene has a strong impact on the viewer, who feels directly involved in the sacrifice. The second scene I have in mind plays on a different level. In this case Andy, who has become mad because his wife's ghost keeps on haunting him, walks around the market, harassing street vendors and digging into the rubbish bins in search of food. The absence of professional extras and of artificial lighting, the shaky camera movements, and the people's reactions to Andy's behaviour, make the scene, like the previous one, look particularly "true".

Again, we have the feeling that there is no mediation between the scene and the reality that surrounds it. In this case, the way the people in the market react to Andy's movements makes the artificiality of the scene evident (they look into the camera, they crowd around Andy, staring at him in a definitely non-naturalistic way), but as I underlined earlier, this particular artificiality, by marking the intrusion of the behind-the-camera reality into the film, has a powerful effect which makes the scene appear as "real".

In the early years of Nollywood (and to a certain extent still today), the intrusion of the behind-the-camera reality into video film language used to mark video production processes at all levels. As numerous scenes in the existing documentaries about Nollywood evidence, for instance, Nollywood producers and directors have often to deal with unpredictable events that can profoundly condition the production processes and the contents of the videos produced. As a result of this situation, in many cases, directors are pushed to integrate the elements that the reality "imposes" on them into the videos' narrative structure. In *This is Nollywood* (2007), for instance, we see the director Bond Emeruwa forced to cope with power failures, noise from generators, songs and prayers coming from a mosque near the set. All these elements are creatively integrated into the film production, and inevitably find their way into the final result, thus participating to the creation of the specific "realistic aura" of Nollywood films.

Conclusion

As Calvino wrote in the lines I quoted at the beginning of this essay, the real and the represented cities "are not equal [...]. Every face and gesture [are] answered, from the mirror, by a face and a gesture inverted, point by point. The two [cities] live for each other, their eyes interlocked; but there is no love between them" (54). Lagos and its screen-mirrored image live with their eyes interlocked. As I described in the first section of this essay, the materiality of Lagos generated Nollywood and constantly participates in shaping its new developments.

On the other hand, early Nollywood films looked inside the heart of Lagos, mirrored its image, but without producing a mirror-like reflection. Nigerian early videos excavated into Lagos feelings and emotions, turning the city upside-down and mirroring its "faces and gestures inverted, point by point". Nevertheless, the city's materiality found its way into the texture of the video films, left its marks on their skin, allowing film directors and viewers to claim that Nollywood videos are nothing less than a pure and realistic representation of the Nigerian everyday life. The megacity and the video industry are involved in an endless negotiation, in which they generate and regenerate each other constantly. Neither of them will ever have the last word. Neither of them will ever fully contain the other. But together they will allow us to better understand the material and emotional dimensions of everyday life in Nigeria.

Notes

[1] A previous version of this article was published in *Proceedings of the 3rd International Conference on Hausa Studies: African and European Perspectives*, edited by S. Baldi and H.M. Yakasai (Naples: Studi Africanistici, Serie Ciado-Sudanese, 2011, pp. 183-198). It is republished here thanks to the kind authorisation of the volume's editors.

[2] For an account of the use of the metaphor of the mirror in film theory, see Elsaesser and Hagener (2010: ch. 3).

[3] For a penetrating representation of this period of economic, infrastructural and social decline, see Sefi Atta's novel *Everything Good Will Come* (2008).

[4] As Jonathan Haynes puts it, Nollywood videos do not represent "any particular pure indigenous tradition of melodrama" or any unfiltered acceptance of foreign melodramatic models: they are rather the result of "layers of influence and adaptation going back a long way, of which contemporary televised forms are only the most recent" (2000: 23).

[5] The Nollywood director Bond Emeruwa, for instance, during the documentary *This is Nollywood* (2007), defined Nigerian videos as "edu-entertainment". In a similar way, Teco Benson, another successful Nigerian director, labelled Nollywood as a "message-oriented film industry" (2010).

[6] Brian Larkin's formulation of an "aesthetic of outrage" mentioned above is particularly fitting in this context (Larkin 2008).

[7] As I mentioned elsewhere (Jedlowski 2013b), these documentaries have been shot during a period in which the Nigerian video film industry was going through a difficult production crisis, a period in which probably the contingent technical problems related to low budgets and tight shooting schedules affected Nigerian videos' aesthetics the most.

Works Cited

Achebe, Chinua. *The Trouble with Nigeria.* Harlow: Heinemann, 1984.

Addelman, Ben and Samir Mallal. *Nollywood Babylon.* AM Pictures and National Film Board of Canada, Canada/Nigeria, 2008 (video).

Adejunmobi, Moradewun. "Nigerian Video Film as Minor Transnational Practice". In *Postcolonial Text* 3(2), 2007, 1-16.

____________. "Charting Nollywood's Appeal Locally and Globally". In *African Literature Today* 28 (2010): 106-121.

Akyeampong, Emmanuel and Charles Ambler. "Leisure in African History: An Introduction". In *The International Journal of African Historical Studies* 35 (1) 2002, 1-16.

Amenechi, Andy. *Mortal Inheritance,* Silverscreen Studios (English), Nigeria, 1996 (Video).

Anikulapo, Jahman. Personal Communication, Lagos, 19th of January 2010.

Atta, Sefi. *Everything Good Will Come.* Melbourne: Spinifex Press, 2008.

Bakhtin, Mikhail, *Rabelais and His World.* Bloomington: Indiana University Press, 1984.

Barber, Karin, *The Generation of Plays: Yoruba Popular Life in Theatre.* Bloomington: Indiana University Press, 2000.

Barrot, Pierre (ed). *Nollywood: Le phénomène Video au Nigeria,* Paris: L'Harmattan, 2005.

Bazin, André. *What is Cinema?* Vol. 2, Berkeley: University of California Press, 1971.

Benson, Teco. Personal Communication, Lagos, 19th January 2010.

Brooks, Peter. *The Melodramatic Imagination: Balzac, Henri James, Melodrama and the Mode of Excess.* New Heaven and London: Yale University Press, 1976.

Calvino, Italo. *The Invisible Cities.* London, Secker and Warburg, 1974.

Elsaesser, Thomas and Malte Hagener. *Film Theory: An Introduction through the Senses.* London and New York: Routledge, 2010.

Esan, Oluyinka. *Nigerian Television. Fifty Years of Television in Africa.* Princeton: AMV Publishing, 2009.

Ferguson, James. *Expectations of Modernity: Myths and Meanings of Urban Life on the Zambian Copperbelt,* Berkeley: University of California Press, 1999.

Gandy, Matthew. "Learning from Lagos", *New Left Review* 33 (2005): 36–52.

Haynes, Jonathan. *Nigerian Video Films,* Athens: Ohio University Press, 2000.

___________. "Nollywood in Lagos, Lagos in Nollywood Films". In *Africa Today* 54(2): 2007a. 130-150.

___________. "Nnebue: The Anatomy of Power". In *Film International* 28 (5.4): 2007b, 30-40.

Haynes, Jonathan and Onookome Okome. "Evolving Popular Media: Nigerian Video Films". In *Research in African Literatures* 29(3) 1998. 106-128.

Imasuen, Lancelot Oduwa. Personal Communication, Lagos: 12th of February 2010.

Jedlowski, Alessandro. "When the Nigerian Video Film Industry became "Nollywood": Naming, Branding and the Videos' Transnational Mobility". In *Estudos Afro-Asiaticos* 33 (1, 2, 3) 2011. 225 – 251.

____________. "From Nollywood to Nollyworld: Processes of Transnationalization in the Nigerian Video Film Industry". In *Global Nollywood: Transnational Dimensions of an African Video Film Industry.*

Matthias Krings and Onookome Okome (ed). Bloomington: Indiana University Press, 2013a. 25-45.

Jeyifo, Biodun. "Household and Neighbourhood Mini-municipalities: The Unquantifiable, Epiphenomenal Costs". In *Talakawa Liberation Courier* 132, in *The Guardian Nigeria*, 21st of February 2010. 83.

Koolhaas, Rem. "Fragments of a lecture on Lagos". In Okwui Enwezor (ed). *Under Siege: Four African Cities. Freetown, Johannesburg, Kinshasa, Lagos.* Ostfildern-Ruit: Hatjie Cantz Publisher, 2002. 173 – 184.

Larkin, Brian. "Degraded Images, Distorted Sounds: Nigerian Videos and the Infrastructure of Piracy". *Public Culture* 16 (2) 2004. 289-314.

___________. *Signal and Noise: Media, Infrastructure and Urban Culture in Northern Nigeria.* Chapel Hill: Duke University Press, 2008.

Mbembe, Achille. *On the Postcolony.* Berkeley: University of California Press, 2001.

Miller, Daniel. "Materiality: An introduction". In Daniel Miller (ed). *Materiality.* Durham and London: Duke University Press, 2005.

Nnebue, Kenneth. *Died Wretched,* NEK videos, Nigeria, 1998 (video).

Obiechina, Emmanuel. *An African Popular Literature: A Study of Onitsha Market Pamphlet,* Cambridge: Cambridge University Press, 1971.

Oha, Obododimma. "The Visual Rhetoric of the Ambivalent City in Nigerian Video Films". In *Cinema and the City.* Mark Shiel and Tony Fitzmaurice (eds). Oxford: Blackwell, 2001. 195-205.

Okome, Onookome. "Writing the Anxious City: Images of Lagos in Nigerian Home Video Films". In *Under Siege: Four African Cities. Freetown, Johannesburg, Kinshasa, Lagos.* Okwui Enwezor, Ostfildern-Ruit (ed). Hatjie Cantz Publisher, 2002. 315-336.

____________. "Nollywood: Spectatorship, Audience and the Sites of Consumption". In *Postcolonial Text* 3(2) 2007. 1-21. http://journals.sfu.ca/pocol/index.php/pct/article/view/763/425,

Okoye, Gabriel Onye (aka Gaboski), Personal communication, Lagos: 25th of June 2014.

Olukoju, Ayodeji. "'Never Expect Power Always": Electricity Consumers' Response to Monopoly, Corruption and Inefficient Services in Nigeria". In *African Affairs* 103 (410) 2004. 51–71.

Rapu, Chris Obi. *Living in Bondage,* NEK videos, Nigeria, 1992 (video).

Sacchi, Franco. *This is Nollywood.* Center for Digital Imaging Arts and Eureka Film Productions, USA/Nigeria, 2007 (video).

Simone, AbdouMaliq. "The Visible and Invisible: Remaking Cities in Africa". In *Under Siege: Four African Cities. Freetown, Johannesburg,*

Kinshasa, Lagos. Okwui Enwezor (ed). Ostfildern-Ruit: Hatjie Cantz Publisher, 2002. 23–43.

______________. *For the City Yet to Come: Changing African Life in Four Cities.* Durham and London: Duke University Press, 2004.

Sundaram, Ravi. "Recycling Modernity: Pirate Electronic Cultures in India". In *Third Text* 13 (47) 1999. 59–65.

UNESCO, *Emerging Markets and the Digitalization of the Film Industry: An Analysis of the 2012 UIS International Survey of Feature Film Statistics,* Montreal, UIS, 2013.

Vasudevan, Ravi, *The Melodramatic Public: Film Form and Spectatorship in Indian Cinema.* New Delhi: Permanent Black, 2010.

CHAPTER TEN

Charting Moral Geographies: Nollywood and the Concept of the Nation

Nomusa Makhubu

Abstract

The fascination with Nollywood resides in the fact that, as an expression of local agency, it formulates a new paradigm, a new way of looking and seeing. One should be reminded of Sylvester Ogbechie's proclamation that Nollywood is "the first global pan-African film medium to cut across social, cultural, economic and national boundaries" (2009). As Ogbechie explains, "Nollywood films played a major role in the social and economic recovery of Liberia after its civil war". However, the "political" positioning of Nollywood as a cultural commodity "in service of the nation-state" or in engendering peace, religious toleration or pan-Africanism, raises many questions. Furthermore, this kind of positioning conceals the initial rejection of Nollywood by scholars as a phenomenon that bore little artistic or historical significance. This initial rejection stemmed from a conventional view that saw Nollywood as a "gaudy visual style that robs the productions of memorable pathos and artistry" (Adesanya 1997: 19). The paper questions the reductionist idea that Nollywood is "essentially Nigerian". I suggest that the filmic narratives are difficult to "place" within the construct of nationhood, in the light of debates on the problematic nature of the categorisation of national cinema. The paper also explores how these filmic narratives both affirm and subvert moral principles assumed to be the architrave of nationalist objectives. Using the Halleluiah thematic category, I discuss the concept of redemptive spaces simulated in the church and state.

Introduction

"The proletariat has no country"– Marx and Engels

In relation to the idea of "nation", Nollywood is a complex form of cultural politics. A variety of questions arise: is Nollywood a national product? What would it mean to define Nollywood as a national product? In what ways could Nollywood be seen as a 'national cinema'? In asking these questions, one has to consider who regulates Nollywood's industrial infrastructure, as well as the ways in which Nollywood constructs or projects identities which may or may not form part of a 'national' character. Furthermore, it would be necessary to compare popular cultural forms vis-à-vis 'legitimised' or state-sanctioned cultural forms, to ascertain the ways in which they are entrenched in the nationalist rhetoric in Nigeria. This paper seeks to focus on popular and populist film and to initiate further dialogue through a selection of issues regarding experiences of public and private "national" space in Nollywood. Taking its discursive cue from David Harvey's "historical-geographical processes of place and community construction" as well as Edward Said's notion of symbolic territories that chart a "cartography of identities", the paper will unpack various politics of representation in the myriad of images of the national space of Nigeria as projected by Nollywood.

Where does one place, for a start, the claim that Nollywood "mis-represents 'us' as a 'nation'" and that Nollywood's "ideologically misguided esotericism" "primitivises national culture"? Hope Eghagha articulates this dismissal, stating that "We may need to state for record purposes that there are many Nigerians who have refused to buy into the culture of watching Nollywood movies because of the strong presence or motif of 'ritual and juju'..." (Eghagha 71). Although there is a sense that Nollywood delineates an "essence" of Nigerian-ness or social and cultural life in Nigeria, there is also on the other hand the general perception that it does not mirror Nigeria or Nigerian cultural dynamics.

Considering that thematic categories of Nollywood are named through ethnic and religious indices, the concept of an existing 'national' character (the "us") that is "misrepresented" should urge inquiry. Abubakar Momoh (2) reminds us that "the national question [in Nigeria] ultimately requires to be posed as an ideological question" as it is "the (un)evenness in the distribution of or access to power... in the context of *deliverables* and what advantage co-ethnics or a fraction of them take of one another in the process". The national question for Momoh is "basically a problem of the realisation of human essence". What becomes important to debate are the ways in which Nollywood reflects and constructs intricate and complex identities which aptly question and problematise the implication of the national question as a "lived essentialism".

Nollywood has long traversed borders. It is defined by Sylvester Ogbechie as "the first global pan-African film medium to cut across social, cultural, economic and national boundaries". It is produced and consumed globally. "Nollywood" production is no longer logistically dependent on the geographical specificity of Nigeria or of Africa for that matter (that is, there are producers who reside in Ghana, the U.S. and the U.K. amongst other places which are more than just filming locations and make Nollywood films there). Nonetheless, these films draw largely from social and cultural practices that are specific to the Nigerian context.

Nollywood has also been described by Moradewun Adejunmobi (2007) as a "minor transnational product" which African Diasporas recognise as a product from "home". It is generally perceived as a form of self-narrativisation that Hamid Naficy (121) delineates as a characteristic of transnational film. For Naficy (121), the transnational genre "allows films to be read and reread, not only as individual texts produced by authorial vision and generic conventions, but also as sites for intertextual, cross-cultural, and transnational struggles over meanings and identities". Thus, the ways in which the stereotype in Nollywood is conceptualised may be specific to local conventions but is liberated from fascist ideals. Rather than conscientising the nationhood idea, it can be argued that Nollywood is an exploration of the inequitable material conditions that people find themselves in, across boundaries.

Nollywood video films are principally a working class product. Nollywood is an industry that is primarily conceptualised, manufactured, distributed and consumed by the working class (This is by no means to say that it is not consumed by the bourgeois at all but that it is necessary to note the ambiguous nature of [cultural] value of Nollywood). The predominance of fantastical wealth and power as themes in Nollywood is aptly described by Jonathan Haynes (145) "as a figure for the mysterious, unearned wealth of the oil boom". These themes also draw out narratives of domination and marginalisation, alienation and displacement where people seek to move from one place to another (from the village to the city, from being local urbanites to being cosmopolitans, from poverty to riches, from earth or hell to heaven).

Stories of migration and movement through transformation or deliverance suggest a complex way in which constructions of real, fictional or simulated spaces are circumscribed with an intersection of morality with politics, the economy and culture in the mapping of identities. This is evident from the ease with which "evil" is easily relatable to the "forest", "the village", "the city" and ultimately "the nation". I discuss moral geographies in Nollywood as the ways in which relations of power are inscribed in certain places (or spaces) where moral values that may or may not form part of the architrave of nationalist objectives are performed and, at times, subverted. In discussing moral geographies, I am reminded of Ogbu Kalu's observation that "In Africa, the political realm is sacralised or enchanted and politics is a religious matter precisely because it is a *moral performance*" (12, own emphasis).

By using the Halleluiah thematic category of Nollywood, I intend to discuss the ways in which the idea of "nation" is made elusive. The Halleluiah film category speaks more directly to the notion of moral performance which illuminates a theological economy between politics, religion and cultures that is ever-present in Nollywood film. Furthermore, it seeks to unpack the construction of precolonial utopias in which pastoral spaces seem to exist without the possibility of a city or of a nation. These spaces appear in Nollywood films as self-governed and self-defined, ruled by traditional leaders who seem to bear no relation with a larger polity other than the immediate community. Traditional leaders, however, are sometimes constructed as a parody of national government or as caricatures of national leaders.

Parameters of National Cinema and the Surfeit of Nollywood

It seems inappropriate to define Nollywood as a national cinema for reasons stated earlier, as well as because the industry has been independent of ideological nationalising cultural forms. Governmental support in any form has been very recent. Nwachukwu Frank Ukadike asserts that in the 1960s, the conservative, bureaucratic and 'traditionalist' class blocked the establishment of the cultural policy needed "to expand and strengthen creative potential... and [concretise] the nation's cultural identity" (141). The formation of the National Film Corporation (NFC) in the 1980s did not adequately support the development of film archives, film production and distribution. Faced with this, Nollywood has had to carve its own space and draw on its own resources.

But given this, how would one conceptualise a national cinema. Andrew Higson (36-37), in his four-tier discourse on the concept of a national cinema, suggests firstly an economic approach, supported by a text-based approach, an exhibition-led or consumption-based approach and a criticism-led approach. The economic approach looks at questions such as the ownership and control of the industry; the text-based approach is concerned with the construction of "nationhood" in the film narratives; the consumption-based approach analyses audiences by comparison to foreign films (such as American films) and the criticism-led approach reduces "national cinema to the terms of a quality art cinema… or modernist heritage of a particular nation state" (Higson 36-37). For Higson, "to identify a national cinema is first of all to specify a coherence and a unity; it is to proclaim a unique identity and stable set of meanings" (37).

Using these prescriptive approaches, Nollywood is anything but a national cinema. Nollywood does not only denote various filming practices but is also delineated across ethnic and religious categories. For instance, we speak of Igbo films, Yoruba films and Hausa films (amongst others). Furthermore, Christian films are generally located in Southern Nigeria, whereas Muslim films (mostly Hausa films) are associated with the Northern parts of the country. Jonathan Haynes points out that the term 'Nollywood'

> […] refers principally to southern Nigerian, English-language films, whose distribution is largely controlled by Igbo marketers, but which are made by people from the full range of southern Nigerian ethnicities. *Nollywood* has come into general use as the name of the Nigerian video film industry, but when used in this way, the term obscures the Hausa branch and Yoruba-language video production based in Lagos, though the Yoruba production partly overlaps with that of Nollywood.

The "first Nollywood film", *Living in Bondage*, was made on cassette by an Igbo businessman, Kenneth Nnebue, with Yorùbá travelling theatre performers (Haynes 2007:286). Although it would be erroneous to over-emphasise socio-linguistic classifications, the use of such categories as heuristic device can be limiting and flattening. The slippage between "ethnic" identities and socio-linguistic classifications has implications for contextualising Nollywood. While the Igbo-Yoruba-Hausa distinction is generally used to define language differences alongside English and Pidgin films, one has to question if these distinctions go beyond language usage. For example, does the Yoruba film category merely convey the language in which a film is made or does it delve deeper into the film's expression or interrogation of Yoruba socio-cultural identity? What happens to this specificity in English and Pidgin-based films (and are the English and Pidgin mediums more dominant)?

Yoruba films, such as Tunde Kelani's, seek to serve a historicising purpose and seek to "re-educate" through presenting "a compendium of Yorùbá history, literature, and science" (Kelani ctd in Esonwanne 25). Kelani's *Arugba* is a narrative of the Arugba, the chosen virgin who is tasked to carry the basket of offerings from the King's palace to the river stream during the Osun Osogbo festival in the South-West of Nigeria. The Osun festival in Osogbo is a celebration of a female Orisa who arrived in Ile-Ife with the first male-dominated batch of seventeen Orisas (Abímbọ́lá 2006: 126-7). Kelani has often rejected the term "Nollywood" to describe his films because he feels that his *oeuvre* is at a different artistic level.

Igbo films such as *Odudu Kingdom* represent constructions of Igbo 'traditional' societies governed by 'traditional' leadership structures made up of kings and chiefs. Hausa films form part of moralist storytelling traditions fused with "Islamic ethos and aesthetics" (Adamu 2). The majority of English and Pidgin films explore socio-economic issues faced by (aspiring) urbanites or cosmopolitans. Some of these distinctions are simplistic and overlap but this chart, although generalised, is representative of some reality and makes it unseemly to conceptualise Nollywood (in its general terms) as a national cinema.

Linguistic distinctions have an important implication for various constructions of a unified "national character". In colonial Nigeria, Diri Teilanyo argues, "nationalists had the attitude of 'revelling in their own command of English'" (Mazrui qtd in Teilanyo 1975:150). Ali Mazrui claims that "Resistance to foreign rule in Africa… did not become 'nationalistic' until its leaders became English speakers" (Mazrui 1975:48 qtd in Teilanyo 2003:82). However, Moradewun Adejunmobi (74) points out that there is an assumption that cultural products made in European languages (such as English) have less appeal to Nigerian audiences on the whole as they "are considered [to be] intelligible only to elite audiences and operate in African cultural practice mainly as signifiers of colonial experience". If this is true, then films made in indigenous languages form part of an "authentication" process, but do not enable a nationalising function. The English language in Nollywood films is perceived as a medium that cannot "authenticate" the syncretism of urban-based African popular culture. This operates under appropriated separatist *practices* of speaking and performing English as local or specifically Nigerian (Adejunmobi 2002). Furthermore, variations of English construct hierarchical relations between speakers.

An interview with film producers Zeb Ejiro, Ajoke Jacobs, Tunde Kelani and Aquila Njamah alludes to varying power relations and the precariousness of the Nigerian socio-economic space in the ethno-nationalist political framework.

> **Ejiro**: The Yoruba is watching the Hausa, and the Igbo is watching the Hausa. People are very careful. Everything you do, people are looking for their political angle.
>
> **Njamah**: Exactly. That is why we need political censorship. Until things stabilise, "a hungry man is an angry man."
>
> **Kelani**: We can't have movies that say all Muslims are bad. It would tear Nigeria apart. You can't say all Christians are lazy.
>
> **Ejiro**: If you make a movie that abuses the Yoruba ways, it cannot go. And if you say all Nigerian policemen are corrupt, it cannot go. But you can say this policeman is corrupt. You cannot say the government is corrupt, but you can say a minister in the government is corrupt. It's when you generalise—

Internally, films are made and interpreted in relation to each other. Yoruba films are read in relation to Hausa films; Hausa films are read in relation to Igbo film and so on, in a process of differentiation. The notion of a 'national' cinema is similarly a process of differentiation in which the local film industry is viewed in relation to films made in other countries. Externally, Nollywood generates stereotypical images that inform the ways in which Nigeria is imagined. While the national question is the process of constructing moral values, Nollywood might best be characterised as a process of creating redemptive spaces.

Redemptive Religion and the Preservation of the Imagined City

Jonathan Haynes locates Lagos as the epicentre of Nigeria's filmmaking and film distribution. Nollywood concurs with "a new *visibility*… of the Lagos metropolis—or 'megacity'" (Haynes 11). This implies that Nollywood contributes to the visibility of the city-life. The city is a place of danger, chaos and moral decadence; it embodies experiences of inequality, displacement and alienation. Nollywood movies deal with urban elites whose lives are traumatised by traditional forces – deities, witches, rituals, many based on distinctive ethnic practices. In addition to traditional religion however, the Halleluiah thematic category of film has a strong Christian basis.

The popularity of the Halleluiah video film theme, described by Onookome Okome as "a narrative of redemption through the intervention of Jesus Christ whose earthly agent is the thaumaturge… has soared, mostly due to the depleting economic resources of the poor who now seek solace in the promise of a heavenly *polis* of bliss and eternal happiness" (Okome 14). In Nollywood, magic or "divine power" is made visible, even though it remains fictional and therefore transforms space into partly simulated space. The notion of staging "divine power" is linked by Achille Mbembe "with the process of reinventing the self and the polis, in its twofold sense— earthly polis and heavenly polis (the Kingdom)".

The construction of a heavenly city in Nollywood is not merely an imagined utopia, as it exists precisely to address the real conditions in the lived national space. The term 'utopia' is a combination of the Greek terms *outopia*, which means 'no place', and *eutopia*, which means 'good place' (Mumford 1). If the heavenly city in Nollywood offers moral transformation, or redemption as stated by Onookome, then it is conscientised, not as a fictional place, but as an existing virtual or simulated space. Onookome defines these transitive spaces as spaces of production and reproduction when he argues that, in Nollywood, human agency finds salvation "not in the production of goods and services but in the production of heaven and earth". The heavenly polis is as much a place of negotiations and exchanges as is the earthly city. The notion of transformation or redemption sets a hierarchical relation between the earthly and heavenly cities.

In *40 Days and 40 Nights in the Wilderness*, directed by Ugo Ugbor, the demarcation of moral spaces follows the superficial dichotomy of "village" and "city". It is a narrative about a pastor who operates in the city, performing miracles on people with various physical ailments. Through Pastor Jerry's prayers, those who cannot walk begin to walk, those who cannot hear gain the sense of hearing and so on. Based on the biblical narrative in which Jesus experiences temptations from Satan, the title illustrates the forty-day evangelising mission in a rural village that Pastor Jerry and a group of male disciples embark on. To get to the village, they must cross a dense forest. On their way, they are attacked by a monstrous supernatural force and some of the men die.

When they eventually reach the village, they are welcomed by the traditional leaders or elders and allowed to stay in the village for forty days and forty nights. In his instructions, the pastor tells the men to accept the food and drink of the villagers because they must not be like strangers. The men convince the villagers to become Christians by performing miracles in public spaces. Here, they learn of the local god worshipped by the villagers, Kubala. The similarity that this narrative bears to colonial evangelising missions takes a turn when two of the men find out that Pastor Jerry serves Kubala – the source of his healing powers. Two of the disciples discover that the real reason they have been brought to the village is to receive power from Kubala so that they can perform miracles, but they must offer human sacrifices. The men that died in the forest were Pastor Jerry's offerings to Kubala. The two disciples survive because they kept their Christian faith and did not eat the food offered by villagers since "the more you eat their food, the more you become possessed with Kubala's power".

While the film takes place in three main spaces: the city, the forest/wilderness and the village, it alludes to a fourth space which is demonstrated through pointing or waving towards the sky as the "heavenly *polis*". Although it is the place of magic, redemption and transformation, it becomes indexed in the same way as the place of Kubala who also hovers in a sphere above the earth but is visually represented "on earth" as a dark hairy creature. The construction of a theo-political city is demonstrated by Pastor Jerry's acquisition of a heavenly language - speaking "in tongues". When the film climaxes, Pastor Jerry's use of a foreign 'heavenly' tongue during deliverance sessions is replayed to show that he was in fact using an incomprehensible language to harness power from Kubala. Communication between agents that inhabit the invisible (heavenly polis) and the visible earthly polis in Nollywood is invariably the illusion of a process of empowerment.

It can be argued that the allegorical city is materialised into the space of the church. The church maintains characteristics of the heavenly and earthly cities. It is illustrated simultaneously as a place of virtue and malevolence. The church ground, argues Okome (2007:4), is "an important locale in this narrative because it is here that the drama of the earthly polis is transported into the realm of the heavenly polis and the final resolution of all earthly schisms is given meaningful ending after the timely intervention of the spiritual actor". The "transportation" between realms implies a transformative process achieved in the church. Rather than being part of the ideological process in the state, the church can be interpreted as a polity which has a "coherent" administrative system.

Nollywood video films form a large part of an intriguing theological economy, which alludes to the church as either a polity or as prosthesis. By this I mean that the church in Nollywood is at times seen to be a remedy where the state fails. Helen Ukpabio's assertion that "In a country like this, if you don't have Jesus, you can't survive because the government does not offer us anything… whatever you are, you are self-made" (Ukpabio 2007), is a reverberation of the general sentiment. Ukpabio is the head of Liberty Gospel Church, with over 50 000 members and 78 branches in Nigeria. She is also a successful Nollywood producer. This view is echoed in Odia Ofeimun's argument that "The evangelicals have taken over the film culture in a way that is very representative of the nature of the Nigerian society today but at the same time a deviation from the more enlightened approach to national building and society building that had become dominant up to the 70s". Ofeimun continues:

> Between Oregun and Oba… there were twenty-five factories that closed down over the early years of the structural adjustment program. Well now about fifteen of them are churches. The first question you want to ask is: the people who now go to those churches to pay tithes, to pay ten percent of whatever money they have made, were they not the ones who used to work in those factories as labourers, as technicians and what not? The church promises you wealth. If you stay in the church, you will have prosperity. The very prosperity already denied you by the fact that the factories died. The poorer people get, the less hopeful they are, the more they wish for that extraordinary power that will take them out of the doldrums, out of penury. The

> churches provide it. You ask yourself, how come? In spite of the grand erection of mosques all over the place, how come there's still so much corruption in the country? It begins to tell you what the churches are for. They are therapeutic agencies. Not religious or moral intent. And since a strong segment of the population is involved in this, if the films do not minister to them, they will be throwing away the source of their income.

Nollywood video films, particularly the Halleluiah theme, reveal a portion of this political economy. The two main actors in *40 Days and 40 Nights* are young disempowered and unemployed men for whom joining the church's evangelising mission will become a source of income. In this sense, theology is political or carries out political functions.

In Nigeria, a church-state separation policy was forged by the former head of state Yakubu Gowon. However, this partition between religion and politics is also viewed as "a quasi-separation" (Kalu 6). As noted by Kalu, religion "has been given a front seat in the Nigerian public sphere" (13). The God of Africa, Kalu contends, "was a part of the nationalist rhetoric and propaganda". The moral polarisation that Nollywood illustrates between Christianity (as morally upright) and traditional beliefs (as debauched or as a source of witchcraft) constructs an axis on which the nation-state is perceived as corrupt and the church, its counterpart, as ethical. These dichotomies are superficial but exist to highlight social inequality.

Performing "moral codes" in Nollywood is part of the process of transforming and constructing ideal living spaces. Kalu asserts that "Political theology is about what the people are really saying on the moral quality of the exercise of power among them and not about the pronouncements of the elites..." He continues: "What the people are… doing at the level of infra-politics provide[s] clearer guides and these implicate the church because the wide range of the associational life of the church makes it the leader of civil society in most parts of Africa" (Kalu 5).

There is a debatable assumption that Nollywood takes on religious themes because of its financial dependence on church patronage. The general response to this observation is that religion is a medium of infra-politics. Nollywood producer and director Rotimi Ige Emmanuel proclaims: "The church does not go to Nollywood, Nollywood goes to church!" (Personal communication). A number of Nollywood producers are pastors. For Faruk Lasaki, a producer and director, "In this country...uhm... we believe in God and as I say it's either you're a Muslim or a Christian" (oral interview). In his argument, Lasaki states that "There are other smaller gods which I don't believe in. So my question is... why would the smaller god bring out something that is bigger than that?" A majority of church-sponsored Nollywood productions are confronted with the criticism that in revering Christian ideals, they cast 'traditional' beliefs as evil and create a dichotomy between the city and the village.

In *40 Days and 40 Nights*, what lies in the forest is manifest in the village and in the city. Whether in the city or in the village, lepers, blind and mad men are equally punished and delivered by the same supernatural creature that dominates the forest. The pastor who heals the sick in the city does so as a worshipper of Kubala rather than of the Christian God. In the forest and in the village, Kubala can appear in the form of lightning to cause death or illness. In the city, Kubala is an implausible beneficial source of power for young men to carry out divine miracles. What becomes apparent in the film is the dearth of *visual* difference between the city and the village. The village is the city, inasmuch as they can both be defined as wilderness ("concrete jungle"), and both appear inhospitable.

The city (Lagos in particular), defined by Onookome Okome's as "a huge slum really" in which "the community of people who suffer… is huge". In many ways, the village can be interpreted as a metaphor of the imagined city, the kingdom. There is hardly any visibility of a judicial system. Death is not punishable by law since it is a sacrifice to Kubala. In an essay that addresses horror movies from Ghana and Nigeria, Tobias Wendl proposes that

> The dichotomy of "village" and "city" is a central issue in most of the videos; and it is, of course, a transformation of the older topographic dichotomy between "wilderness" and "village," with the difference that the village, which is now constructed and represented from the perspective of the city, appears itself in the position of the wilderness (4).

The village, Wendl (5) argues, "forms part of the 'uncanny', of what the city has repressed, and what now returns from time to time into the consciousness of the city-dwellers as the 'horror of traditions'".

In the film, Christianity is seen as an opposing force, or, as one of the elders proclaims, "the visitors, some of them have opposing powers". The village is constructed as a precolonial heterotopia. It is both a space of identification as it is a space of otherness. Nollywood constructs villages as ethnic-specific spaces covered by "universalising historicism" (Said 6). Films such as *Odudu Kingdom* and *Soul of a Maiden* are located in remote spaces. Characters are dressed in "traditional" batik fabric and beads. The village is re-cast as an imagined city which is "contaminated" by the Christian urban visitors.

Conclusion

In *Out of Place*, Edward Said remarks that "Just as none of us is outside or beyond geography, none of us is completely free of the struggle over geography. That struggle is complex and interesting because it is not only about soldiers and cannons but also about ideas, about forms, about images and imaginings" (Said 7). The construction of the ideal space in Nollywood implies dissociation from the local. It is part of being able to imagine the freedoms over geography.

It weaves reality and myth to create simulated experiences of the cultural landscape of Nigeria. However, it seems to function outside of the myth-making process that is part of the nationalising process. Nollywood reproduces the past and present in such a way that history and mythology seem almost indistinct. It can be interpreted as a kind of emancipating process from which economic conditions can be turned into knowable visual forms. If one considers Karin Barber's (109) argument that "third-world texts" (if we are to consider the ways in which Nollywood reproduces meaning textually) "are necessarily [...] allegorical [...], they are to be read as [...] national allegories" that were "deployed to 'imagine' what is usually held to have been the nation state". Nollywood, it can be argued, forms imagined constructions of "baseline" identities rather than national identities. Where Nigeria is said to "drift across our television screens and into the world's public consciousness, only to fade to back out again"(Maier xvii), Nollywood aids in illuminating lived experience and imagining as a process of dissociation.

Since its inception, Nollywood has been regarded as an illegitimate cultural *objet d'art* insofar as it has been perceived as a product for popular audiences. Bogumil Jewsiewicki articulates this: "[In] the African context, even more than in the West, a non-ethnic popular artefact that is mainly thought of a *lumpenproletarian* (in ethnic as well as elite cultures) disqualifies ideas, practices, and behaviours" (343, own emphasis). The debate about Nollywood's aesthetic echoes the familiar Eurocentric dichotomy of popular and high art forms. Even within the European critical theory, de Certeau has argued that this dichotomy is characterised by "a confrontation between the rural and urban working people's tactics, aimed at the production of an autonomous culture (identity), and the institutions' and elites' strategies of dampening their old and odd cultural elements".

For Jewsiewicki, "only in this way can the term 'popular' be used, from time to time, as a reservoir for national ideology production" (343). The term *popular* gains political meaning if used in the context of the traditional and modern contradistinction and assumes populist ideology. Although Nollywood is perceived as apolitical, its use of populist ideology gives it a political edge. The delimitation of Nollywood as popular culture requires a nuanced analysis of how it forms part of historicising processes.

The premise of this paper is to incite debate in a process of re-conceptualising the interception of identity and spatiality in Nollywood. Nollywood is not a national cinema and can, in fact, be seen as a mode of interrogating "national identity". Its ideological function can almost be read as counter-cultural. Nollywood is the use of mass culture ideology to publish a social commentary in simplistic terms. Since the social and political is entrenched in religious principles, the Halleluiah thematic category illuminates some of the struggles in the theopolitics of Nigeria.

Notes

[1] From the International Workshop held at the Kwara State University in Ilorin during 2010 under the theme "Nollywood: A National Cinema?" for which the briefing blatantly states that "if Nollywood is so ubiquitous in the global marketplace of cultural commodities, there is a need to discipline it so that it does not misrepresent 'us' as a 'nation'. Its sloppy narrative regimes must be disciplined".

[2] Referenced from a conference Paper delivered in 2011 at the University of Lagos. In this paper, entitled "Re-reading Nollywood: Neo-Primitivism and Tunde Kelani's Quasi-Movie", Awosanmi questionably

classifies some Nollywood films as "quasi-movies" whose "technological banality and misrepresentational neo-primitivism project Nollywood as an artistic parody of Nigeria's globally distressful crippled-giantness".

[3] This term has also been used to denote video film but is also used recently to incorporate celluloid films that relate to Nigerian cultural dynamics.

[4] These designations (Halleluiah film, Epic film, Campus film) have been called genres. I find some of them particularly derisive but I have used them because they are recognised categories. I have called these designations thematic categories as opposed to genres. Genres, as Hamid Naficy (120) points out, are not neutral structures but are "ideological constructs masquerading as neutral categories". These themes overlap and are used flexibly in this discussion.

Works Cited

_______________ "Video Boom: Nigeria and Ghana", *Postcolonial Text*, 3.1 (2007): 286-296. Print.

Adejunmobi, Moradewun. "Nigerian Video Film as Minor Transnational Practice", *Postcolonial Text*, 3.1 (2007): 320-336. Print.

Eghagha, Hope 'Magical realism and the 'power' of Nollywood home video films', *Film International*, 5.4 (2007): 71-76. Print.

Esonwanne, Uzo. 'Interviews with Amaka Igwe, Tunde Kelani, and Kenneth Nnebue', *Research in African Literatures*, 39.4 (2008.): 24-39. Print.

Falola, Toyin and Agwuele, Augustine (Eds.) *Africans and the Politics of Popular Culture.* New York: University of Rochester Press, 2009. Print

Hackett, Rosalind (Ed). *New Religious Movements in Nigeria.* New York: The Edwin Mellen Press. 1987. Print.

Harrow, Kenneth W. *Postcolonial African Cinema: From Political Engagement to Postmodernism.* Bloomington: Indiana University Press. 2007. Print.

Harvey, David. "Cosmopolitanism and the Banality of Geographical Evils", Public Culture, spring 2000: 529-564. http://www.davidharvey.org/media/cosmopol.pdf

Haynes, Jonathan and Onookome, Okome "Evolving Popular Media: Nigerian Video Film." *Research African Literatures*, 29.3 (1998): 106-128. Print.

Haynes, Jonathan. "Nollywood in Lagos, Lagos in Nollywood Films", *Africa Today*, 2007: 131-150. Print.

Kalu, Ogbu "Faith and Politics in Africa: Emergent Political Theology of Engagement in Nigeria". McCormick Theological Seminary, Chicago, 2003. Print.

Marston, S. Woodward, K. Jones, J.P. "Flattening Ontologies of Globalisation: The Nollywood Case", *Globalisations*, 4.1 (2007): 45-63. Print.

Momoh, Abubakar and Adejumobi, Said (Eds) *The National Question in Nigeria: Comparative Perspectives.* Burlington: Ashgate. 2002. Print.

Murray, Martin and Myers, Garth (Eds). *Cities in Contemporary Africa.* New York: Palgrave MacMillan. 2006. Print.

Okome, Onookome. "Nollywood: Spectatorship, Audience and the Sites of Consumption", *Postcolonial Text* 3. 1 (2007): 383-404. Print.

Okome, Onookome; Ukpabio, Helen "'The Message is Reaching a Lot of People": Proselytizing and Video Films of Helen Ukpabio', *Postcolonial Text,* 3.2 (2007): 1-20 http://postcolonial.org/index.php/pct/article/view/750/419 (accessed 14/02/13)

Okoye, Chukwuma. "History and Nation Imagination: Igbo and the Videos of Nationalism", *Postcolonial Text* 3.1 (2007): 352-362. Print.

Shiel, Mark and Fitzmaurice, Tony (Eds). *Cinema and the City: Film and Urban Societies in a Global Context.* 2001. Print

Wendl, Tobias. "Wicked Villagers and the Mysteries of Reproduction: An Exploration of Horror Movies from Ghana and Nigeria", *Postcolonial Text* 3.1 (2007): 263-285

Wilson, Rob and Dissanayake, Wimal (Eds). *Global/Local: Cultural Production and the Transnational Imaginary.* Durham: Duke University Press, 1996. Print.

CHAPTER ELEVEN

Binaries and Ambivalence: An Analysis of Two Nollywood Actors' Spatial Discourses

Ogochukwu C. Ekwenchi and Allen N. Adum

Abstract

It is quite safe to say that Nollywood owes its existence to globalisation processes. Widely available and affordable video technology, the ease in air travels and a nose for lucrative business have combined to create the industry that has toppled Hollywood as the premier provider of audio-visual entertainment in Nigeria. Video technology equally gave birth to other 'woods' in sub-Saharan African countries such as Ghana, Kenya and Malawi and is the engine behind the revitalisation of Nigeria's and Ghana's previously comatose national film industries. The accounts of globalisation have, however, largely marginalised the subjective dimension of the impact on these countries' culture industries on the globalisation of the video technology and of culture. This paper highlights this aspect of the impact of globalisation, especially as it concerns the issue of identity. Using Segun Arinze and Steph-Nora Okere, two well-known Nollywood actors, as cases, and drawing also from interview excerpts with both actors, the paper employs critical discourse analysis to argue that a contradictory structure of feeling has developed in the actors in relation to Nollywood and social practices elsewhere, symbolised by Hollywood. This tension comes mainly from the reality of working in the country's video film industry and the global ideals as imagined by the actors. The paper concludes by arguing that imagination has combined with wide availability of foreign cultural materials to foster mental migration in the two Nollywood actors.

Introduction

A key argument in the globalisation dialectic is that culture has become untied from its national moorings (Featherstone 1995). Robertson has equally pointed out that this disembedding instantiated by globalisation processes has led to the intensification of our consciousness of other societies but warned, however, that such a consciousness of other places "may well be grossly misinformed" (5). When awareness of other societies is based on partial information, the pitfall then becomes that abstract social spaces are treated as real, concrete spaces resulting in what Lefebvre (93) has called a fetishisation. Partial knowledge of Hollywood that generates the ambivalent attitude displayed by the two actors towards their industry, and illustrates the mental state that Lefebvre has warned about, is rooted in Nollywood in general and acting in particular. But what is it about acting in Nigeria and in the video film industry itself that could, in some cases, predispose some people in the industry, as the two actors, to hold unsubstantiated and exaggerated views of elsewhere?

Acting was previously seen in the country as something that one took up in addition to 'normal' employment. With the birth of Nollywood, though, acting is fast becoming the number one 'profession' of choice for many, especially the young, as can be seen by the many new faces in video films in the recent times, and those are not discouraged by the fact that few actors ever succeed in the industry. The rising popularity of acting in Nigeria is also, in large part, the reason that many producers never hold auditions for roles in their productions. As one actor [1] put it, every Nigerian would then turn up to be auditioned! The claim is perhaps an exaggeration, but it does serve to highlight the scale of the challenge which actors face within the industry.

This could as well account for the enduring image problem of Nollywood productions in general and of the professional status of acting in particular. Productions are, in many cases, hurriedly put together. For producers on slim budgets, it becomes a case of economy of scale in which quality loses out to the more overriding need of wrapping up every aspect of production within the shortest possible time, sometimes in as little as a fortnight. Besides, where competition for roles is as cut throat as it is in the acting profession in general, and where some Nollywood producers would rather pay less to hire an 'upstart' with no training than hire a 'star' with formal training, professionalism is bound to suffer. The net effect is the comparing and contrasting that characterise the ways the two actors spoke about their social context and other places.

Nollywood and Elsewhere

In the two actors' conversations, such binaries as standard/sub-standard, professional/unprofessional and exploitative/humane were used interchangeably to describe existing conditions in the industry and the way the actors imagined similar conditions to be elsewhere. In such discourses of approbation, 'standard' or 'professional' practice was used to stand for places where the actors believed that the best practices obtain, practices which Nollywood would do well to follow. The comments of the actress, Steph-Nora Okere, when asked about the changes she would like to see in the current practices and attitudes in Nigeria's video film industry, capture aspects of this particular way of looking at the world.

> *Ms Okere*:
> I need the working environment to be different. I need the pace to be different too. I need everything to be different. I need the Nigerian movie industry to actually follow the ideal situation, not playing to the Nigerian thing. Home movie is not a Nigerian thing. We are copying, so let's copy right.

Mr. Arinze continued on this theme of the global as a place of 'ideal', 'standard' practice where things are done in the 'right', 'professional' manner, in his response to the question of how he got his roles. The actor had been asked whether his agent negotiated his roles or whether the actor negotiated his roles and fees with the video film producers himself. Mr. Arinze's answer was at once self-deprecatory and serious but it again highlights the tension between local reality and global ideal.

> *Mr. Arinze*:
> Hump, (*in self-mockery*) when you speak of agent, you're speaking as if you're in Hollywood. Please, there is no agent. Here, the actor is his own manager, the agent, PA. He negotiates his roles and his fees by himself, which is very unprofessional indeed. It is unprofessional because then a lot of sentiments get in the way. Unfortunately for us here in Nigeria, the actor is his own everything. He even provides his own clothes on set because we are more on interpersonal relationship here. We haven't yet got to the highest level of professionalism in the business.

Apparently, production practices considered to be 'standard' are still at the rudimentary stage, if not a distant prospect in Nollywood, when compared to places that have perfected the practices, such as Hollywood. Through the standard/sub-standard binary, the actors have also highlighted interpersonal relationships and sentiments as aspects of the local that drag down filmmaking practices in Nigeria into the 'sub-standard' zone. Sentiment is seen to interfere with practical matters of finance. This structure of feeling, a postcolonial condition, marked by the unfavourable comparing of the local context with a global one, exemplifies the nature of the shadow that colonialism does still manage to cast on the thinking of some Nigerians, more than five decades after independence. Morley's argument regarding the way European imperialists constituted the notion of modernity during the colonial era supports the above position in accounting for the Nigerian actors' ambivalent attitude:

> In the context of imperialism and colonialism, the centre as the site and source of modernity, progress and metropolitan advance is thus set up as the power node of a binary opposition with the periphery—as the site of traditionalism, regionalism and provincial backwardness. In this binary, the centre acts as a model – or point of originary reference—while the periphery can only ever be a poor copy, a reflex extension condemned to the reproduction and imitation of a succession of original moments (165).

For the above Nigerian actors, Nollywood, which has yet to attain the 'professional' standard of the centre, is thus a "site of traditionalism, regionalism and provincial backwardness." This opposing conceptualisation of the global as the centre of excellence and "the realm of `eventfulness", and the local as a work in progress, could not be unconnected with the harsh criticisms which Nollywood video films have drawn in Nigeria in relation to technical quality. Although quality has generally improved since he made his observation, Shaka (2003) has blamed the poor technical quality which has continued to plague the industry on the take-off technology (VHS) which led to a high rate of depreciation after post-production. Writing separately, the authors Robert Allen (1992) and Jeremy Tunstall (1977) also see one consequence of the globalisation of popular culture and wide availability of foreign films of all sorts in developing countries such as Nigeria as being the capacity of such films to accustom film audiences in these countries to expect too much from their own culture industries.

In fact, as Allen (25) puts it, such foreign programmes are likely to cultivate in their local consumers "standards against which that country's domestic programs will find difficult to compete." Barber (1997) is, however, a lot more direct in her observation about the Nigerian elite and university-educated class, like the two actors, generally preferring foreign films and television programmes to those produced locally. Hollywood has set the bar which Nollywood can never match. Therefore, the actor who wanted Nigeria's video film producers "to copy right" may discover that she may still have some time to wait before the local video film industry can attain the level, if ever, to which Hollywood has accustomed her.

For the two Nollywood actors, other places are not only constituted as models of standard practice but are equally seen as some sort of guide or teacher. Described by Lull (2007) as a relationship at a distance and by Thompson (1995) as a non-dialogical and non-reciprocal relationship, individuals from other places, usually Hollywood movie stars, incidents that have occurred elsewhere and plots from Hollywood films, provide points of reference, ideas and tips on human behaviour. These external resources also increase the range of available options for Mr. Arinze on how to handle real life interpersonal relationships within his local context. Mr. Arinze had, while relating his experience with a Nigerian publication which alleged that the actor had contracted some disease, referred to a Hollywood film he had watched. Apparently, tips from the film had influenced his reaction to the provocative story, as Mr. Arinze's answer, when asked why he never considered legal action against the magazine, clearly illustrates:

> *Mr. Arinze*:
>
> I won't fight them. What I've learnt to do in the past years is ignore it; it will go away. I watched a movie, *Double Platinum*. They were talking about something and this guy said, 'hey, listen, this is the media, it sucks, let it go.' That's the attitude, ignore it and it will die. That's what I've learnt to do. Because, immediately you start to make a noise about it, you blow it out of all proportions. And, of course, everybody begins to look at your objection. So, I've learnt to ignore the press.

Thus, his relationships with plots and characters in a Hollywood film have combined to become for the above actor a script for imagining his own life (Appadurai 255) and invariably those of Hollywood stars. For the actor and others like him, one consequence of this imagined affinity with other people and places has become an overvaluation of elsewhere and the construction of the local as a site of deprivation.

In such a "deprived and sub-standard" social context as Nigeria, not even human and business relations escape "contamination" or comparison with other places, it would appear. When asked what his experience of working in the industry has been, Mr. Arinze's response is an open criticism of certain production practices in Nollywood and an implied comparison with other societies:

> My experience has been a mixture of everything: the good, the bad, and the not-so-good. Sometimes you work with people who are highly professional, who know what they are doing. Sometimes you work with people who don't at all know what they are doing. And sometimes we celebrate mediocrity and that is the worst ailment you can ever think of, when we celebrate mediocrity.

Ms Okere's criticism of the 'unprofessional' practices in the video film industry, when asked whether she was happy with her earnings, was even more damning, as she considered Nollywood in comparison with other places very far behind:

> *Ms Okere*:
>
> No, I won't say I'm happy and I won't say I am sad. You know, the regular African wants to rip you off, if he can. Not because he doesn't know your worth, he knows alright but wants to get around it. The pay to me, when compared with when we started, is a whole lot different. It's a whole lot better but it's still not right. And why it happened like that was because of what I said earlier. Some people who were money-minded capitalists came into the industry and now they are doing it as if you're trading things: buy tomatoes, sell and make a little profit. But they are not being truthful about their profits, their sales. So they are not paying us what we're supposed to be earning.
>
> And that saddens my heart because some people want to keep all the money for themselves. Honest producers too. But a regular producer finds it difficult to produce a film because he is scared of losing his money because some people might just not level up with him when it comes to the sale of the movie. So, you find some people have just commandeered the market. It's got to an era of writing, producing, directing, and acting. People are not doing the normal work because some aspects of the industry are not being truthful about what really is the situation. We are made to believe sales are poor.
>
> Yet the man who tells you sales are not good, why are you still in the industry, why are you building houses, why are you buying new

> cars, why are you attaining new grounds? You don't want the man next to you to grow. So the pay is alright as you can feed your family relatively, you can buy this one car that you've been pushing around, pay your rent and the rest of it. But entertainment is more than that. We have more than 150 million people in Nigeria and people are telling us that they can't even sell up to 200,000 copies. I think that's sheer robbery. I'm not happy about it. And even when some people came out and took the bull by the horn and said, 'pay us a little more than you pay us,' they got slammed with a ban. I find that very insulting.

The privileges accruing to actors in other places are also knowingly or unknowingly exaggerated in these discourses of deprivation and affluence. The two Nollywood actors used comparison to highlight what they perceived as the big divide in their working conditions in comparison to Hollywood. Such comparisons are also based on the assumption that the situation spoken about in these other places exists literally. Successful Hollywood actors also represent what the appropriate reward for working in a film industry should be, in these comparisons. While talking about their fee, a subject which some Nollywood actors are extremely cagey about, due, perhaps, to its paltriness, Mr. Arinze had said that Will Smith was previously earning about $20 million to star in a film but now commands as high as $40-$60 million for a starring role in a single film. However, no account of the Hollywood actor's fee or any other Hollywood A-list star in scholarly literature or entertainment media has credited any actor, male or female, who played only a lead role in a production, with earning as high as $50-60 million.

Some background facts about Nigeria's video film industry in relation to Hollywood will perhaps help contextualise Mr. Arinze's claims about the Hollywood actor's fee. It will, as well, support the argument that it is mainly to emphasise in a most unmistakable manner Nollywood's poverty when seen alongside Hollywood, rather than envy of the Hollywood star that is behind the Nigerian actor's claim. Haynes (2007) has estimated the total yearly worth of the Nigerian video film industry at about $200 million. Nollywood's annual net worth, however, pales into insignificance when understood against the backdrop of the value of US films' global sales in 2004 which Thussu (2006) estimated at $25.24 billion, with $9.54 billion generated within the US domestic market alone. The fact that Will Smith earns $20 or $40 million for appearing in a film, it is important to point out, is not a problem for Mr. Arinze. The American star's supposed earnings have, instead, been used by the

Nigerian actor to highlight the "sub-standard and unprofessional" video film production practices that exist in Nollywood.

Mr. Arinze is also a star in his country's entertainment industry but was being paid about $300 in 2006 for his starring role in the Wale Adenuga Productions' *A New Song.* Lefebvre (93) would further argue that people such as the above-mentioned Nollywood actor, who erroneously equated the abstract with the familiar, have turned themselves, their presence, their lived experiences and their bodies into abstractions too. While it is safe to say that Will Smith will no doubt welcome the idea of commanding $50 million to star in a film, Mr. Arinze has failed to separate reality from the false picture of Hollywood stars' earning prowess that only exists in his imagination. It is this failure, coupled with the reality of the context of video film production in Nigeria, which has given rise to the fetishisation of America, apparent in these actors' positions about Hollywood. The two actors are thus transformed into 'armchair émigrés', imagining the existence and possibilities of a better life elsewhere, which could probably be theirs with as little as a one-way ticket and a plane ride to Hollywood.

Counting their Blessings, Nonetheless

Apparently, those other sites of standard practices are not always worthy of emulation. In fact, elsewhere is also seen as a site of negative practices, while the local, though as yet developing in such a sense, is preferred. In this discourse of innocence versus corruption, the local is portrayed as being spared some of the negative consequences of the 'standard' and 'professional' practices that are often features of the West. For instance, practices like stalking, associated with places of "professional standard practices" like Hollywood, are almost unknown in Nigeria. When such comparisons are made, local video film production practices that are considered rudimentary and lacking in professionalism tend to carry a positive charge. Lack of professionalism is then seen as something of a shield for the video film producer.

This is a protection which their counterparts in other places have forfeited, living as they do in a context where the positive healthy intercourse that characterises interpersonal relationships at the local, has become corrupted for material gain. Mr. Arinze, when asked about how he dealt with the issue of overenthusiastic fans, spoke about actors in Nigeria being spared false allegations of sexual harassment and abuse that their better known counterparts in 'developed' countries sometimes suffer at the hands of their fans:

> It is such a good thing we have going for us in our society. Our society has not got to that advanced level of blackmail. We have no problem of blackmail, unlike places where if a female fan manages to gain access to you and talks to you and says one or two things and you get carried away, the next thing you know, she has reported to the police that you've sexually harassed her. And then the police will pick you up. We're lucky we've not got to that level.

His view of the global as not being an entirely benign space is, perhaps, the reason for the resistance to certain globalising tendencies that is apparent in this interview.

Mr. Arinze did not like the idea of Nigeria's video film industry being called Nollywood. In his words:

> I hate calling it Nollywood, because there is no reason why I should call it Nollywood. I prefer to call it Nigawood, if it has to be any 'wood' at all.

The suffix 'wood', derived from Hollywood, which has become synonymous with film production, is employed by many a national film industries to give visibility as well as credibility to their industry. Although Mr. Arinze's affirmation of the "right to be different" is incomplete, seeing as he still retained 'wood' in his preferred "Nigawood", the actor's objection could be understood as a reaction to what is increasingly looking like an appeal for legitimation that is implicit in the use of 'wood' by many Third World national film industries and the universalisation of the name Hollywood. India's film industry alone has spawned other 'woods' such as Kollywood (Tamil) and Tollywood (Telugu) besides the more famous Bollywood. Pakistan cinema industry goes by the name Lollywood. And there must be other 'woods' besides these better known ones, if one looks hard enough.

Despite their expressed dissatisfaction with certain practices within their industry, Nollywood producers are not exactly voting with their feet out of the industry. If anything, in the same breath that despair is expressed, expressions of hope and optimism would usually soon follow. The actors interviewed expressed the hope that things would improve with time. Ms Okere, who said that she had thought of quitting at some point because of what she considered the influx of mediocrity whose "unprofessional" practices and activities resulted in the lowering of standards in the industry, was glad that she reconsidered her decision and stayed on. According to her, "things are getting into shape now." Mr. Arinze was equally optimistic that things were improving in the industry, particularly with regard to what he saw as the wide appeal of the Nigerian popular culture within the country itself. According to him:

> We are going on smoothly. Well, I won't say smoothly, but, of course, every country has its own problems. We are all staggering, we are all stumbling, but of course we'll perfect it as we go along. Who would have ever thought that in Nigeria, we would see something like *Big Brother Nigeria* showing on television? That Nigerians would actually want to watch their own movies, Nigerians listen to their own music? Before, it was, 'please, can we have Michael Jackson, Lionel Riche?' Now, whenever you play any Nigerian music, everybody goes crazy. If you doubt me, go to any night club. It's Nigerian music they want to listen to, Nigerian Jamz. Everybody wants to watch Nigerian home movie.

Conclusion

Such notes of optimism about future improvements in Nollywood notwithstanding, prevalent poverty in the industry will continue to ensure that only few actors will ever manage to achieve relative financial success. Working also in an industry whose yearly net worth of $200 million is easily outgrossed by one Hollywood blockbuster, imagination has, understandably, become the actors' means of escaping the largely impoverished condition which generally characterises the video film production in Nollywood. For the majority, clinging on to the uncertain hope that the industry would one day reward them with the kind of lifestyle and fees which Hollywood guarantees its successful practitioners, imagination offers the only viable escape route out of the reality of video film production in Nigeria. For this vast band, a fetishisation of Hollywood has also become a worrying legacy of the globalisation of video technology and culture.

Notes

[1] Video technology, initially used by affluent Nigerians to document such ceremonies as christening, wedding and chieftaincy title conferment, was first introduced into Nigeria from the Asian markets by Igbo electronics dealers.

[2] In 2006, one of the authors, Ogochukwu Ekwenchi had, as part of fieldwork for her doctoral research at the University of Westminster, UK, travelled to Lagos in order to study video film production and used Wale Adenuga Productions Ltd as her research site. The original intention had been to provide an account of video film production in Nigeria by observing location shooting and interviewing the practitioners. This the author did between March and July of the same year by travelling to Ikorodu and staying at Papa Ajasco House with the cast and crew of Wale Adenuga Productions' *A New Song.* It was, however, while analysing the data that she noticed these comparisons that the actors and other crew members would, without being asked direct questions about film industries elsewhere, make about video film production practices in Nigeria and other countries. That was what informed the author's position that accounts of Nollywood would be more productively rendered within the debate on the impact of globalisation. Mr. Arinze and Ms Okere, both graduates of theatre arts and actors with many years of experience in the industry, had been the stars on the set and they had played the lead characters in *A New Song.* The two actors were used in the discussion to provide views of the industry from male and female perspectives.

[3] The actor, Mr. Biodun, also worked as the soundman on the set of Wale Adenuga Productions' *A New Song.*

Works Cited

Allen, R. C. (ed). *More Talk about TV: Channels of Discourse, Reassembled.* London: Routledge, 1992.

Appadurai, Arjun. "Disjuncture and Difference in the Global Cultural Economy". In R. Robertson and K. E. White (eds). *Globalisation: Critical concepts in Sociology.* London: Routledge, 2003.

Barber, Karin. *Readings in African Popular Culture.* London: The International African Institute, 1997.

Haynes, Jonathan. "Video Boom: Nigeria and Ghana". Retrieved May 2008 from Postcolonial Text Website: postcolonial.org/index.php/pct/article/viewPDF Interstitial/522/422, 2007.

Lefebvre, H. *The Production of Space.* Cambridge: Blackwell, 1991.

Lull, J. *Culture-on-Demand: Communication in a Crisis World.* Oxford: Blackwell Publishing, 2007.

Morley, D. *Media, Modernity and Technology: The Geography of the New.* London: Routledge, 2007.

Robertson, R. *Globalisation: Social Theory and Global Culture.* London: Sage Publication, 1994.

Shaka, F. O. "Rethinking the Nigerian Video Film Industry: Technological Fascination and the Domestication Game". In F. Ogunleye (ed). *African Video Film Today.* Manzini, Swaziland: Academic Publishers, 2003.

Thompson, J. B. *The Media and Modernity: A Social Theory of the Media.* Cambridge: Polity Press, 1995

Thussu, D. K. *International Communication: Continuity and Change.* London: Hodder Arnold, 2006.

Tunstall, J. *The Media Are American: Anglo-American Media in the World.* London: Constable, 1977.

CHAPTER TWELVE

The Healing Word: The Significance of Orality in Nigerian Home Videos[1]

Nkechinyere Mbakwe

Abstract

In remembrance of Nigeria's 50th anniversary, this study explores the healing of the African word. The history of the African word has been greatly affected by the history of the colonisation of Africa, for the implementation of the Latin alphabet in many parts of Africa dramatically changed communications. Thus, the colonial impact on the evolution of the African word is relevant in the modern age; there is clearly a correlation between the so-called crisis of the Nigerian word and the collective trauma experienced by West Africans. The nature of the Nigerian word is therefore explained using the example of Nollywood. The recovery of a pan-African experience is the subject of discussion in interviews conducted in Nigeria and in the African Diaspora with some forty experts including Nigerian filmmakers, producers, actors and viewers. Nigerian home videos effectively support not only the decolonisation of Africans everywhere but are also instrumental in healing collective traumas. Thus, this study links postcolonial theories with the history of the Nigerian word. This is a story of healing.

Introduction

Nollywood today is of great importance in Nigeria as well as in the African Diaspora. This is not only because of its impact on media structures, but equally because of its socio-cultural implications. As one critic has observed, "The rise of video culture is […] part of a new era in Nigerian media production" (Larkin 238). By exploring the Nigerian home video industry, the history of the Nigerian word becomes evident.[2] Nigerian home videos therefore reflect a collective trauma which is significant for African peoples all over the world. At the same time, these stories effectively support the healing process of a pan-African experience. Hence Nigerian home video productions represent one of the most successful stories ever told by modern Nigeria.

Regarding its terminology, Nollywood faces major challenges. The term invented by the United States press in order to represent the Nigerian video film phenomenon was first used in 2002. Meanwhile, Nigerian film-makers and producers have fully adopted the term initiated by the Western world. However, *Nollywood* clearly does not represent the video film industry from the North, also known as Kannywood.[3] The term was designed in order to address the Nigerian home video industry in totality but it actually refers to the Southern video film industry and not necessarily to the Northern equivalent. In an attempt to describe the underlying principles of an overall Nigerian film phenomenon, I name the Nigerian video film industry 'Nigerian home videos' or simply 'Nigerian video films'. Nevertheless, most works referred to in my analysis essentially celebrate Nollywood.

It is important to note that the approach of my analysis is formalistic. Instead of analysing single productions, I examine the structure behind Nollywood, following Marshall McLuhan's approach of a medium as the extension of man. The use of any kind of medium alters the patterns of interdependence among people, "as it alters the ratios among our senses" (McLuhan 80). An exploration of the Nigerian home video industry therefore illuminates continental conditions. Interviews with some forty experts including Nigerian filmmakers, producers, actors and viewers conducted in Nigeria and the African Diaspora moreover nurture a discussion on the recovery of a pan-African existence.

On Orality

Regarding all this as background information, the core of this paper is on the history of the Nigerian word, focusing on the aspect of orality. Translating the term "orality" into colonial German, it merely means "Mündlichkeit" – a term linked to a notion of culture and tradition. But orality is basically a mnemonics, a storage system of knowledge, whereby wisdom is preserved over generations. With time, this storage system gets altered. Today, the "cultural book" (Havelock, Preface vii), which contains all the information of a people, is stored in various ways. According to Walter J. Ong, who depicts orality as the source of modern communication, the word has gone through transformations. Initially, the word was spoken, later it was written, and today the word is technologised. So, we actually find ourselves within the age of new or secondary orality.[4]

Naturally, all three stages bring along different implications. The stage of the spoken word refers to a notion of the word as sound, momentary and fading:

> The unrecorded speech act is always in a context and therefore surrounded by a time, a place, an event and an audience. No sooner is the unrecorded speech act articulated than it is embedded in a history, a real social and communicative context from which it cannot be extracted. It can be remembered and it can be reconstructed by those who were there using the fiction that the reconstruction matches the original, but it can never be reconstituted in its original context (Furniss 72).

This concept of primary orality however does not imply that literacy had not existed. Referring to this stage as the era of the spoken word means that existent writings primarily functioned as aide-mémoires. They rather activated wisdom than stored it. The actual storage of knowledge prevailed aurally.

During the second stage, all wisdom was stored through scripts. Culture then became essentially visual. The denatured word gave man "an eye for an ear" (McLuhan 27). What happened with the emergence of alphabetic typography was not "that man discovered the use of his eyes but that he began to link visual perception to verbalisation to a degree previously unknown" (Ong 50). The so-called warehouse of storage, no longer acoustic but visibly material, was now extensible. The collective archive of wisdom therefore became obsolete. The solipsistic act of reading and thinking eventually transformed the consciousness of human societies. The word became fixed, and all spontaneity, mobility and improvisation of the spoken word vanished (Havelock 70).

Today, the word is technologised. This stage is characterised by the use of electronics for verbal communication (Ong 87). Therefore, secondary orality generates a sense for groups immeasurably larger than for those of primary oral cultures. The "tribal village" (Ong 88) became a "global village" (McLuhan 31). But most remarkably, the transition of the word transformed the consciousness of people.

Regarding the Nigerian context, the transformation of the word has been shaped by colonialism. A system operating on oral mnemonics, pictographics and syllographics was painfully interrupted and a smooth transition of the word discouraged. The introduction of the Latin alphabet literally replaced the fundamental oral encyclopaedia and twisted the consciousness of people by making them use a previously unknown storage system of knowledge. I refer to this as the *crisis of the Word.* What does all this have to do with the Nigerian video film industry? The *crisis of the Word* is revealed in its evolution as well as its productions. This paper nevertheless focuses on the actual structure of the films.

Methodology and Findings

In order to qualitatively evaluate the nature of Nigerian home videos, I interviewed some forty experts of the Nigerian home video industry between April 2007 and March 2008. Interviewees were scholars, journalists, filmmakers and producers, actors and actresses and audiences, in Nigeria, Germany, Ghana and Zanzibar. These interviews were conducted in colonial English and colonial German. The average interview took 60 minutes. It was recorded in mp3 format and later transcribed and analysed.

Study Unit	Numbers
Scholars and journalists	**10** (9 male/ 1 female)
Filmmakers and producers	**8** (male)
Actors and actresses	**8** (4 female/ 4 male)
Audience	**9** (8 male/ 6 female)
Group interview	**1** (4 female and 1 male student)
TOTAL	**36**

Nollywood's Social Encyclopaedia

According to Eric A. Havelock, the social encyclopaedia stores the wisdom embedded in a culture of primary orality. It is "a sort of encyclopedia of ethics, politics, history and technology which the effective citizen was required to learn as the core of his educational equipment" (Havelock 27). Nollywood successfully re-enacts this principle. Thus, Nigerian home videos effectively store wisdom, while educating on traditional values.

This very principle was crucial to the people interviewed. By watching Nigerian video films, viewers either learn about their own culture or that of other Nigerian communities. Filmmakers and producers today become modern day poets, the voice of the voiceless. Emmanuel U. C. Ezejideaku links the function of the playwright to serve the society as the "watchdog, visionary, teacher, chronicler and moral custodian" to that of the modern video artist (1-2). The filmmaker, who is part of the audience and deeply rooted in the audience's cultural and social behaviour, is also part of the making of a new urban culture. Therefore this filmmaking practice narrates a vibrant part of a new social meaning (Okome 108). Filmmakers therefore imbibe the function of fulfilling a didactic axiom as demonstrated below through their statements:

Mr. Don Pedro Obaseki: I recognise my role as a culture-connoisseur, as an opinion-moulder.
Mr. Bond Eyinnaya Emeruwa: I seek to educate. I seek to inform.
Prof. Aderemi Raji-Oyelade: There is a tradition in the local industry which sees the scriptwriters and film producers as poets. Traditional poets see themselves as the conscience of the people of the society, individuals who have to tell the stories, who have to tell the truth. They are saying what nobody would like to talk about, so they use the film medium as a means of educating, as a pedagogical means of teaching and moralising.
Prof. Durotoye Adeolu Adeleke: Using Aristotle's poetics as our basis, you must have a message to pass. Whatever you are saying must be of benefit to humanity. So, most of the Yoruba films, I can say, are didactic. They have a message to say. And they are daring, most of the time. The axiom "A sinner will not go unpunished" is there. "Law of karma" or "retributive law", "Whatever you sow, you'll reap." So, the corrupt officers are caught, the armed robbers are killed and so on. All these things you find in Yoruba films.
Mr. Victor Okhai: The African filmmaker is probably the modern storyteller in the African society. So, after watching my films, I'd like the audience to be able to go home with something. A lesson of sorts, something to take away, to make you think, to ponder.
Mr. Jeta Amata: There's always that message at the end of it. This is the reason why the leopard has spots, or this is the reason why the tortoise has that big black stone on top of it. There's always that thing that you must learn from any of my films. At the end of the film, there is always that last line, I can't do without it.

Moreover, Nollywood works as an electronic archive of values and traditions. Nigerian home videos serve as a living archive which adopts functions generated by primary oral-aural cultures. Therefore, children living in the metropolis get accustomed to the village life respected in former times. Mr. Zack Orji refers to Nollywood as a means of "modern world preservation".

Re-Enactment of Principles of Primary Orality

There are seven different principles of oral-aural cultures which Nollywood re-enacts successfully: recycling, spirituality, stories of everyday life, conservatism, variability, the spoken word and tempo.

Recycling

Nigerian home videos re-enact diverse principles of primary orality. These principles represent a vital part of oral-aural cultures in order to store knowledge. Nollywood recycles themes, motives, titles as well as costumes.

> **Mr. Alex Usifo:** They're recycling the stories. Also they recycle costumes a lot. So in different movies, you see the same costumes. Especially if you're able to take note of the costumier, you find out the costumier parades the same costumes almost in all the movies.
> **Mr. Osa George Ehiorobo:** It is always the same story. Unfortunately. There have been so many films whereby, before a guy meets a girl, her car has a flat tire. So, this girl's vehicle has a flat tire and a guy passes by in his car. He stops. They start talking, and so on.
> **Mr. Ekpenyong Bassey-Inyang:** If you close your eyes and watch some films and see those actors in ten movies, they're the same. They sound the same, they act the same.
> **Mr. Akinola Famson:** If you are a producer producing, let's say, three films in a year, and you are using more or less the same location, you're using more or less the same titles in your production, you're using the same actors and actresses. It's like you're just working in one circle. I mean, Nigeria is a vast country; there are lots of areas one can go and shoot films. But it maybe because they are lazy, maybe because they don't really care.

Although most experts refer to this principle as the laziness of producers or the ignorance of filmmakers, they actually ignore a vital feature of the re-enactment of orality in Nollywood. Repetition is a significant mnemonics of primary oral cultures. This principle enables the survival of oral-aural thought. The retelling of the same story makes it possible to remember it, "and so be able to retell it in whole or part, and so, relish it. The repetition is linked with a feeling of pleasure, a factor of primary importance in understanding the spell of oral poetry" (Havelock 71).

Spirituality

Spirituality in Nigerian video films is omnipresent, most times antagonistic: the good versus the evil.

> **Prof. Remi Raji-Oyelade**: Most of these filmmakers have a mission. They have a message. Especially those who have a religious mission usually teach towards the Christianisation of the populace, the Christianisation of the typical viewer or the audience of the Nigerian home video industry. I have watched so many films that I can always predict the end. I mean it goes back to all these morality tales, you know: good versus evil, the satanic versus the one who is godly, the born-again who always has to triumph at the end of a struggle.

This antagonistic principle is a fundamental mnemonics of oral-aural cultures in order to secure the recollection of knowledge. "Praise goes with the highly polarised, agonistic, oral world of good and evil, virtue and vice, villains and heroes" (Ong 45).

Stories of Everyday Life

Nigerian video films are generally based on everyday life experiences. This phenomenon enables the audience to identify with what is shown on screen. The success of the Nigerian video industry was due to the fact that Nigerians could identify with it (Ogunsuyi 60). Regarding the history of the Nigerian film, Nollywood is therefore of great significance. "Video culture has thoroughly altered the landscape of Nigerian media" (Larkin 209).

Prof. (Mrs.) Akachi T. Ezeigbo: They take their themes from things happening in the society. I noticed that a lot. What drives these home videos is what they see and hear around them. Most of these home videos are based on everyday experience, ordinary experience. So, the oral culture is very healthy and strong here. Sometimes it is based on experiences of people. There's so much of these rituals, and kidnapping, and going to native doctors and *babalawos* in our films, issues of childbirth, not having children, mother-in-law. So, orality is very much alive in our home video.

Mr. Ibiajulu Onyemaechi Amuro: Die [Filmemacher] haben jetzt nicht unbedingt das Bedürfnis einen richtig tollen Film zu machen, sondern einfach einen Film aus ihrem Leben. Und das finde ich einfach einzigartig. *[Those filmmakers don't really feel like making a great film. They just make a film inspired by life. And that to me is unique.]*

Mr. Bond Eyinnaya Emeruwa: Now the thing is that the Nigerian movie industry was born out of oral tradition. Oral tradition is our history; it's all about telling stories. So, if you notice, most of our movies are actually story-movies. So, we are not into all of this Hi-fi, that's science fiction and all that. It's mostly story-movies. And there's this emphasis on detailing the stories. So, that's actually because of our background, which comes from oral tradition.

Mr. Ekpenyong Bassey-Inyang: Most of the Nigerian stories borrow heavily from true-life happenstances. So, most of all the stories are narratives of the events that have happened in the past, and people can easily identify with that.

This characteristic is a crucial factor for oral-aural communities, since "Oral cultures must conceptualise and verbalise all their knowledge with more or less close reference to the human lifeworld, assimilating the alien, objective world to the more immediate, familiar interaction of human beings" (Ong 42). Through this means, knowledge is preserved.

Conservatism

Furthermore, Nigerian video films express a conservative mind-set. While Mr. Kepy Bassey-Inyang believes this aspect to represent predominant characteristics in Nigeria, Prof. (Mrs.) Akachi T. Ezeigbo considers those transmitted images not to match the present status quo. To her, "The woman's role in various situations as the wicked stepmother, the envious or jealous co-wife, the betrayer of family or village secrets to an enemy, and the eternal gossip whose evil pastime is to sow seeds of discord" (Ezeigbo 116), all this is outdated. The re-enactment of clichés in Nigerian films however is a precious mnemonics of primary oral thought. Since, in a primary oral culture, conceptualised knowledge that is not repeated aloud soon vanishes, oral societies "must invest great energy in saying over and over again what has been learned arduously over the ages. This need establishes a highly traditionalist or conservative set of mind" (Ong 41).

Principle of Variability

Experts interviewed link the spontaneity and flexibility displayed in Nigerian home videos to a lack of creativity, complexity and continuity. Hyginus Ozo Ekwuazi asserts that "from production through distribution to exhibition, nothing is properly structured: virtually everything is on an ad hoc basis" (131). Don Pedro Obaseki even refers to Nollywood as "accidental". Jonathan Haynes notes that "many of the films [...] being made now are shot [...] as rapidly as possible, with minimal rehearsals or attention to script" (10). Once more, principles of oral-aural cultures have not been recognised. Instead of Nollywood being accidental, it rather re-enacts formulaic modes of expression. Generally, the spoken word represents itself by redundancy, simplicity and situativity. Oral cultures tend to use concepts in situational, operational frames of reference. "[They] live very much in a present which keeps itself in equilibrium or homeostasis by sloughing off memories which no longer have present relevance" (Ong 46).

The following characteristics, which are relevant for Nigerian home videos, are equally crucial principles of the spoken word: loopholes, lack of continuity and proficiency, improvisational ingenuity, mistakes and informality.

The Spoken Word

Nigerian home videos are highly oral. "Even at the electronic level, it is still a talk show'" (Havelock 63). Don Pedro Obaseki refers to them as "talkie". Events taking place within the totality of the film are often reported orally instead of being depicted visually. Dialogues are more crucial than action, and often redundant.

> Dialogue in these films is often tedious, lacking the crisp realistic pattern in most advanced film cultures. Movement is sluggish, winding and monotonous, leading to overstatements and many repetitions. It is reasonable to trace this character to the oral nature of the theatre, with its emphasis on spontaneous improvisation. It is not uncommon to find lengthy dialogue scenes in these films. The audience tolerates this because it is used to this speech pattern in its everyday existence (Okome, Cinema 97)

> **Mr. Cornelius Eze Onyekaba:** Nigerian films remain the ones that we can still describe as heavily wordy, in terms of use of words. There are some American movies, when you score the words said in the movie, you'll discover that they've not used up to 2,000 words in the whole film. And when you average that against a Nigerian film of the same duration of one hour for example, you'll be shocked that the Nigerian film of one hour used 50,000 words.
> **Mr. Don Pedro Obaseki:** When you watch a basic Nigerian movie, the first thing you will find is the preponderance of words. So, it's not really a movie, it's more like a talkie. But I don't blame the average Nigerian movie maker because the background that he is coming from is very wordy. We are a talking people. And the country that gave us birth celebrates so much of speech. And then we have a huge storytelling culture that has been grafted onto the movies. They will keep talking about the obvious, talking and talking and talking about the obvious, talking, talking, talking about the obvious. So, they want you to tell the story rather than watch the story.
> **Mr. Zack Orji:** I could tell you something that happened to me in a flashback, or I could tell it to you by reporting an event that had already happened. Sometimes you find in our films, instead of depicting an event that actually took place, we prefer to report that event, we prefer to report it orally, have a third party telling the story of what happened, without the audience having been given the benefit of seeing it really depicted.

However, redundancy has a clear purpose. The public speaker's need "to keep going while he is running through his mind what to say next [...] encourages redundancy. In oral delivery, though a pause may be effective, hesitation is always disabling" (Ong 40). Hence, it is better to repeat something in an artful way rather than to pause while fishing for the next idea.

Tempo

Durotoye A. Adeleke states that the tempo of Nigerian films is "slow and dragged". Film-edits are usually long.

> Emphasis is retained on specific actions and sequences, and shots are delayed for far greater time than it happens in the fast cutting of conventional cinema. This shows a deviation from the standard Western format of editing. This slow paced technique cannot be divorced from the dialogue pattern which indigenous film has come to adopt. Because dialogue is slow and elaborate, actions tend to take longer on screen. To behold the full significance of the *word*, it is necessary to keep editing at a slower pace (Okome 96).

Words in an oral-aural culture are inseparable from action for they are always sounds (Ong 112-113). The spoken word, therefore, determines the dynamics of the film. Speech itself, as sound, is irrevocably committed to time.

The African Diaspora

Although most experts I spoke to question the simplicity of the films, the re-enactment of principles of the spoken word is one of the major reasons why Nigerian home videos are so successful. They are the refraction of their peoples. This aspect, in particular, reconnects Nigeria with the African Diaspora. Hence, Nollywood becomes a connector of African peoples. It allows peoples in the African Diaspora to stay in contact with home. Nigerian home videos reconnect "Nigeria's transnational community" and its "homeland" (Okome 5). Nollywood therefore creates a pan-African unity. It unifies Africans worldwide.

> **Mr. Bond Eyinnaya Emeruwa:** For Nigerians, there's something that happens on their streets every day. It's something that happened that their forefathers experienced and told them about. They heard about the story and passed it on. So, they now take it, add here a little bit and turn it into a movie. So, they can relate with it. And the same thing with every other African country, not just Nigeria. Witchcraft for example is an African fear. Go to the West Indies, there is witchcraft. Because it's from Africa. Then go to South America. Some people say the Black man everywhere in the world has his roots in anything from the same

> place. So, when you tell an African story you're appealing to every Black man anywhere in the world. They are still Africans, they are Nigerians, they're Ethiopians, they're South Africans, even when they've changed their citizenship. Let me tell you something. Actually it's a population of 900 million people living in Africa. Now, let's go to the Caribbeans, let's go to South America, let's go to Africans in the Diaspora. So, Nollywood is definitely worth a production of well over one billion. That is the market. These are the people that each story you will tell touches their lives. And that is the basis for the success. Because there was a market and all we did was to try to meet the need of this market. A market searching for their roots. A market that people have begun to forget their history. A market that was going to forget their background. So, the hunger was always there.

The Healing Word

So far we have explored the mechanisms of the spoken word. We have looked into various principles of oral-aural thought within Nigerian home video productions. So far, we have learned that Nollywood successfully re-enacts principles of the spoken word. We are yet to investigate its function.

The re-enactment of oral principles in Nigerian home videos actually expresses the *Crisis of the Nigerian Word* we have spoken about earlier. The evolution of the Nigerian word hence is represented within the totality of home videos. Why is that? In the psychological sciences, re-enactment is an essential metaphor to describe a trauma. The technique of re-enactment is used to overcome former helplessness in order to finally make a better experience (Kühner 49). A notion of glorification supports this aspect. Epic movies in particular are considered authentic. The notion of an authentic culture therefore marks the past as the optimum, although the return to an "oral state of mind" (Havelock 41) has already become impossible.

Principles of re-enactment and authenticity support the individual by (re)compensating existing disproportions. They individually assist the recovery from a collective crisis. An oral-aural mind-set therefore is recurrent in order to embed the missing into the existing. The precolonial past thereby becomes idealised. Orality here becomes a metonymy for African (Papaioannou 147). These principles actually support the healing of the word.

Nollywood therefore represents and enables the recovery of (post-) colonial thought and act. According to Stuart Hall, the so-called African Cinema generates an imaginary completion of events (136). This makes Nollywood a powerful means of decolonisation of Africans all over the world. The word is healing. And new orality encompasses modernity and tradition at the same time in order to create a new future.

Interviewees

Ms. Zuwera Abdullahi Mr. Ahmed Muhd. Aboud Prof. Durotoye Adeolu Adeleke Ms. Bimbo Akintola Prof. Maffam Al-Bishak Mr. Mahmood Ali-Balogun Mr. Jeta Amata Mr. Ibiajulu Onyemaechi Amuro Mr. Israel Opeyemi Ayansola Mr. Sola Balogun Mr. Ekpenyong Bassey-Inyang Mr. Madu C. Chikwendu Ms. Happy Dablu Prof. Ademola O. Dasylva Mr. Patrick Doyle	Ms. Johni Esther Echa Mrs. Mary Ehiorobo Mr. Osa George Ehiorobo Mr. Zeb Ejiro Mr. Bond Eyinnaya Emeruwa Mr. Justus Esiri Prof. (Mrs.) Akachi T. Ezeigbo Mr. Akinola Famson Muma Gee Ms. Ogechi Mbakwe Mr. Ulonna Mbakwe Ms. Envorh Mayo Mercy Mr. Don Pedro Obaseki, Ph.D. Mrs. Kassandra Odita Mr. Abiodun Odukoya Mr. Doyin Odukoya	Mr. Olufemi Odukoya Mr. Kingsley Ogoro Mr. Zik Zulu Okafor Mr. Victor Okhai Ms. Mabel Okosuns Mrs. Ahuruchi Okwulehie Ms. Folayemi Blessing Olafusi Mr. George Oluwole Mr. Cornelius Eze Onyekaba Mr. Ikechukwu Orji Mr. Zack Orji Ms. Joy Okuchi Osuagwu Prof. Aderemi Raji-Oyelade Mr. Alex Usifo Ms. Tari West Mr. Muhd. Bashir Yusuf

Notes

[1] This paper is an English summary of my PhD dissertation titled "Die Heilung des Wortes: Zur Bedeutung der Oralität in nigerianischen Homevideos" [translated: The Healing Word: The Significance of Orality in Nigerian Home videos].

[2] Since Kenneth Nnebue's Living in Bondage (1992), Nollywood's first major commercial success, this movie industry has advanced to one of the major film industries worldwide exclusively shooting direct-to-video.

[3] Whereas Nollywood grew out of Lagos, Kannywood grew out of Kano.

[4] Walter J. Ong's concept of orality, clearly discussed controversially, marks a significant stage in the conceptual study of orality. His pathos is apparently drawn from a white-hegemonic, Jesuitical school of thought.

Works Cited

Ahmad, S. 'B. "From Orality to Mass Media: Hausa Literature in Northern Nigeria". *Afrika und Übersee.* 86 (2003): 223–234.

Alexander, Jeffrey C., et al. (eds). *Cultural Trauma and Collective Identity.* Berkeley, Los Angeles: University of California Press, 2004.

Angela Kühner. *Kollektive Traumata: Konzepte, Argumente, Perspektiven.* Reihe Psyche und Gesellschaft. Gießen: Psychosozial-Verlag, 2007.

Barber, Karin. "Orality, the Media and New Popular Cultures in Africa". *Media and Identity in Africa.* (eds). Kimani Njogu and John Middleton. Edinburgh: Edinburgh University Press, 2009. 3–18.

Ekwuazi, Hyginus Ozo. "The Igbo Video Film: A Glimpse into the Cult of the Individual". *Nigerian Video Films.* ed. Jonathan Haynes. Africa Series. 73. Athens: Ohio University Press, 2000. 131–147.

Ezeigbo, T. Akachi, (ed). *Gender Issues in Nigeria: A Feminine Perspective.* Lagos:
University of Lagos Press, 1996.

Ezejideaku, Emmanuel and Ubaka Chidolue. "Protest and Propaganda in the Igbo Video Film". Being a Dissertation Presented to the University of Ibadan, März 2004.

Furniss, Graham. *Orality: The Power of the Spoken Word.* Hampshire/New York: Palgrave Macmillan, 2004.

Hall, Stuart. "Zur kulturellen Identität im Kino der afrikanischen Diaspora". *Afrikanisches Kino.* (eds). Marie-Hélène Gutberlet, and Hans-Peter Metzler. Arte Edition. Bad Honnef: Horlemann-Verlag, 1997. 136–150.

Havelock, Eric A. *Preface to Plato.* Cambridge, Massachusetts: Harvard University Press, 1963.

Havelock, Eric A. *The Muse Learns to Write: Reflections on Orality and Literacy From Antiquity to the Present.* New Haven/ London: Yale University Press, 1986.

Haynes, Jonathan. "Nigerian Cinema: Structural Adjustments". In Onookome Okome, and Jonathan Haynes (eds). *Cinema and Social Change in Nigeria.* Ibadan: Printmarks Ventures, 1997. 1–25.

Jeyifo, Biodun. *The Yoruba Popular Travelling Theatre of Nigeria.* A Nigeria Magazine Publication. Lagos: Emaconprint Limited, 1984.

Larkin, Brian. "Hausa Dramas and the Rise of Video Culture in Nigeria". *Nigerian Video Films.* Jonathan Haynes (ed). Africa Series. 73. Athens: Ohio University Press, 2000. 209–241.

McLuhan, Marshall. *The Gutenberg Galaxy: The Making of Typologic Man.* Toronto: University of Toronto Press, 1962.

McLuhan, Marshall. *Understanding Media: The Extensions of Man.* London/New York: Routledge, 1964.

Ogunsuyi, Steve Airehenbuwa. "The aesthetics of traditional African theatre: A gestalt for television drama production". Beind a Dissertation Submitted to the University of Ibadan, 2001.

Okome, Onookome. "The Character of Popular Indigenous Cinema in Nigeria". In Onookome Okome and Jonathan Haynes (eds). *Cinema and Social Change in Nigeria.* Ibadan: Printmarks Ventures, 1997. 92–109.

Okome, Onookome. "Women, Religion and the Video Film in Nigeria". *Film International.* 1.7 (2004): 4–13.

Ong, Walter J. *The Presence of the Word.* New Haven and London: Yale University Press, 1967.

Ong, Walter J. *Orality and Literacy: The Technologizing of the Word.* London and New York: Routledge, 1988.

Papaioannou, P. J. "From Orality to Visuality: The Question of Aesthetics in African Cinema". *Journal of African Cinemas.* 1.2 (2009): 141–157.

Pasch, Helma. "Competing Scripts: The Introduction of the Roman Alphabet in Africa". *International Journal of the Sociology of Language.* 191 (2008): 65–109.

CHAPTER THIRTEEN

Film and Literature: Connections and Disconnections

Tunde Onikoyi

Abstract

The transition from literature to the visual form of films and now video films is a path rarely trodden in the Nigerian literary society, due to the strict division between literary pursuits and film. Literature is most often considered as a more serious domain of popular culture, reflecting as it does a poetic interpretation of life. Film, on the other hand, is often considered as a pure entertainment medium. Filmmaking also constitutes a form of discourse and practice that is not just artistic and cultural, but also intellectual and political. The video medium provides a very special opportunity for studying the transition of the same spectrum of creative arts. This paper will consider the relationship between film and literature, and also argue that both film and literature constitute aesthetic, cultural and (in the case of film) popular cultural discourse. It also seeks to investigate why many Nigerian literary texts have not yielded themselves to adaptation, and why people prefer the film medium to that of literature.

Introduction

The introductory section shall involve three sections. The first section involves a brief discussion on the relationship between film and literature. The second section looks at the theory of connection and disconnection in the context of film and literature. An attempt to discuss the relationship between the two media will offer a general survey, so that we can put them in proper perspectives. The third section will attempt a diachronic discussion on the evolution of the Nigerian film industry in relation to literature. Our major point of historical investigation will refer to the classics that have been written and transformed into film.

Film and Literature: What is the Relationship?

Writing about the relationship between film and literature deserves more than a cursory look, because the two media occupy a central place in the discourse in the areas of literary studies and performing arts. In academic circles, there is an enormous interest in exchanges between film and literature, which are critically studied from various perspectives. Debates have addressed such relations and exchanges between the two media since the beginning of the twentieth century. Examples including the historical evolution of the relationship between film and literature and the various methods and issues surrounding those relationships, constitute discourse[s] on issues of genres and practices such as poetry and movies, film scripts as literature, or the relations between adaptation and popular culture, which are currently taking centre stage within academic circles.

Recent writings by individual researchers and debates in organised seminars or conferences around the world have tilted towards the link between film and literature, showing new directions and approaches for thinking about the inextricable connection between the two fields. Much attention is drawn to the impact of the two media through the adaptations of literary works to film form.

One major way of describing the two is that they are both *imaginative communication of significant experiences* (Bowskill 3). The two also have the potential to explore the essential depths of human conditions through their *individual* and unique processes of narration. Discussing film or literature also involves studying crucial materials that will enrich our understanding of any particular work of film or literature. They could also include materials about film forms that clarify the connections between film and literature and the various approaches used to analyse film and literature as forms of art (Corrigan ix).

The interest which some Nigerian critics have shown for the study of film and literature and their mutual relationship has become overwhelming. Some of the reasons for that range from the cultural enquiry of artistic hierarchies and canons to the increased diversity of media involvement in both literary and film practices. Another reason is based on the sociological import of the two media. Several discussions and publications on the sociology of art include the development of the sociology of various art forms: literature, film and fine art by critics and art historians on how they impact on scholarship and life (Bamidele 1).

Through the means of presentation peculiar to each of them, they illustrate various aspects of socio-political life and situations, which are further subjected to critical studies. As critics pay more attention to the study of film and literature, it becomes an opportunity to think about their social implications. They both treat the subject of social values. This has been made possible over the years because, they have, through their aesthetic potentials "reflected or fostered social trends and encouraged social values" (O'Brien 15).

If we take a broader look at the relationship between film and literature, it become clear that such a relationship is as old as film itself, as, for more than a century, films have depended on stories, plots, characters, roles, narrative and rhetorical devices from literary works. Novelists, playwrights and screen writers have adapted literary texts and have written scripts based on established literary genres and styles. Moreover, cinema's debt to literature is not limited to the innumerable adaptations of novels and plays.

The intersection of film and literature can be viewed from a variety of angles - the angles of the different exchanges between literary works and films. Novels, dramatic literature, short stories or poetry, all have particular counterparts in film forms. Film influences literature and vice-versa. It also influences literary imagery in many ways, and each of these parts leads to other issues - about the production of the films, their reception, the production of the literature, its reception, writing and scripting, reading and viewing.

These practices, however, create a kind of interesting relationship between film and literature. The sociological impact achieved by films results from the quality of available literature. It leads to a shift in spectatorship and literacy, resulting in cinema's demand of equal time and attention when one argues about the relative value and meaning of film and literature (Corrigan 3). Both film and literature afford spectators and readers the opportunity to make sense of their experience before a page or screen. The art of script writing versus story writing, as well as acting techniques, are part of the resonant perspectives through which we pay meticulous attention to their relationship. They both lend themselves to more than one method of analysis, and draw the spectator's and reader's attention to the diversity and range of opinions which they offer. In other words, "Methods used to study both film and literature include: a structuralist approach, psychoanalytic theory, feminism…and a literary/textual approach [which] have made their presence felt in contemporary study of both film and literature" (Nelmes 1).

Film and literature can be discussed on the common ground that has been provided by interdisciplinary studies. They can also be seen as businesses, as well as industries. Both engage in matters of gender, race and class which contribute immensely to critical and cultural perspectives. Because of their heterogeneity, their relationships thrive and they have the ability to draw in contemporary thinking and to apply what is relevant to their analyses. These constitute for us reasons why discussions and debates about the relationship between the two media become more compelling and topical in Nigeria today, and why issues on the two continue to claim the attention of critics.

Through their interaction, both film and literature have special relevance to our cultures. By this, we mean to say that they both constitute cultural discourses. They are also cultural materials and in this regard, the opinions of scholars who have commented on cultural identity, Nigerian literature and film, cannot be left out of the mainstream of culture.

Louis Luzbetak (13) has observed that there are as many definitions of culture as there are writers on it. As a result of this myriad of definitions, there have been several conflicting views on the subject, and this has complicated matters over the years. However, according to Ibanga Ikpe, from these many definitions of culture emerge two distinctive approaches to the analysis of culture. The first can be gleaned from the definition of culture as "the totality of knowledge and behaviour, ideas and objects that constitutes the common heritage of the people (Ikpe 3)."

In this connection, culture can be seen as something that has to do with the experiences of a people in their interaction with one another and with the environment. We can then say that both literature and film share that common potential as purveyors of culture because they illustrate anything that an individual or a group of individuals have undergone or lived or perceived or sensed (Ikpe 4). Film and literature have served as a barometer for questions about class, human intelligence, political action, the different statuses of races and genders, and the use and abuse of leisure time.

The Theory of Connection and Disconnection in the Context of Film and Literature

In considering the theory of connection and disconnection in film and literature, we shall pay close attention to the various aspects of both film and literature and their interactions. Connections and disconnections involve similarities and dissimilarities between film and literature. But the question we may want to ask is: what kind of similarities and dissimilarities are noticed in these art forms? Daniel Barnes, in his assessment of the similarities and dissimilarities between film and literature, identifies two broad categories which we should consider. He argues that when comparing the two media, emphasis should be laid on material and technical similarities and dissimilarities. In other words, when we think of the theory of connection and disconnection in the context of film and literature, we think of the material and technical similarities and dissimilarities between them (Barnes 3). Barnes goes on to define both the material and the technical. He defines the material as the simple visible features that form the whole essence and production of the literary text as well as the visual text (film) in their unique form – features made clearer to the reader and the viewer by their contrast (3-4). Barnes tells us that when we look at the material differences and similarities between film and literature, we are to pay attention to those aspects that make up the literary text and the film text in words and images, respectively.

He then defines the technical as those human and mechanical aspects which create the entire essence of both the literary text and visual text, in order that we become familiar with the way they were created (4). Barnes' explanation has given a clear approach to the study of another branch of the relationship between film and literature. The material similarities and dissimilarities help us to see what is created, while the technical similarities and dissimilarities help us to see the conditions in which they were made. We shall consider some of those material and technical similarities and dissimilarities briefly for purposes of clarity.

The Material Similarities between Film and Literature

Both literature and film texts are appreciated by their individual audiences. Film and literature, especially enacted dramatic literature, are public and commercial spectacles addressing audiences rather than only individuals; both can also be watched. Today, dramatic literature is written, not to be read alone but in such a way to meet stage demands. The novel cannot be watched in a physical theatre like dramatic literature, except when it is adapted. Both dramatic literature and film share production materials - sets, costumes and actors. As these materials are used in theatre, they are readily available for developing the entertainment potential of films.

Another similarity is that both have contents. The roots of dramatic literature in conflict continue in classical film, as both drama and film foreground confrontations between individuals and other individuals and between individuals and societies. History has it that nineteenth century western drama and its paradigm of the "well-made play" provided film with one of the most durable formulas "for structuring film action as [an] organised dramatic (theatrical) action according to exposition, complication, crisis, climax and resolution. These remain standard developmental structures in much theatre and film today" (Dudley 47).

Literature of any kind comes to us mainly in form of books, while film comes to us in form of cassettes and CDROM. We read literature, whether novel, play text or poetry, while the film is meant to be watched, whether at home or in cinema halls. When dramatic literature is enacted, the set design is constructed in such a way that the different locales are seen positioned at different areas of the stage. In film, on the other hand, we are made to observe as if we were experiencing reality in the real sense of the word. In other words, these locations, as created in film, are observed as true to life. As Corrigan puts it, sets and settings in the film naturally gravitate more towards realistic locations; and the possibilities for constructing space and time are significantly different in the two media (Corrigan 18). The form in which language is transmitted in literature and film is equally different. While, in literature, it is transmitted through the written word, film comes in the form of recorded pictures and sounds.

The Technical Similarities between Film and Literature

Adaptation is involved in both literary and filmic works. We could adapt the text of a novel or drama for the screen and vice versa. For instance, over a decade ago, Hyginus Ekwuazi adapted the film script of Eddie Ugbomah's *The Great Attempt*, and he observes: "I also did a novel (same title) based on the script and film" (Ekwuazi 2). Our mass mediated cultures of the screen and the novel so influence each other that, not only do novelists write as if they were writing film scripts, but any well received novel is likely to end up on the screen. This is equally true of the play text.

Both film and literature share in narrative motifs. By narrative motifs, we refer to characters, events, motivations, consequences, contexts, viewpoints, imagery and so on. Although the structure of narrativity adopted by the two media can still be compared, storytelling is the most solid median link between literature and film and the most pervasive tendency of both verbal and visual languages (Cohen 4).

While literature goes through the process of publishing, film goes through the process of editing after shooting. Literature usually employs printed words, and often requires longer reading time than the way we access stories through images on screen, which are usually presented in a 90 or 100-minute format. Dramatic literature likewise distinguishes itself from film performance, most clearly through the difference of an actual physical performance versus a performance recorded on celluloid or video tape.

Another difference in this category is that literature (for example the novel) organises words through sentences, chapters, or stanzas (in the case of poetry), while plays use acts, scenes or more recently movements whose breaks are, in most cases, clearly evident (Vardac 2), Film may borrow from these structures but usually works to make cinematographic and/or scenic shifts.

Literature is written most of the time by only one person (except on rare occasions where you have more than one person co-authoring a text). But the shooting of a film involves a large crew. Perhaps, we could refer to Ekwuazi again when he succinctly argues that it is for this reason that literature appears to be more compact than the film: "Film is not literature. Literature is not film. Literature expresses a purely personal universe. Film does not, and cannot. For it takes some 253 different trades and professions to accomplish the move from script to screen" (Ekwuazi 1). Although critics may single out a predominant signature in any film and go on to assert the auteur theory and principle, such privileging of one professional in a long chain of trades and professions does not in any way shrink the universe expressed in the film, which is anything but personal.

Another technical difference is that while literature is longer and accommodates longer speech, film, in adapting literature's subject, does a lot of cutting and shrinking if it is to be recreated in the shorter temporal format of film. Dialogue in film is usually shorter and more economical as it mostly depends on camera shots and movements. It is very challenging trying to compare and contrast literature and film. Studying them critically and keeping them in mind may be the best starting point in the examination of what film and literature finally have or do not have in common. What we have done is to take a cursory look at some of the similarities and differences between the two media through the theory of connections and disconnections.

The Evolution of Film in Nigeria: From a Diachronic Angle

An attempt is being made in this section to look at the evolution of film in the Nigerian nation from a critical point of view in relation to literature. Many critics and scholars have, from very different perspectives, attempted to survey the history of the Nigerian film industry from its earliest beginnings. Many texts and critical essays have been published in this direction and have further elicited critical enquiry into the nature, context, and, to use the words of Adesokan, "the…politics of Nigerian Video Films" (2004).

From "Theatre and the Emergence of the Nigerian Film Industry" (Wole Soyinka), to *Film in Nigeria* (Hyginus Ekwuazi 1997), *Nigerian Video Films* (Jonathan Haynes 1997), *Cinema and Social Change in Nigeria* (Okome and Haynes 1997), *The Cinema in Nigeria* (Francoise Balogun), *The Nigerian Film* (Afolabi Adesanya), *The Development and Growth of the Film Industry in Nigeria* (Opubor, Onuora and Oreh), and to recent and thought-provoking essays by Ola Balogun, Lanrele Bamidele, Abdulla Uba Adamu, Josef Guglar, Biodun Jeyifo, Ajose Adelakun, Akin Adesokan and Sola Osofisan, all have at various points of their works taken a deep and strategic look at various perspectives of the development of the Nigerian film industry.

Some of these works however have given room for further studies which have tried to fill up spaces uncovered. But what we intend to do here is to attempt a brief survey of the development of film in Nigeria in connection with literature. For the purpose of what this paper seeks to achieve, we shall begin on a note of specificity, which is to trace the evolution of Nigerian films from a number of eras: Nigerian films in the colonial era, Nigerian films between the mid-60s and 80s and recent Nigerian home videos from the 1990s and beyond.

Nigerian Films: The Colonial Era

The development of film in Nigeria is very interesting. Its progress was built upon the backdrop of the combined efforts of the colonial government and the Church. The colonial government did not fully go into the cinematography business until the beginning of World War II when the Colonial Film Unit (CFU) was established. According to Ekwuazi,

> The foetal stirrings of what has become today the Nigerian Film Industry must be traced to the frenetic documentary activities of the then British Colonial Film Unit, which at its demise, had succeeded in bequeathing to the Federal and Regional Film Units a strong tradition of the narrative documentary (Ekwuazi 3).

It was this unit which was charged with the responsibility of the colonial film production, with the objectives of such films linked with what Ekwuazi has again highlighted as the following:

> [t]o show/convince the colonies that they and the English had a common enemy in the Germans: to this end, about one quarter of the films made by the CFU were war-related; to encourage communal development in the colonies and to show the outside world the excellent work being done in heathen parts under the aegis of the Union Jack (*Daybreak in Udi* 1991:2).

The Colonial Film Unit was sponsored by the Colonial Development Welfare Act. The Church (as earlier stated as a co-collaborator) was also discretely a face of the government of the civiliser and coloniser. The various European missionary groups were able to capitalise on the acculturation potential of the film. This invariably led to Biblical and religious films being brought into the country, heavily supplemented with films from the colonial government. These films were of course non-religious but since they were generally made to condition the audience to "civilisation", they were deemed suitable. A typical example of such films was *Mr. English At Home*. At that time, the Colonial Film Unit was the main producer and distributor of films. Films came from the British Council, London and from the Crown Film Unit - both, like the CFU, under the Central Office of Information, London.

Nigerian Films between the Mid-60s and the 80s

Some major factors influenced the film-making industry during this period. These factors, as identified by Jide Malomo, included the growing nationalistic fervour among Nigerian artists before and after independence in 1960, the advent of television, and a flourishing theatrical tradition that later shifted its focus from 'live' theatre to filmmaking as a result of economic pressures (6). It is important to note at this juncture that since we are dealing with the Nigerian film in relation to literature, we shall be very careful to concentrate more on those literary works that were adapted into film.

Although, Nigerian literature had started before the exit of the coloniser (Griffiths, Tiffin and Ashcroft 3), it was readily available to filmmakers for production possibilities. The desire to make indigenous films was largely influenced by the vibrant nationalistic fervour among theatre artists after independence. Film was considered a powerful medium for cultural emancipation and a potent instrument for the creation of a national consciousness and identity. An indigenous film industry reflecting Nigerian culture was intended to help to curtail the unsavoury effects of foreign films, which continued to promote violence and a new era of cultural imperialism.

During the mid-60s, efforts were made by practitioners of the folkloric and the literary theatre (7). The leading exponent of the literary theatre is Wole Soyinka, the winner of the 1986 Nobel Prize for Literature. In his attempt to research into the evolution of the Nigerian film industry, Ekwuazi explains that several filmmakers who had started from the stage came from the south-west region of the country, where it is believed that a vibrant theatre tradition began (20). He also mentioned that some of these filmmakers had initially become popular before going into film.

Among the first few films made in the country are *Culture in Transition* (1963) and *Kongi's Harvest* (1970). *Culture in Transition* integrates into its structural and thematic framework an abridged version of Soyinka's stage play, *The Strong Breed* directed by Bart Lawrence. *Kongi's Harvest* was adapted from his stage play of the same title. These two films have become the precursors of later works. For instance, *Shehu Umar* had progressed from the prose narrative medium, as a novel of the same title by Nigeria's late Prime Minister, Sir Abubakar Tafawa Balewa, through the stage adaptation by Umaru Ladan and Dexter Lyndersay, to the screen (20).

What emerged as a film culture seemed to replicate the stage in technique and plot. What is more crucial is that, at that time, some important features of the stage hovered over the film. This means that indigenous films were heavily indebted to the stage for their personnel and technique. *Kongi's Harvest*, which was to be the first feature film in Nigeria, was produced in 1970 by Francis Oladele, who formed a company known as Calpenny Nigerian Films, and directed by an African American, Ossie Davies, who was to have appeared in the early scenes of the film version as the narrator (Gugler 115). According to Josef Gugler, history has it that during the period, Wole Soyinka also made efforts to produce a film version of his shorter play *The Swamp Dwellers* directed by Norman Florence. With the growing nature of film in Nigeria, Francis Oladele also decided to try his hands on Chinua Achebe's *Things Fall Apart.* The title of the film was changed to *Bullfrog in the Sun* because of government pressures.

While the literary filmmakers were putting some texts on screen, the Yoruba theatre practitioners themselves also thrived with film adaptations of a majority of their stage plays. These films in Yoruba grew straight out of the Yoruba Travelling Theatre, and this form of popular drama was created by the late Hubert Ogunde out of the Alarinjo Theatre, with additional elements from the Ghanaian Concert Party. His first film, *Aye* (1979), in which he played the lead role - a common practice among travelling theatre troupes - was directed by Ola Balogun. Another film was *Ayanmo* (1988), which turned to be better than the first due to its metaphysical themes and dimensions. They appeared cultural, social and religious, and their thrust was conveyed through a continuous aesthetic heightening (Okome 7).

The transition from stage to film continued and Ola Balogun, another prominent film practitioner from the seventies, made his first Yoruba film *Ajani Ogun* in 1977, with Duro Ladipo and his troupe starring great actors like Adeyemi Afolayan (Ade Love). Ola Balogun also worked with Hubert Ogunde and other main stars of this tradition like Moses Olaiya (popularly known as Baba Sala). Ola Balogun's *Bisi Goddess of the River* was also adapted from a play of the same title in the same year 1977.

Not all the films of that period between 1960 and the 1980s were adaptations of novels and plays. Others could be directly linked to some significant events that occurred in the country. For instance, Eddie

Ugboma's *Death of a Black President* was based on the wanton assassination of the military head of state, General Murtala Muhammed. Ade Love's *Taxi Driver 1* and *2* also depicted the life of taxi drivers in metropolitan areas. These works were inspired from urban life, political crises and violence. Other films were *The Rise and Fall of Dr Oyenusi* (1976), *The Mask* (1979), *Oil Doom* (1981), *Bolus80* (1982), *The Boy is Good* (1982). *Ija ominira*, though filmed in Yoruba, was one of the most successful films in the history of the Nigerian film industry. Directed and produced by Ade Afolayan, it enacts the successful revolt of serfs and pariahs against a tyrannical king of the old Oyo Empire, undoubtedly a major lesson for our contemporary society. The film was readily embraced by the already extensive audience of the travelling theatre (Malomo 8).

Television was however a major factor which encouraged indigenous filmmaking (and still does). The first television was established in 1959 by the Western Region of Nigeria and at its inception, over 90% of televised programmes were foreign films. This was largely due to the initial non-existence of locally-made films. This situation was unsatisfactory and the emerging TV stations determined to increase the local content of their programmes, if not totally indigenise them. Malomo's account comes in handy:

> The travelling theatre contributed a lot to this effort through their local drama programmes, as their plays were often adapted to television and some of them were actually serialised for the screen. Initially, the plays were produced and transmitted from the studios, but later they were recorded at appropriate locations just in the manner of filmmaking (9).

Leading Travelling Theatre Troupes, under the auspices of practitioners of that period like late Ogunde, Duro Ladipo, Oyin Adejobi and Akin Ogungbe, earned considerable income on television, which increased their audiences. Perhaps, this is why Lanre Bamidele, in his criticism, constructively argues for television drama as one of the gate-keepers through which a literary work passes to the audience (42).

By the mid-1980s, most of the travelling theatre practitioners were involved in filmmaking. New stories were created, which dealt with the prevailing social and political matters. Some of them were Olaiya's *Omolagbe 1* and *2, Mosebolatan, Are Agbaye,* and Jimoh Aliu's *Omo Orunkan.* Others which centred on more contemporary social and political issues were *Eri Okan* and the most striking of them all, *Ireke Onibudo*, based on D.O. Fagunwa's novel of the same title. Several other films had been produced on video cassettes and shown on the new video projectors with large screens, and we can say that this kind of practice still thrives in Nigeria today.

Recent Nigerian Home Videos: 1990s and Beyond

Discussions on the recent Nigerian home videos straddle between the 1990s and now. Although some may appear more recent than others, this period marks the beginning of the commercialisation of Nigerian home videos. It was a period when a lot of unprofessional marketers and distributors flooded the market and dabbled in the film business, fancying themselves as filmmakers, producing sub-standard films for monetary gains with fantastic stories and miserable technical professionalism.

Pioneer films were *Living in Bondage* and *Circle of Doom* (1990). These films were not adapted works from novels or plays. Few works of literature were turned into films in the 1990s, because of the commercial orientation which this so-called new breed of filmmakers had. One of them was Ogunde's adaptation of *Mr Johnson* in 1990. Okome's account reveals that during his later years, the late Hubert Ogunde co-produced *Mr. Johnson* (an adaptation of a novel of the same title) with an American director, Bruce Beresford, with the support of an American film company (2). This was imbibed by a number of entrepreneurs and artistes. Anyone with a nose for quick money made a bee line for the industry. It was as if the industry had a *peculiar paradigm* of power, which led to the emergence of the marketer-producer (casting) potentate.

But while the home video began to take shape, with some English language films springing up, artists like Jimoh Aliu continued to make films. *Fopomoyo*, which was of a traditional setting, was produced in 1991. *Agbo Meji*, a film that infused most of the aesthetics and technical import which Ogunde's works contained, was produced by Ola Makinwa. Yoruba film production was by now highly professionalised in acting and camera work. For instance *Eri Okan*, directed by Tunde Oloyede, and Babatunde Balogun's *Orogun Orun*, were produced in 1990 and 1992 respectively. *Ose Sango*, entirely devoted to occult matters, was produced by Afolabi Adesanya. Moses Olaiya's *Agba Man* (1992) and *Return Match* (1993) were produced in the Yoruba language despite their titles.

English language films by notable directors cannot be left out of the mainstream. Directors like Amaka Igwe, Lola Fani-Kayode, Peter Igoh, Zeb Ejiro and Zak Amata have made a tremendous impact on the industry in spite of the overwhelming criticism which followed the adoption of western patterns by some of the films. Films like Amaka Igwe's *Violated* (1992), Andy Amechi's *Mortal Inheritance* (1993) and Chico Ejiro's *Shame* (1993) are all tailored after western patterns. Others like *Onome, Glamour Girls 1 and 2, Rattle Snake 1 and 2* and *Rituals* are also from the same mould.

Conclusion

We can still count on our fingertips the number of good adapted works by those who consider our literatures as the best option to enjoy good adaptations. *Sango*, an adaptation of Duro Ladipo's *Oba Koso,* was produced by Even Ezra Studio in Lagos and directed by Femi Lasode in 1997. The film featured very prominent actors like the late Wale Ogunyemi.

Oduduwa (2002) and *Obafemi Awolowo* (1998) are other adaptations, based on texts written about the life and times of these great men. Albert Egbe's adaptation of Neville Ukoli's play, *Home to the River* was also produced in 2001. He equally made an adaptation of Rasheed Gbadamosi's *Trees Grow in the Desert* (2003), a play which was transformed under the same title. These works are typical challenges that were able to revitalise the practice and praxis of proper filmmaking in Nigeria.

Tunde Kelani's efforts at picking up good literary works written mostly in Yoruba language, whether plays or novels, has marked him out among his contemporaries as being quite exceptional. He is the foremost cinematographer of home video (Ayorinde 37), whose vision of what filmmaking should look like is based on his inspiration, which comes from his cultural background and experience. *Agogo Ewo* (2001), *Saworoide* (1999) and *Ole Ku* (2000) are works written by Akinwunmi Ishola, including the famous *Efunsetan Aniwura.* Another work is an adaptation of Adebayo Faleti's *Magun, The Whore with Thunderbolt AIDS* which was produced in (2001) to further buttress the author's love for culture, taking cognizance of some of the socio-cultural matters as reflected in our society.

Works Cited

Ashcroft, Bill, Griffiths, Gareth and Tiffin, Helen. *The Empire Writes Back: Theory and Practice of Postcolonial Literatures.* New York: Routledge, 1989.

Adesokan, Akin. "The Politics and Aesthetics of Nigerian Home Video Films". *African Drama and Performance.* Bloomington: Indiana University Press, 2004.

Ayorinde, Steve. "A Millennium in Motion". *Comet Newspapers*, Saturday, January 1, 2000.

Bamidele, Lanrele. *Literature and Sociology.* Ibadan: Stirling and Horden, 2000.

Barnes, Daniel. *The Interface between Film and Literature.* New York: Routledge, 2002.

Bowskill, Derek. *Acting and Stage Craft Made Simple.* New York: Newton 1972.

Cohen, Keith. *Film and Literature: The Dynamics of Exchange.* New Haven: Yale University Press, 1979.

Corrigan, Timothy. *Film and Literature: An Introduction.* New Jersey: Simon and Schuster, 1999.

Dudley, Andrew. *Concepts in Film Theory.* Oxford: Oxford University Press, 1984.

Ekwuazi, Hyginus. *Film in Nigeria.* Jos: Nigerian Film Corporation, 1991.

______________. "To the Movies Go-Everything Good Will Come". Keynote address at the 24th International Convention of the Association of Nigerian Authors (ANA), on the theme: 'Literature and the Developing Film Industry' November 10-13 2005.

Gugler, Josef. *African Film: Re-Imagining a Continent.* Bloomington: Indiana University Press, 2003.

Ikpe, Ibanga. *Culture and Societal Values.* New York: Routledge, 2000.

Luzbatak, Louis. *The Concept of Culture.* New York: Howard University Press, 1993.

Malomo, Jide. "The Folkloric Film in Nigeria". A Paper Presented at the International Symposium on African Theatre and Film at the Graduate Centre For Study of Drama, University of Toronto, Canada, 1993.

Nelmes, Jill. *Introduction to Film Studies.* New York: Howard University Press, 1999.

O'Brien, Tom. *The Screening of America: Movies and Values from Rocky to*

Rainman. New York: Continuum, 1990.

Okome, Onookome and Haynes, Jonathan. *Cinema and Social Change in West Africa.* Jos: National Film Institute, 1997.

Book Review

"...an important contribution to the emerging field of Nollywood studies. Taking questions of nationhood, language, culture and modernity into consideration, the essays assembled here ask how Nollywood video films can positively impact and transform Nigerian society...and cultural landscape. The essays also make a key intervention in the field by examining video films made in indigenous languages and asking the pointed question, "What is the language of Nollywood?" This is a must-read for anyone interested in African screen media studies."
- **Prof. Lindsey Green-Simms, American University, Washington DC**

"This collection of sophisticated essays takes up, in the context of Nigerian video films, the grand themes of African literary criticism: the role of orality and oral traditions in contemporary art forms, relations with international models and audiences, women's issues, and—the encompassing concerns in this volume—language, modernity, and the nation. The essays are remarkably various in their methodological and theoretical equipment and in their concerns. Some drill down deeply into indigenous resources: Hausa folktales, the healing power of the oral tradition, and filmmaking in minority languages. Others are concerned with globalisation in several dimensions. The sum of the collection is greater than its parts, making it a stimulating book that should push Nigerian film criticism forward."
- **Professor Jonathan Haynes, Long Island University, Brooklyn, NY**

"What the home video has basically done is precisely what its antecedents (cine and reversal filmmaking) by their very nature, could not have done-- that is, democratize the storytelling space. Thus, today, we can distinguish the GREATER Nollywood (Hausa, Igbo and Yoruba films) from the LESSER Nollywood (e.g. Edo and Tiv films); and the OLD Nollywood (home video films) from the NEW Nollywood (cine films).

This is the background against which this collection of essays must be read. Without prejudice to the intrinsic value of each essay, taken as a whole, these highly illuminating essays do remind one of the proverbial saying that the masquerade is best viewed from different positions. This

book is a many-angled look at the Nollywood film."
- Professor Hyginus Ekwuazi, University of Ibadan, Nigeria

Index

J

K

L

M

Y

Z

www.ingramcontent.com/pod-product-compliance
Lightning Source LLC
LaVergne TN
LVHW020051110826
845155LV00021B/62

9781909112742